Oracle 8*i*
Data Warehousing

Oracle 8*i*
Data Warehousing

Lilian Hobbs
Susan Hillson

Digital Press
Boston • Oxford • Aukland • Johannesburg • Melbourne • New Delhi

Butterworth–Heinemann supports the efforts of American Forests and the Global ReLeaf program in its campaign for the betterment of trees, forests, and our environment.

ISBN 1-55558-205-2

MS-DOS, MS Windows, MS Windows NT, Microsoft, Excel, and Microsoft Access are registered trademarks and Windows is a trademark of Microsoft Corporation. Netware and Novell are registered trademarks of Onvell, Inc. ORACLE is a trademark of the Oracle Corporation. All other trademarks are the property of their respective holders.

British Library Cataloguing-in-Publication Data
A catalogue record for this book is available from the British Library.

The publisher offers special discounts on bulk orders of this book.
For information, please contact:
Manager of Special Sales
Butterworth-Heinemann
225 Wildwood Avenue
Woburn, MA 01801-2041
Tel: 781-904-2500
Fax: 781-904-2620

For information on all Butterworth–Heinemann publications available, contact our World Wide Web home page at: http://www.bh.com/digitalpress.

10 9 8 7 6 5 4 3 2 1

Printed in the United States of America

Composition: Lilian Hobbs/Diane DeMarco

To my mother, without whose support and encouragement I would have never written books like this.

Lilian

To my mother and father, who taught me to work as hard as I could, and to my mother and father-in-law who believed I could do anything.

Susan

Contents

Foreword

Chuck Rozwat, Senior Vice President, Oracle Server Technologies

The Internet has the potential to make as significant a change to today's society, as the industrial revolution did 200 years ago. Success in this new economy is dependent on how well information is leveraged.

The Internet has redefined the rules of competition, making the need for accurate, timely information more critical than ever. The data warehouse can be used to identify ways to attract new customers, retain existing customers, and increase profitability, e.g. customer profiling, buying history, and patterns. It can also be used to gain insights into daily operations, identifying potential areas to reduce costs so your business can operate more efficiently.

The Web provides the infrastructure needed to access data from anywhere in the world, making it easier to conduct business on-line with suppliers, customers, and partners. Using a warehouse, data published via the Web, can be accessed from anywhere through a Web browser interface. The number of users of the data warehouse may be a few hundred or thousand today, but could easily could grow to the hundreds of thousands in the next few years. The above business drivers create an ever increasing need to retain more history and greater detail to make better business decisions. As a result, the size of data warehouses continues to grow rapidly.

Oracle 8*i* is designed for data warehousing. It provides robust data management capabilities, fast performance for interactive query processing, high availability, continuous operation, and the ability to survive catastrophic failures. Oracle 8*i* provides the infrastructure necessary to significantly scale both the number of users and the amount of data. Materialized views significantly improve performance, by precomputing frequently accessed summary information. A summary advisor provides advice on the best set of summaries to create. New data partitioning schemes simplify the management and availability of large data warehouses. When moving data between Oracle systems, transportable tablespaces facilitate fast movement of data into the warehouse by eliminating the need to extract and reload the data.

Database management systems are at the core of every application that supports business decisions. Building a successful data warehouse requires understanding the underlying DBMS technology. Using it to obtain strategic value requires sophisticated business intelligence tools. Written by Susan Hillson and Lilian Hobbs, this book offers a thorough coverage of the tools and techniques used to design, build, manage, analyze, and Web-enable your Oracle 8*i* data warehouse. Whether you are building an enterprise data warehouse, a departmental data mart, or looking for techniques to improve performance and scalability as you Web-enable your existing warehouse, this book will serve as a useful guide with many examples.

Preface

Data warehousing has grown out of decision support systems, which, as their name implies, are computer systems built to help people make better decisions. There was a time when the data warehouse, or decision-support system, as they use to be known,was something that only a major corporation could develop—despite being invaluable to an organization to help them better understand their business and, therefore, profit from the information they extract from it. Only recently has it been possible for anyone to build and maintain a data warehouse or smaller scale data mart.

This book introduces the reader to the subject of data warehousing and data marts with respect to implementing on an Oracle 8*i* database. It has been designed so that anyone new to the subject can gather a basic understanding of data warehousing and what is involved in designing, creating, implementing, and managing that solution using Oracle 8*i*.

The authors have endeavored to make the book easy to read and have provided lots of examples to illustrate how features are implemented. If you are not yet using Oracle 8*i,* this book is still appropriate, but then obviously, all of the features presented in this text will not be available.

Each chapter focuses on a specific topic, and, where possible, they have been written to follow the logical flow of designing, building, and managing a data warehouse. The structure of the chapters is as follows:

- Chapter 1 provides an introduction to the subject of data warehousing, introducing terms, and the need for a data warehouse or data mart.

- Chapter 2 shows how to design a data warehouse and illustrates how to create dimension and fact tables. At this time, the database used for all the examples in the text is introduced, illustrating how the warehouse can be created.

- Chapter 3 describes the various techniques and objects that you can create in your data warehouse and advice is given on how to make the best use of features such as indexes, partitions, and materialized views.

- Chapter 4 is devoted to explaining the techniques you can use to load data into the warehouse.

- Chapter 5 describes how to use the Data Mart Suite to create a data mart or your data warehouse.

- Chapter 6 looks at some of the Oracle tools you can use to report on the data in your data warehouse. Specifically described are Oracle Discoverer, Express, and Time Series.

- Chapter 7 discusses the techniques you can use to manage your data warehouse. Many of the tasks are illustrated using Oracle Enterprise Manager, but they do not have to be completed using this method.

- Chapter 8 describes how you can Web-enable your data warehouse so that the contents can be accessed from a browser and how you can drive reports off of the database.

Acknowledgments

When one is writing a book, there are many people who are involved at various stages of the production cycle. The extremely important but often silent contributors are those people who give up their valuable spare time to review the book. For this book, the authors would like to thank the following excellent technical reviewers:

Jay Davison, a consulting member of the technical staff at the Oracle New England Development Center.

Jay Feenan, a consulting member of the technical staff at the Oracle New England Development Center, was a major contributor to the Summary Management Project.

James Lear, from the Discoverer Development team in the UK, who has been developing the Discoverer product for many years, and contributed greatly to this book.

Lory Molesky, one of the Developers for the Oracle Time Series at the New England Development Center.

Simon Oxbury, a Developer at the Oracle New England Development Center and a member of the Web development and services team.

Michael Schmitz, Vice President of Data Warehousing of Magma Solutions who specializes in multidimensional design and building data warehouses.

Dennis Murray, a Senior Principal Consultant for Oracle U.K. who is an extremely experienced data warehousing consultant. Dennis has experience in building warehouses that occupy tens of terabytes, and we welcomed his perspective on the issues regarding building huge data warehouses.

Mike Rubino, a Director of the Oracle New England Development Center's Web development and services.

We also need to say a big thank you to:

Max Hillson, whose E-commerce site, coolstuffcheap.com, served as the inspiration for many of the shopping examples.

Chuck Rozwat, Senior Vice President of Oracle Data Server Technologies Division, for his support in starting the book.

Steve Hagan, Vice President of the New England Development Center, for his encouragement throughout the writing of this book.

Finally, this book is dedicated to the software developers of the Summary Management, Data Mart Builder, WebDB, Oracle Express, Oracle 8*i,* and VLDB Utilities teams, both in New England and Redwood Shores, and, of course, the Discoverer team in the UK.

Everyone at Butterworth-Heinemann has been marvelous in making this book happen. Phil Sutherland, Karen Pratt from the U.S. and everyone on the production team who made this book possible.

1   Data Warehousing

1.1   ORACLE 8*i*

Data warehousing is the enabling technology that facilitates improved business decision-making. By using the information you already own, you can react smarter, quicker, and more efficiently than your competitors.

A data warehouse contains a wide variety of data used for decision support and analytical processing. It contains data from multiple operational systems that have been integrated, aggregated, and structured so that they are easy to use.

In this book, we will show you how to best use Oracle 8*i* in your warehouse. By understanding the design principles used in building some of the features and what scenarios are optimized in Oracle 8*i*, you can build a better performing data warehouse.

For example, it is assumed that new data is loaded into the warehouse in batch mode on a periodic basis, using SQL*Loader's direct path option, and only occasionally will you need to update individual rows. Thus, features in Oracle 8*i*, such as fast refresh of summaries, will expect this style of use. This book gives you the unique opportunity to learn the design principles behind the software development of Oracle 8*i* warehousing features from some members of the development team.

With Oracle 8*i*, you can now add multimedia data to your warehouse. In addition to the product description, you can also add a picture or image of the product to your dimension table. We'll also show you how to Web-enable your warehouse, both what you can do using tools today and what will be possible in the future.

1.1.1   Why Do You Need a Data Warehouse?

Is all the information needed to run your business available when it's needed, in the form in which it's needed, and in sufficient detail and with accuracy to base decisions upon?

1

Or, do two users arrive at a meeting with reports that don't match. One thinks sales for March is $500,000, and another says it's $524,000. After much analysis, you determine that different data has been used to calculate the sales in each report, and you spend considerable time trying to figure out why, and correcting the problem.

Does your company have multiple systems for the same function—the old inventory system and the new one you just spent millions of dollars building? Do you need to get data from both of these to combine together for reporting purposes? How well is this working? Do users need to understand the differences between the two systems to query them on-line? If this requires custom programming, do you still have an application backlog?

Do you have sufficient historical detail for analysis purposes? How many months of history are you able to keep on line? Did you even save all of the historical data? Are you able to analyze the sales for each product for each geographic region before and after a major reorganization of the sales force reporting structure? Data warehouses are built to help address these problems.

1.2   WHAT IS A DATA WAREHOUSE?

1.2.1   Where Does the Data Come From?

The primary source of data for the warehouse is the many operational systems used in production to run the day-to-day business operations of a company. These are usually on-line transaction processing (OLTP) systems. Order processing, order entry, inventory, general ledger, and accounting are all examples of operational systems.

In an inventory application, there are transactions to insert new items into the inventory, delete items when sold, and update the quantity on hand, always maintaining the balance on hand. OLTP systems represent the state of a system at a current point in time. A limited amount of history is retained. It is easy to determine how many of product 111-45-222 is on hand, for example, or on what date order number 45321 was shipped.

In addition to the data you already own, you can purchase data from external data providers, to add to your warehouse. You can buy information about the weather, demographics, and socioeconomic data.

Examples of usage would be:

- Adding data that tracks regional weather events on a daily basis. This way, you can determine which products show an increase or decrease in sales when there is a snowstorm.

- Adding customer demographic data. Selective marketing can be performed, targeting those customers most likely to respond to a sales promotion.

- Knowing what types of customers buy what types of products, you can anticipate demand and increase profitability. Demographic data can be used to help choose a location to place a new retail store.

1.2.2   The Data Warehouse Contains Historical Data

Management needs to view the business over time, and spot trends. Typical warehouse queries involve reporting on sales for a product over the last two years or looking at the impact of a major snowstorm on retail sales vs. Internet sales.

Because warehouses hold a large amount of history, they tend to grow rapidly and become very large databases. In order to determine and analyze trends over time, the warehouse contains historical data. Generally, multiple years of data are needed, particularly when the business is seasonal.

Not all levels of history needs to be kept at the same level of detail. It might be necessary to keep the detail of all sales transactions for a year. After two years, it may only be necessary to keep the data as a monthly summary. Today, we may need to know that Mary Smith bought a lava lamp. Two years from now, we need only to know how many lava lamps we sold in November 1998. As time goes on, the detail of any one transaction is less interesting than a summary of the transactions.

On-line transaction processing (OLTP) systems are used primarily by the clerical staff or people who are responsible for tasks such as order entry. Data warehouses are used by *decision-makers*. OLTP systems automate processes; data warehouses provide decision support.

Data warehouses are designed for quick retrieval, when the access path is not known in advance. Information is often derived from other data, by rolling up data into summaries, drilling down to get more detail, or looking for patterns and trends.

1.2.3   The Data Warehouse Lives on a Separate Dedicated System

You may already be wondering why you can't use your operational production systems for your data warehouse. You already have databases that are accessible through your corporate network, so why can't you just use those to get the information you need to run your business more efficiently? Why do you need to copy data from one system to another to build a warehouse? Because operational systems do not contain historical data, the information is not available to analyze.

It is impossible to run decision-support queries that require a large amount of computing power to sort and summarize millions of rows without impacting the performance of your operational system. And to make it even more difficult, usually the many different operational systems are running on different hardware platforms, with different operating systems and database-management systems. Some applications may have been purchased, and others built in-house. On some, the source code may no longer even be available to make changes to, and many of the systems could be several years old.

It was once believed that distributed databases were going to allow you to issue one query and that location transparency would find and retrieve the data, returning it to the user fast enough so he never realized it was located on a machine in a different geographic location. As a result, data needs to be moved from the operational systems into a separate data warehouse, where they are stored in a common format on a different machine for analysis.

1.3   STEPS IN BUILDING A DATA WAREHOUSE

In this book, we'll take at a look at the operations in a warehouse:

- Designing the warehouse (logical, physical, processes)
- Building the warehouse
- Using the warehouse for analysis, reporting, On-line Analytical Processing (OLAP), and data mining
- Managing the warehouse

1.3.1   Logical Database Design

In an OLTP system, entity relationship diagramming techniques (e-r) are used to design the database schema. Each entity becomes a table, attributes become columns, and relationships are represented by primary/foreign keys that are joined together at runtime.

A normalized design provides optimal performance for OLTP systems, which support high volumes of transactions that frequently update data. Normalization ensures the tables are correctly formed by putting related data together in one table and eliminating redundancy. By having only one copy of the data, *update anomalies* are avoided. You have only to update the data in one place, and consistency is maintained.

Sometimes designers of OLTP systems reintroduce some redundancy for performance reasons. Whenever you have multiple occurrences of an item that needs to be updated, you have a potential problem. Invariably, you are bound to forget to update one occurrence.

In a data warehouse, the primary activity is querying, or reading the data. New data is generally batch loaded into the warehouse on a periodic basis— at the end of the day, week, or month. In order to optimize performance for a warehouse, dimensional modeling techniques are used.

The dimensional approach to modeling organizes data into fact and dimension tables. It was developed by General Mills and Dartmouth College in the 1960s and was commercialized in the 1970s by A.C. Nielsen. The goal of

Figure 1.1 Star Schema

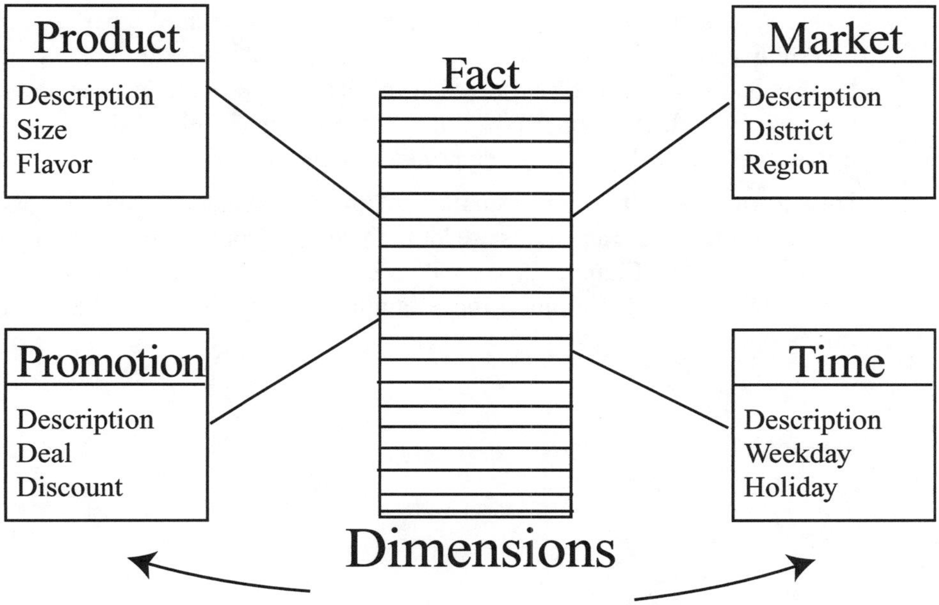

dimensional modeling is to represent data in a way that is easily understood by users. Business users often ask for reports of sales results on a quarterly basis broken down by store and geographic region. The sales numbers are the facts. Store, region, and quarter are the dimensions the data is analyzed by.

With dimensional modeling, redundancy is introduced. The database is designed as a star schema, as illustrated in Figure 1.1, with one or more large fact tables surrounded by many dimension tables.

The fact table contains points to be analyzed about the business, such as the total sales for each store. The dimension tables contain additional descriptive attributes, such as the city where the store is located. Many companies have reference or lookup tables already, which become the dimensions in the warehouse. The dimensions contain the constraints for the SQL queries.

Many dimensions are hierarchical in nature. Individual products may be grouped into product families. Product families may be grouped into brands and brands, associated with specific divisions. Geography is also hierarchical. Stores are located in cities, which are located in states, which roll up into countries. Another example is time. Many companies use a fiscal calendar, where days roll up into weeks, which roll up into fiscal quarters, which roll up into fiscal years. Reports often represent each level in a hierarchy as a subtotal—product sales with subtotals for each day, week, quarter, and year followed by a grand total of all sales.

Each level is logically connected to the levels above and below it in the hierarchy. Values at a lower level aggregate into values at the higher level. The hierarchy can be viewed as a family tree structure. A value at the next higher level is its parent; at the next lower level, its children. Hierarchies are often used when drilling up or drilling down to different levels of detail as illustrated in Figure 1.2, where we can see a sample time hierarchy.

Dimension tables are usually small, containing anywhere from under 50 to a few thousand rows. Fact tables are large in comparison, often containing millions of rows. In Chapter 2, we will see how to actually create a physical design for our Easy Shopping Inc. example, which will be used throughout this book.

Figure 1.2 Sample Hierarchies

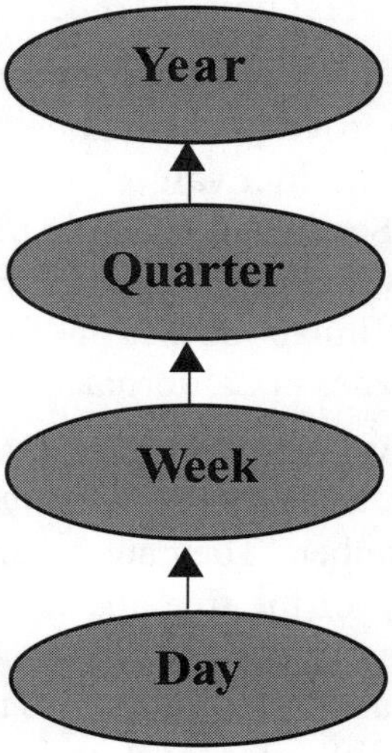

1.3.2   **The Physical Database Design**

Most data warehouses grow faster than planned, with more data and users being added to the system sooner than expected. As time goes on, warehouses store increasing amounts of historical data. In addition, both detail and summarized data is stored in the warehouse. Terabyte databases are becoming common. As warehouses are used as the underlying technology to distribute information to customers, employees, and suppliers, the number of users is expected to grow from a few "knowledge workers" to thousands or millions of people accessing information over the Internet. Designing the database for scalability, as the amount of data and number of users grows, is critical.

The logical design is converted to a physical representation that will best optimize performance and manageability. Tables, constraints, indexes, and partitions are defined. Many capabilities not yet implemented by other vendors are available in Oracle 8*i* which improves performance and manageability of a data warehouse.

Tables are the basic units of storage in an Oracle 8*i* database. All user data is stored in rows and columns within a table. Indexes provide an efficient method for retrieving specific rows from a table. An index is similar to an index in the back of a book. When you are looking for a topic, you look in the index and find the page the topic is located on. If a column on a table has an index,

Oracle will look in the index to find the rows of the table that have the value specified for that column. Several types of indexes are available.

Bitmap indexes have been designed for data warehousing and decision-support applications to improve performance of retrieving data where, in a column, the number of distinct values is small compared to the number of rows in the table. "Sex" is an example of such a column; there are only two possible values, "Male" and "Female." States of the United States are another good example. Bitmap indexes are optimal for answering questions such as "How many females in California bought lava lamps last month?"

B*tree indexes have been available in database and file systems for many years, and are most effective when there are many possible values, such as a customer name or phone number. They are organized like an upside-down tree, with the root at the top of the tree and the leaves at the bottom. The bottom level holds actual data values and rowids, or pointers to the physical location of the data. B*trees are useful for queries that retrieve a single row or a range of rows, such as "Find all sales for store xyz." When multiple columns will be frequently used together in a query, one index may be defined on that set of columns concatenated together.

Rather than checking to ensure data is valid in application code, constraints can be defined that Oracle uses to prevent data from being entered or modified that would violate data integrity. By using constraints in the database, the rules are coded once as part of the table definition and will apply to every transaction against that table.

Constraints should always be used in OLTP systems, but their role is somewhat different in the warehouse. Because the data is entered through large batch loads, often the data is validated, transformed, and cleansed prior to loading. Therefore, checking constraints as data is added may be redundant. However, constraints are very useful in the warehouse to document the relationships among the tables.

Each dimension table is related to the fact table by primary/foreign key constraints. For example, the primary key product_id in the product dimension uniquely identifies each item a company may sell. The purchases fact table also contains the product_id of the item the customer purchased. The foreign key ensures that we do not record the sale of an item that is not in the product table.

When a primary/foreign key relationship exists between two tables, the join criteria for any query that references both tables can be utilitzed by query facilities. Oracle provides a mechanism to define the constraints but not enforce integrity checking, when enabling them using the NOVALIDATE and RELY options.

In a data warehouse, you will have one or more very large fact tables. Partitioning makes it easier to manage very large tables and indexes by dividing them into smaller parts. Partitioning can also improve availability and query performance. All the data for a single partition can be moved as a unit.

In Oracle 8*i*, a single table can be created with multiple partitions. Data in each partition is grouped together based on a range of key values in a column. A common partitioning scheme in a warehouse is to group all data for a time period, such as a month, together in its own partition. Oracle 8*i* supports a variety of partitioning schemes, including hash and composite, which are discussed in detail in Chapter 3.

Because of the large volume of detailed data, data is often summarized to reduce the need to store and process the same data repeatedly. In some warehouses, detail data is never stored. Light summarization can be done as part of the extraction and transformation process, reducing the network transfer and load times. The appropriate level of data granularity may be a summary by day or week. However, if you need to drill down to the finest level, all the detail data is required. In Chapter 3, we will learn more about how to create summaries using Oracle 8*i*.

1.3.3   Designing the Process

While designing the data warehouse, you must also design several other processes:

- Data extraction from the operational systems
- Transformation and cleansing
- Procedures for initial load to populate the warehouse
- Procedures to add new data on a regular basis (end of day, week, month)
- Procedures to update the internal structures to reflect the newly loaded data (update indexes and optimizer statistics, refresh summaries)
- Utilization monitoring
- Managing users security and access
- Developing a backup strategy to protect from possible failures
- Data retention (developing purge/archive procedures)

1.4   BUILDING THE WAREHOUSE

Building a warehouse involves extracting data from operational systems, sometimes combining it with additional information from third parties, transforming it into a uniform format and loading it into a relational database.

Once data is entered in the warehouse, it almost never changes, since it records the facts of an event or state that existed at some moment in time, such as a particular sale of a product that happened on 23-Dec-1998. If there was another sale of a similar product on 24-Dec-1998, it would be recorded as a separate event.

The data in the warehouse is generally not updated in real time. New data is added to the warehouse on a periodic basis. They are usually loaded in batch in the evenings or at another time when the warehouse is not being used heavily by the analysts.

1.4.1   Extraction Process

Operational data must be extracted from the source operational systems and copied to the staging area, a temporary location where the data is cleansed, transformed, and prepared for the warehouse. Sometimes you have direct access to the source systems; however, often access is severely restricted, and you can only get files of data that have been extracted for you. The operational systems frequently must be running on a 24x7x365 basis, and performance cannot be impacted in any way.

1.4.2   Transformation

Data from multiple systems need to be transformed into a common format for use in the warehouse. A knowledge of the meaning of the data in the operational system is required.

Each operational system may refer to the same item by a different name. For example, a tool company in the U.S. might call product_id "1234" a "wrench," where a company in another country may call the same product "1234" a "spanner." Each system might use a different encoding scheme. The product_id may be represented as three characters separated by dashes (xxx-xx-xxx) in one system and characters separated by spaces (xxx xx xxx) in another. The data must be transformed to a common encoding scheme in the warehouse.

An attribute of a table may have different names. One system might refer to a column in the customer table as gender, represented by values "0" or "1." Another system may call it sex, represented as "M" or "F."

Different systems may use different units of measure. The sales amount might be in dollars in the U.S., and pounds in the U.K. The data must be transformed to a common measure in the warehouse.

In designing the transformation process, you map these different column names from the operational systems into the common name chosen in the warehouse. You transform it to a common encoding scheme, equating the values of sex, "0" and "1," in the operational system to "M" and "F" in the warehouse.

1.4.3   Transport

Once the data is transformed, it is ready to be loaded into the warehouse. Often the transformation area is on a separate machine from the warehouse, thus the data will need to be transported or moved to the machine the warehouse is located on.

If the transformed data is stored in a flat file, it may be transported using FTP, and then loaded using the SQL*Loader utility.

If the data has been transformed in an Oracle database, a new Oracle 8*i* feature, transportable tablespaces may be used to move a tablespace from one database to another.

Often up to 80 percent of the work in building a data warehouse is devoted to the extraction, transformation, and transport (ETT) process: locating, extracting, filtering, cleaning, transforming, and loading the data warehouse. Tools are available to help automate the extraction, transformation, transport, and load aspects of the process. Sometimes the steps in the process are done in different orders. We may extract, transport and then transform the data. We'll take a further look at the extraction and transformation process and tools in Chapter 4.

1.5   ACCESSING THE WAREHOUSE

1.5.1   Ad-hoc Query and Reporting

Many decisions require being able to look beyond the details of today's operations and take a broader view of the business. They often look at trends and correlations over time.

Types of queries include: In what month do we sell the most lava lamps? Are we spending more money on advertising than last year? When people buy lava lamps, do they also buy Titantic posters? Therefore, we are looking at how values have changed over time and what else also changed, and possibly discover connections.

In order to perform this type of analysis, data in the warehouse is retained for long periods of time, often five to ten years.

1.5.2   OLAP

On-line analytical processing, or OLAP, facilitates business analysis. It assumes queries will be posed iteratively, where the results of asking one question leads to asking many more questions.

OLAP was first defined by Dr. E.F. Codd, the father of relational databases. OLAP software is used to analyze business data in a top-down hierarchical fashion. Codd stated that relational databases were not originally intended to provide data synthesis analysis and consolidation, functions being defined as multi-dimensional analysis. Many enhancements in Oracle 8i facilitate OLAP queries.

It's not enough to know just the profit made this year; analysts also need to know profit over time of each product for each geographic region. This is a three-dimensional query—the dimensions are products, time, and geographic region.

Or an analyst may need to compare this month's sales to the same month last year for each store versus the newly opened e-commerce site. He discovers that the e-commerce site has gained a phenomenal 130 percent, whereas the retail outlets only gained on average seven percent. He may drill down to get more detail on individual stores to determine which ones are most profitable and which may have lost money.

Common OLAP functions include:

- Finding the top and bottom (five best and worst selling products)
- Period-to-period comparisons (sales compared to a year ago)
- Drilling down from aggregate data to examine more details
- What-if analysis
- Rotating and pivoting columns in a spreadsheet

In Chapter 6, we will take a look at using Oracle Express to perform multi-dimensional analysis.

1.5.3   Data Mining

Data mining is part of the knowledge discovery process. By using statistical techniques, vast quantities of data can be transformed into useful information. Data is like the raw material extracted from traditional mines: when turned into information, it is like a precious metal.

Data mining extracts new information from data. It allows businesses to extract previously unknown pieces of information from their warehouse and use that information to make important business decisions.

The discovery process typically starts with no predetermined idea of what the search will find. Large amounts of data are read, looking for similarities that can be grouped together to detect patterns and trends.

OLAP and DSS tools look at predefined relationships among the data. These are represented by constraints and dimensions. Data mining detects relationships that are not yet defined, such as which products are most likely to be purchased together, known as market-basket analysis. When analyzing data over time, it can be used to detect unexpected patterns in behavior. The likelihood of an activity being performed sometime after another activity can be determined.

Common applications for data mining include customer retention, fraud detection, and customer purchase patterns. Data can be mined looking for new market opportunities.

OLAP tools allow you to answer questions such as "Did sales of lava lamps increase in November compared to last year?" Data mining tools answer questions such as, "What factors determine the sales of lava lamps?"

With OLAP tools, analysts start with a question or hypothesis and query the warehouse to prove or disprove their theory. With data mining tools, the work is shifted from the analyst to the computer. Data mining tools use a variety of techniques to solve a number of different problems.

Market-basket analysis uses a technique called "association." Sets of data are studied to determine how they are associated with each other to determine purchase patterns. Which products are purchased at the same time? The output is expressed as a rule. You may discover that "50 percent of the customers who purchases diapers will also buy beer." Grocery stores have been doing this type of analysis for some time to determine shelf placement. Since customers often use lemons on fish, a basket of lemons is often placed near the fish counter.

Sequential discovery finds patterns between events that occur over time. This can be used to search for purchasing patterns that repeat themselves over time, such as, "A customer who buys a stereo system will be three times more likely to buy a VCR in the next three to six months."

A common use of mining tools today is for classification, which groups data together based on a set of similarities or membership within a class. A predictive model is generated based on historical data, which can then be applied to new cases. The model can be used to predict customer behavior, detect potentially fraudulent transactions, forecast profitability, and identify candidates for certain medical treatments. Is this new customer a good credit risk? What will his lifetime profitability be? What is the probability a patient has a certain disease?

Clustering is a technique that groups similar data sets together. It can be used to find customers with similar profiles. Households with incomes between $60,000 and $80,000 and two or more cars are more similar to each other than households with no children and incomes between 40,000 and $60,000.

One warning: Data mining tools find the correlation among the data. For instance, people who buy diapers also buy beer. They obviously don't tell you why they also buy beer—you still need to figure that out. For example, their kids drive them to drink. Thus, the tools still require a significant level of expertise from users.

1.6   MANAGING THE WAREHOUSE

As large data warehouses are growing to a terabyte or more in size, with 24x7 availability requirements, it is critical to maintain good performance for large numbers of geographically distributed users. Backup and recovery procedures must be established, and both the *data content* and the *usage or activity* in the warehouse must be managed.

The decision support workload is highly variable. In an OLTP system, an application is tuned to process many identical update transactions as quickly as possible. In a data warehouse, performance must be tuned to process as many variable queries as possible.

Usage patterns provide the foundation for tuning the warehouse for better performance. Who is using what data? What levels of summarization are they looking at? What data is not being used? Is the data structured in the most efficient manner, is it indexed on the correct columns? Can the summary tables be used for most queries? If many queries join data from one table with another, it might be beneficial to denormalize the data, prejoining it. Workload information helps determine where indexes should be added, where tables should be combined, and where summaries should be created.

At some point, it may no longer be necessary or practical to keep all the detail data on-line for immediate access. The data may be purged without keeping a copy. Or it can be archived, moved to some low-cost medium such as tape or CD-ROM, where it can later be retrieved if necessary.

1.7   SYSTEM ARCHITECTURE

Choosing a data warehouse architecture is an important decision. In this section, we will look at the components of the system and propose an architecture for your system.

1.7.1   Data Marts

Data warehouses contain detailed, generic, enterprise-wide data. Building a warehouse can be very complex and often takes anywhere from 18 months to three years to deploy. Because a warehouse contains many subject areas and crosses multiple organizations, it can also be highly political. Many of the same benefits of a warehouse could be scaled down to the departmental or line of business, solving a particular business problem.

Data warehouses contain multiple subjects that provide a corporate view across all lines of business. Data marts are subject-specific or application-specific data warehouses and contain data for only one line of business such as sales or marketing. The major difference between a data mart and a data warehouse is the scope of the information it contains. Because the scope of a data mart is much smaller, the data is obtained from fewer sources, and the typical time to implement it is shorter.

Data marts may be dependent or independent, based on the source of information. The source of information for a dependent data mart is an existing data warehouse. A data mart is considered independent when no enterprise data warehouse exists, and the data is extracted directly from the operational systems or external data sources.

Independent non-integrated data marts have many problems. Because independent data marts can be constructed very quickly, many companies have chosen this strategy. Unfortunately, after creating a few data marts, problems begin to arise. Each data mart is its own "island of information." There is nothing worse than two reports with different answers to the same question.

One of the reasons independent data marts can be deployed so quickly is that they postpone some of the critical decisions that later become apparent as the number of marts grows. Only the data needed by an individual department need to be identified and understood.

A complete understanding of all the corporate data is not necessary. Creating independent data marts avoids having to deal with corporate politics on such things as creating common naming and encoding strategies.

Other problems arise from the fact that the individual data marts are often built independently of one another by different autonomous teams. These teams will often select different hardware, software, and tools to use.

Each independent data mart gets its data directly from the operational system. If a company had five different data marts, each needing customer information, there would be five separate programs running to extract data from the customer table in the operational system. You probably don't have enough time in the batch window to run five extract programs today, and you certainly won't be able to run more extract programs in the future as you add more data marts.

Each does its own data cleansing and transformations, possibly each in a slightly different way. It is very easy for the data to become inconsistent. Redundant and inconsistent data leads to different answers, making it difficult to make decisions. Imagine trying to merge these different views at a later point into a common data warehouse.

1.7.2   The Staging Area

The problems of independent data marts can be avoided by the use of a staging area. The staging area provides a place to centralize integration and cleansing processes common to all the data marts.

Figure 1.3 Staging Area with Dependent Data Marts

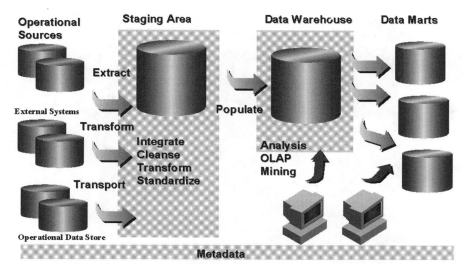

Data extracted from the source operational systems can be put in a temporary location to cleanse it, transform it, and prepare it for loading into the warehouse or the independent data marts. This temporary holding area is called the staging area. Often data arrives at the staging area from different operational systems at different times and in different formats. Some may be in flat files; some, in relational format.

You need to establish an architecture that allows for maximum reuse of data as it moves through its life cycle. Figure 1.3 shows an architecture with a staging area and dependent data marts. It is best to extract the data once from the operational systems, transform and cleanse them once, and load them into the warehouse. The data marts can be built as subsets of the data warehouse.

If you cannot afford to take the time to build a warehouse and want to start directly with data marts, an alternate architecture is illustrated in Figure 1.4. By building the data marts from a staging area, you are performing the data extraction and cleansing processes once for all the data marts.

Figure 1.4 Architecture with Integrated Data Marts

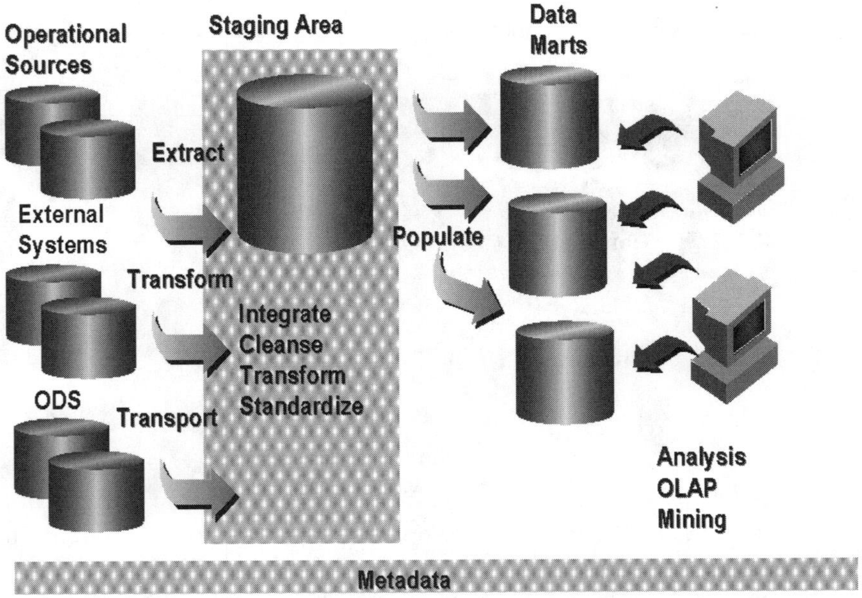

However, just because you are creating a data mart doesn't mean that all of your problems are over. Creating the data mart can involve solving the same problems as if you were building the data warehouse, except that they may be on a smaller scale. However, there is something to be said for gaining experience by building the data mart before progressing onto the full-size data warehouse, and it can also be used as a phased approach to building a centralized warehouse when only a subset of sources is involved. It can also be used as a way to move from independent data marts to a data warehouse.

1.7.3   The Operational Data Store

As discussed previously, there is a major distinction between the data in the operational systems and that in the warehouse. Operational data is about the current state of the company and is used to manage the daily operations. Data in the warehouse is informational, containing a historical record about the past.

If there is a need to provide information about the current state of the business to make tactical decisions to support day-to-day operations, an operational data store (ODS), may be built as part of the information management architecture.

An ODS contains subject-oriented, integrated data that has been validated and cleansed. It is used to support operational queries and reports. For example, customer service organizations need to access current account balances or billing information. The ODS is updated in near real-time, so that it reflects the current state in time. The ODS may serve as the source of data for the warehouse or data marts.

1.8 THE ROLE OF METADATA

Metadata is data that describes the other data and operations on that data. Metadata can be used for either technical or for business purposes. As data flows from the operational systems into the warehouse, they are extracted, transformed, and summarized. Technical metadata is needed to describe this process and is essential for proper "drill down" to finer levels of detail.

Business metadata allows end users to determine what data is available in the warehouse or data mart and how it can be accessed. Metadata provides the integration and uniformity of data across the corporation. It is the place where the different departments describe their use of the term "product."

Metadata is stored in a repository, which is typically a set of tables in an Oracle database. It can then be shared by any user or tool.

1.9 IMPLEMENTATION STRATEGY

Building a data warehouse is just like building software. You cannot do everything in one release, and you will never be able to anticipate all of the possible uses. It is much better to develop an overall architecture, build a framework with components that allows the warehouse to be built in phases. Limit the scope, and plan for enhancements every three to six months.

1.10 THE APPLICATION OF WEB TECHNOLOGY

With the Internet, new companies are starting up competing with established players in electronic commerce. They are able to move quickly, capturing market share from the existing companies via new retail channels. Who would want to fight the throngs of Christmas shoppers at the mall if you could shop from the comfort of your home via the Internet or even telephone?

Last year, one of the author's New Year's resolutions was to automate as many mundane tasks as possible, and top of the list was to start with on-line banking and grocery shopping. The author started to download the bank's application software, but didn't get too far, because she exceeded her available disk space. On-line grocery shopping didn't get very far either, because they don't deliver to many geographic areas yet. Fortunately, nine months later, the bank began offering Internet-style computing, where you don't need to buy disks to store their application. All that is required is an Internet browser and a modem to connect to their server. Therefore, both authors are now keen Internet bank users, one of the big advantages being that they can now access their bank accounts anywhere in the world, provided they have an Internet connection.

With Internet computing, all you need is a low-cost device with an Internet browser, such as Netscape Navigator, and a modem to connect to a server, where all the data and applications are stored. This is often referred to as a thin-client.

In Chapter 8, we'll show you how you can use your Oracle data warehouse with your Web site.

1.10.1   Publishing Warehouse Data on the Company Intranet

Information can be delivered to consumers through ad-hoc queries or scheduled reporting. In the past, information delivery has been mostly passive, i.e. nothing was delivered until the user requested it. Publish-and-subscribe technology provides a more proactive style of delivery. Today, when you subscribe to magazines and newspapers, they are delivered to you when they are published, daily or monthly, for example. Oracle Reports allows you to publish your reports to your subscribers through a Web browser.

1.10.2   Generating Web Content Directly from the Database

The first Web pages were static files that resided in a file in a directory somewhere on disk. The contents were generated using a hypertext markup language (HTML) editor or similar program and did not change. There are many problems with this, however. Whenever you add a new product to your on-line store, you need to create a new Web page describing it. Since it's already in your database in the product table, it would be so much better to query the database for all available products. Dynamic Web pages allow you to do this.

When a hypertext transfer protocol (HTTP) request is received by the Web server, it passes it through a common gateway interface (CGI) to a program that converts it to SQL, which is executed to retrieve the data from Oracle. The result set is formatted into HTML and returned to the Web browser. Thus Web content can be generated directly from the active database.

Using dynamic pages ensures that only the current version of the database is retrieved. Imagine running out of an item in your on-line store during the busy Christmas season? Rather than manually having to go delete the static Web page, by querying the database and determining that inventory is no longer available, you can dynamically stop offering that product.

1.10.3   Multimedia Data

The most popular multimedia applications today involve document management. It is also important for the preparation of marketing and sales materials and for training. Other applications include mapping and product data display. On the Internet, no one will purchase a product if they can't see what it looks like. Today, images can be stored in your product dimension.

By integrating spatial data into the warehouse, additional types of queries are possible. Spatial data is represented by points, lines, and polygons. Any given site, such as a store, can be represented by a point. A river might be represented by a set of points or lines, and a city could be represented by a polygon outlining its boundaries.

An address can provide information about its physical location. By geocoding the address, its latitude and longitude can be determined. This can roll up into streets, cities, zip codes, counties, states, and countries.

Many of the first customers buying over the Internet live a considerable distance from a shopping mall. They don't have a wide variety of stores to choose from. Using the locator function, you can find all of the customers who live more than 60 miles from a shopping mall. Target marketing campaigns can be tailored to these customers.

2 Designing a Warehouse

2.1 DESIGNING A WAREHOUSE

Readers of this chapter probably fall into one of three categories. They have either:

- Never designed a database before
- Designed a database for a transaction processing type system
- Built a data warehouse system

In the later case, the reader could skip this text or use it as a refresher, especially if his or her last database used Oracle. Therefore, this chapter is aimed at readers who fall into categories one or two, which may surprise the person who has previously designed a non-data warehouse database. Why? because the skills and techniques used to create a database for a data warehouse will be different than those required for a transaction-processing-style system. Consequently, you will have a head start, because some of the techniques are the same, however, it is very important to say to yourself, "I am designing a different type of database."

So what is different about designing a database in a data warehouse? In a transaction-processing system, the designer's goal is to make the transaction complete very, very quickly, and the designer also has the benefit of hopefully knowing how the business will interrogate and use the data. Contrast that with a data warehouse, where, although, queries must complete as quickly as possible, they could still take hours.

Another major problem is determining what information should be held in the warehouse and at what level of granularity it should be retained. This book will not discuss the techniques that can be used to determine what should be included in the warehouse and how to go about collecting that data, because there are already many books available that discuss this topic extensively.

However, the importance of trying to determine what should be included in the data warehouse cannot be stressed enough. It is so important because it may not be until a year after the warehouse is in production use that you suddenly discover that the information is either not available or held at an inappropriate level.

For example, a telephone company decides not to hold every call in its database, but instead holds a total of what the customer spent by day. Then someone in the company decides that they would like to offer customers a discount when certain numbers are called. Now if the warehouse had contained every single telephone call made by its customers, then it would be able to find out exactly what this scheme would have cost them if it had been implemented over the last 12 months. Instead, they have no data available and would either have to guess what the cost might be or postpone the planned new system until sufficient data is available to accurately determine the true cost to the company.

One of the difficult decisions for the designer is to determine at what level data will be stored in the warehouse. Often, storing every transaction, such as in our telephone example, may seem rather excessive, and, because it could easily mean the warehouse grows to terabytes, there is a temptation to consolidate the data. Managing a terabytes warehouse requires careful and stringently controlled procedures that must be followed. The bigger the database becomes, the harder it is to manage and query it. Therefore, there is a great temptation to consolidate the information.

Since consolidation is a major design decision, the designer would be wise to seek approval from the users of the warehouse before adopting such a strategy. It should also be clearly explained to these users the limitations that are likely to occur due to consolidating the data.

For instance, in our telephone example, we may decide to consolidate telephone calls by customer, but one of the user departments is interested in calls to specific telephone numbers such as toll-free. Therefore, the information they require is unavailable. With disks being so cheap, hopefully most sites will store all of the data that they require.

2.1.1   Entity Relationship (E-R) Modeling

The typical approach used to construct a transaction-processing system is to construct an entity-relationship (E-R) diagram of the business. It is then ultimately used as the basis for creating the physical database design because many of the entities in our model become tables in the database. If you have never designed a data warehouse before but are experienced in designing transaction-processing systems, then you will probably think that a data warehouse is no different than any other database and that you can use the same approach.

Unfortunately, that is not the case, and warehouse designers will quickly discover that the entity-relationship model is not really suitable for designing a data warehouse. Leading authorities on the subject such as Ralph Kimball advocate using the dimensional model, and the authors of this text have found this approach to be ideal for a data warehouse.

An entity-relationship diagram can show us, in considerable detail, the interaction between the numerous entities in our system, removing redundancy in the system whenever possible. The result is a very flat view of the enterprise, where hundreds of entities are described along with their relationships to other entities. While this approach is fine in the transaction-processing world, where we require this level of detail, it is far too complex for the data warehouse.

If you ask a Database Administrator (DBA) if she has an entity-relationship diagram, she will probably respond that she did once, when the system was first designed. Due to its size and the numerous changes that have occurred in the system during its lifetime, she hasn't updated the entity-relationship diagrams and it is now only partially accurate.

If we use a different approach for the data warehouse, one that results in a much simpler picture, then it should be very easy to keep it up to date and also to give it to end users, to help them understand the data warehouse.

Another factor to consider is that entity-relationship diagrams tend to result in a normalized database design, where, as in a data warehouse, a denormalized design is often used.

2.1.2   Dimensional Model

An alternative to using the entity-relationship model is the dimensional model, which is different from the entity-relationship model because it views data from a different perspective. Instead of considering an entity, which could be a thing such as a product or a place, and the relationships between those entities, a dimensional model describes data using *dimensions* and *facts*, which become actual tables in the database.

2.1.3   Fact Table

The *fact table,* of which there could be more than one, contains factual information. Fact data can usually be identified because it is often numeric and is a value that may be computed in some form. Some examples of fact data are *value of order* and *number of items* purchased.

The fact table is typically where all of the detail data that you want to keep in the data warehouse is stored, such as all of the telephone calls made by a customer or the orders placed with your customer. Therefore, if a customer made 20 telephone calls, then it is likely that 20 rows will be stored in the fact table for this customer. Consequently, the fact table will be by far the largest table in the database, possibly containing hundreds of millions of rows in a large data warehouse.

2.1.4   Dimension Table

The *dimension table* can be seen as a reference table to the fact table, where descriptions and more static information about a piece of data is held. For example, product is considered a dimension because, in this table, everything about the product is held, such as full product name, suppliers, and pallet size. In the fact table, there would be a column called "product_key," which is used to retrieve all of the product information from this dimension table.

If you are uncertain as to whether data is a dimension or a fact, ask this question. "Is the data static?" Typically, dimensions such as a product_id do not change frequently, whereas a fact table would contain the details of the products you had sold.

A fact table will contain millions of rows, where a dimension table could have only a few rows, e.g. the time dimension could have as few as 52 rows if data was stored weekly. Or a region dimension could contain only 15 rows, if the country had only 15 regions. Dimensions don't have to be small in size, because you could sell 50,000 products or have a customer dimension with five million rows. All of these are examples of valid dimensions.

It is hard to say how many dimensions your design will require, but typically there will be less than 20 dimensions and at least four. Therefore, our data warehouse will comprise only a few tables, but it will have huge storage demands because of the number of rows in the fact table.

2.1.5   Is Snowflaking Okay?

It is worth discussing for a moment whether a *snowflake* schema is acceptable. Snowflaking occurs when items in a dimension are moved into another table. This typically occurs when the designer wants to avoid repeating information within the dimension. For example, in a *product* dimension, there could be 25,000 products, but shelf life for that product can take only one of a few values. Therefore, a key is inserted into the product dimension shelf_key, for example, which points to another table called *shelf*, where all of the attributes of that shelf life are stored. Therefore, in the dimension, storage is needed only for the shelf key and not for all of the other attributes, as illustrated in Figure 2.1

Figure 2.1 Snowflaking the Schema

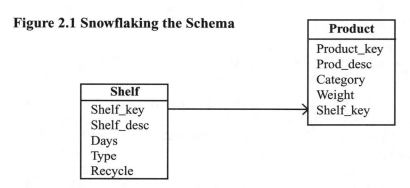

Experienced designers will recognize this as normalizing the design by removing this data into another table. Although this is acceptable, and Oracle 8*i* will accept denormalized dimensions, take care using this approach. One of the disadvantages is that it may impact performance because more joins will be needed in queries, which will take time, and you will not be able to take advantage of bitmapped indexes.

A bitmapped index is designed to index columns that take only a few values. Therefore, this technique allows you to create an index that enables you to identify very quickly which rows in the dimension match the value of interest.

An alternative approach you might like to consider is a *starflake* schema, where two copies of the data are maintained, one in star format and the other in snowflake format. Snowflaking the dimension is a good example of a technique used in transaction-processing systems, which is not always appropriate in the data warehouse.

2.1.6 The Easy Shopping Inc. Example

Throughout this text, we will use an example based on a fictitious company called Easy Shopping. It is a organization that has no retail outlets and sells via its Internet site or via satellite or Cable television. In Figure 2.2, we can see our dimensional model for Easy Shopping Inc.

In this example, we have a fact table called *Purchases*, where we record every item that our customers purchase. Four dimensions have been defined, where we hold customer, product, time, and details of our daily special offers. Although this may be a simple example for the purposes of this book, even the ones that you create will not be that much more complex than the one shown here. However, you will have more dimensions and many more columns in your fact table.

Warehouse schemas are sometimes called *star schemas,* and Figure 2.2 is an example of one. The center point is the fact table and the dimensions sit around the fact table as the points of our star.

As per our entity-relationship diagram, once you have drawn the dimensional model, it can easily be translated into a physical database design since each box represents a table. Although in the text we refer to fact and dimension tables, inside the Oracle database they are all tables and are treated as such. However, before you jump in and create the physical database from this dimensional model, there are a few more decisions to make before the design is complete.

Figure 2.2 Dimensional Model for Easy Shopping Inc.

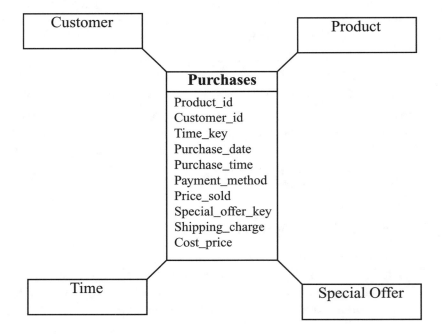

Hint: Readers familiar with Oracle 8*i* may be aware of a dimension object. This must not be confused with a dimension table, described here. Refer to Chapter 3 for an explanation of the Oracle 8*i* dimension object.

2.2   OTHER DESIGN CONSIDERATIONS

When you are constructing a data warehouse, it is easy to become focused on ensuring that queries are processed quickly. However, blindly following this approach could easily result in a database that is difficult to manage or use.

2.2.1   Design to Manage

It's no good building a warehouse that answers all questions in under a minute if the data inside it is at risk because the database cannot easily be backed up. Therefore, always identify the crucial management tasks and determine if they can be easily performed using this design when designing a database. We will discuss in more detail in Chapter 7 the management tasks for a data warehouse, but let us briefly review some of those tasks and see how they affect the design. Some of the important management tasks include:

- Backup
- Loading new data
- Aggregating new data
- Data maintenance activities such as indexing and archiving

All databases should be backed up regularly, and Oracle 8*i* has the *rman* utility, which allows on-line backups and incremental backups of the data that has changed. On the surface, backup may seem a trivial task, but backing up a terabyte warehouse takes time, even if it's an on-line backup. Therefore, the designer should carefully consider the tablespaces where the data is stored to make tablespace backups of read-only tablespaces, or use partitioning so that a full backup can be taken by running parallel backup tasks.

Full database backups are likely to be a luxury in very large warehouses; therefore, you should design the warehouse to allow incremental backups to be taken that contain only the changes to the warehouse data.

Due to the huge volumes of data in the warehouse, any operation that can be performed in parallel will significantly reduce the time required to complete the task, especially if there are many parallel processes running concurrently.

Most of the new data will have to be stored in the fact table; therefore, during the design phase, the designer should ascertain when and how much data is going to be loaded. Then calculate the anticipated load time, and if it cannot all be loaded in the available time, techniques such as partitioning the fact table so that the data could be loaded in parallel should be considered.

When the data warehouse is being tested by the design team, they should not concentrate only on performance testing, which will enable them to advise how long loads will take and discuss with the operations department how backups will be performed and how much time they'll need.

In Chapter 3, we will see how summary management, which was introduced in Oracle 8*i,* can be used to maintain aggregated data. One of the performance techniques widely used in the warehouse is to create summary tables of preaggregated data. Then a query references the summary data instead of having to read all of the detail data. Hence, the performance improvements can be enormous depending on the reduction in rows between the detail and the summary table.

Unfortunately, we get nothing in this world for free and summary tables have to be maintained. This can involve considerable I/O depending on how many new records are added and whether the summary is created completely from the beginning or if only new data is added. A wise designer will ensure that summary tables are placed in different tablespaces on different disks. Failure to do this will result in all I/O occurring on the same disk, thus slowing the refresh process considerably. This an even more important consideration if the refresh operations are to be performed in parallel.

2.2.2   Design for Performance

As we will see in Chapter 3, there are various techniques that can be employed by the designer to improve query performance. Some will involve how queries are constructed, but many are actually in the database design.

For example, all databases benefit from *indexes,* and a data warehouse is no exception. Therefore, do not forget to decide where and how much space is to be allocated for indexes. In a data warehouse, the designer does not have to worry about many users inserting new entries into the index and the associated problems that can result. Instead, the designer is now concerned with the time that is required to maintain or build an index. For instance, re-creating an index on a fact table with 100 million rows will take more than a few minutes to complete!

Oracle 8*i* offers different types of indexes, and the designer should select the one that is most appropriate, which could mean that the design will contain many *bitmapped indexes*.

Physical placement of the data is another important consideration, especially if it is used in conjunction with *partitioning* and parallel operations. If data is physically located on different disks, then queries or tasks can be performed that do not saturate the I/O limits on a specific disk drive.

One of the significant performance gains is when summary tables (material-ized views), which are described in Chapter 3, are used. Since they have to be created and maintained, once again space must be reserved for this data, and the improvement in query response time must be balanced against the time required to maintain this data.

New data for a warehouse often arrives in batches. Hopefully, it will be loaded into the database when it is not in use, but this cannot be guaranteed. There-fore, if during your investigations of the proposed system you discover that data will be loaded into the warehouse while it is in use, review the techniques such as partitioning that allow you to insert data into a different area to the one being used by the users.

2.3   IMPLEMENTING THE DESIGN

Once we are satisfied with the database design, it is time to physically create our database. Initially, one should create a small scale version of the database and test design ideas here before building the full-size production system.

There are various tools available to the designer to help create the warehouse, which will be discussed in other chapters. Here we will see how to create our database using nothing more sophisticated than SQL.

Database designers often prefer to create a script file containing the SQL commands to create the database, and this is perfectly acceptable. However, since the design is likely to contain only a few tables, then consideration should be given to using the Graphical User Interface (GUI) tools in Oracle Enter-prise Manager, which will be illustrated here.

Hint: If the SQL is complex, use these GUI tools to create the SQL, and then paste the SQL into your text file

---

In this section, we will walk through the various stages required to create our data warehouse. First we will see how to create the actual database, then learn how to create the tablespaces and data files where the actual data is stored. That will be followed by illustrations of how to create the tables and a brief introduction on creating the indexes and partitions. Finally, we will discuss summary creation and how to secure the objects in the data warehouse that we have just created.

2.3.1   Which Database?

The data warehouse should be created in its own database. Creating a new database is not a difficult job; it can either be done using an *init.ora* file and the SQL CREATE DATABASE command or via the GUI tool Oracle Database Configuration Assistant. If you have never created a database, then use the GUI tool to create the database, if it is available, selecting the *Custom* option. Once the database has been created, you can then add your own data files and tablespaces using the Schema Manager GUI or via SQL scripts.

Creating a database directly from SQL should be performed with care, because you need to run a number of script files that are required by Oracle 8*i*. If you use the GUI, this work is done automatically.

Using the Oracle Database Configuration Assistant, you can create, delete, or modify a database. You can also specify the type of database that you require, that is, On-line Transaction Processing (OLTP), Decision Support (a data warehouse), or a hybrid that supports both. Select *Decision Support,* because then the database parameters will automatically be set for a data warehouse environment.

Figure 2.3 Using Oracle Database Configuration Assistant

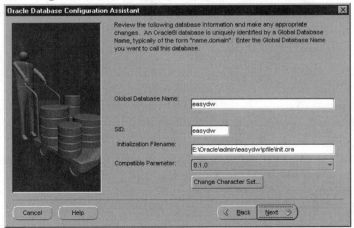

Figure 2.3 shows a sample screen from the GUI, the screen where you name the database. In our example, we have called the database EASYDW.

By specifying that a *custom* database is to be created means that you will be able to control the name and sizes of the default data files generated by this wizard, as illustrated in Figure 2.4.

There are actually five screens available in Figure 2.4, and it may be necessary to customize each one. Here you can specify:

- The size of each file
- Its location
- Its extent size

An *extent* is created for anything that is stored in the database. Therefore, all of data will reside inside a number of extents. When the first extent is full, another extent is created. If you click on the *Unlimited Button,* then you will be allowed to create as many extents as you like. If you are unsure of how many extents you require, then click this button so that you do not get an error telling you that you cannot create any more extents.

Figure 2.4 Customizing the Data files

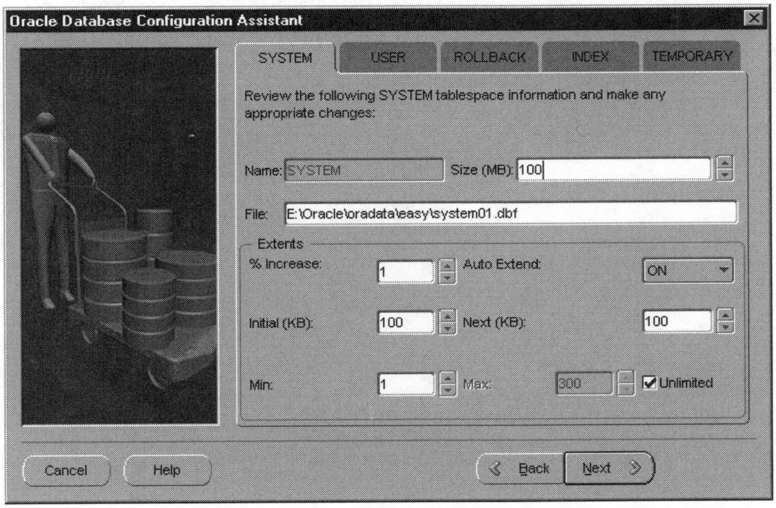

One of the values that has to be set in Figure 2.4 is the size of the area. Once again, it can be very difficult to correctly size a tablespace. If you select AUTO EXTEND to be ON, then the tablespace will automatically expand to occupy extra space on the disk once the initial allocation has be used.

It is a good idea to enable this feature because it will also help to prevent a load operation failing because of insufficient space inside the database. Of course, once the disk becomes full then neither of these options will help you, and you will have to add a data file to the tablespace.

Data is stored in an extent, but within the extent, the actual information is stored in blocks. You can control the size of the block using the screen shown in Figure 2.5. It is recommended that your data warehouse be created with a large block size, and, in Figure 2.5, we have used a value of 16,384 bytes, which means that we can store more data of the same type together, thus helping to reduce our I/O demands.

Figure 2.5 Specifying the Block Size

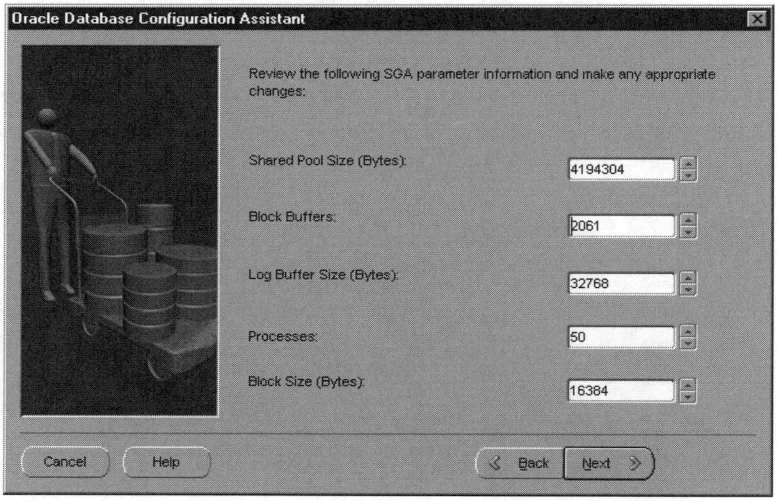

The GUI gives you the option of either creating the database now or running it later via a script that is generated. If you decide to create the database now, you can see how the creation of the database will progress in Figure 2.6.

It was mentioned earlier that, during database creation, a number of scripts are run against the database to provide certain functionality. You can considerably reduce the database creation time by selecting only the functionality that you require. For example, if you don't need JServer or the Time Series cartridge, then deselect it from the option list that is presented by this wizard.

Creating a database will take many minutes, so once it starts, take a short break, or do something else for a little while.

Figure 2.6 Database Creation Progress

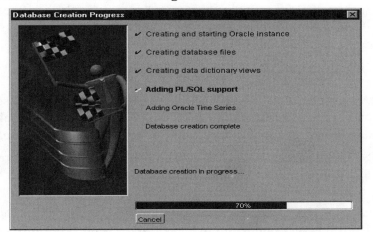

2.3.2   Naming Conventions

Before anything is created in the database, the naming conventions used for all database objects, such as data files, tablespaces, and table and column names should be reviewed. Depending on the tools available to your end users, they may actually see these table and column names. Therefore, if they do not have sensible names, these end users, who are generally not computer literate, could be very confused.

So far we have not discussed the topic of metadata, but in a data warehouse it is very important. There should be one definition of a data item, which in the ideal world would have only one set of values. For example, a region code is supposed to be a three alphanumeric code, and it is in all systems except one, where it is defined as a number.

These are some of the challenges for the team responsible for loading the data into the warehouse, and they will apply all the necessary conversions to the data to ensure that, when it is in the warehouse, all values are the same. But that doesn't help with the column name.

In our Easy Shopping Inc. example, there is a column in the fact table called time_key. Now, for people familiar with databases, it is obvious what that field contains, but to our end users of the warehouse, it means nothing. Therefore, in this instance, a better column name might be, date_time_of_purchase.

The warehouse designer should also avoid classic database shortcut names such as _CD for code, and always provide a more English-like column name if end users will see and use these names.

2.3.3   Which Schema

All objects defined in an Oracle database must reside inside a schema, a logical structure that describes a collection of objects. Therefore, before any tables are created, you should decide how many schemas you require.

Since a data warehouse will contain only a few tables, it is probably a good idea to keep them all in one schema. However, you may prefer to create multiple schemas by subject area.

Hint: It is very important to make this decision at the outset of the design, because the schema name plays an integral part in the naming convention used to retrieve information from the database.

A schema object is created every time a database user is defined. A user is created via the SQL CREATE USER statement or by using the GUI Security Manager which is part of Oracle Enterprise Manager. In Figure 2.9, we can see the window from the Security Manager that is used to create a user.

In our Easy Shopping example, we have decided to create a user called EASYDW. Here we can specify how the user will be authenticated, and we have selected the default mode of by password. This means a password must be specified and is used for all subsequent database access. If in the future this password needs to be changed, then it can be done from within the Security Manager or via SQL.

We must also select a default area where objects created by this user, such as tables and indexes, will reside. In a well-designed database, this is not an issue, because every object will explicitly state in which tablespace it must be stored.

There are a number of options that can be specified for a user, such as a profile of available resources and privileges. It is suggested that you refer to the Oracle documentation for detailed information on how to set these values.

Figure 2.7 Security Manager List of Users

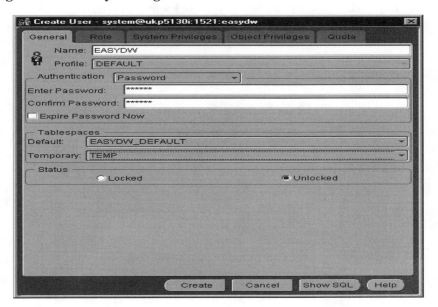

While it is not so important to set the resources that will be used, because the defaults may be satisfactory, you will have to define the privileges for the user; otherwise, they will not be able to retrieve data. As we progress through this book, you will be advised about which privileges are required when a topic is discussed, such as summary management.

When the user is created, a schema is automatically created with that user name. However, you will not be able to see the schema name until the first object, such as a table is defined for that user.

The schema name is very important because it is used to fully qualify an object in the database. For example, we could have a table called TIME in the EASYDW schema and also in our ORDERS schema. To advise the optimizer which table you wish to retrieve data from, you specify the table name as

```
schema name. table name
```

Therefore, to retrieve all the records in our time dimension, the fully qualified table name would be:

```
SELECT * FROM easydw.time;
```

When the Security Manager first starts, the standard navigation window is displayed in the left frame. If you click on *Users,* the right window will display a list of all of the users that have been defined in this database and the status of them, is illustrated in Figure 2.7.

Figure 2.8 Security Manager

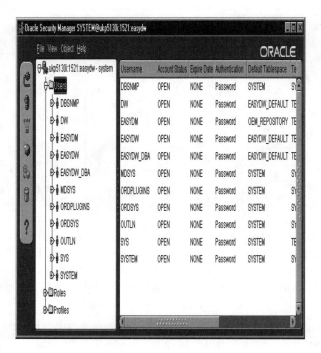

You can create as many users of the database as you require, but only one of them should be used for the purpose of creating metadata, such as tables and indexes. Therefore user EASYDW would be where all of the metadata would reside. The DBA could actually place it in that schema using the user name EASY_DBA which has the extensive privileges required to administer the database. Alternatively, the DBA could connect as EASYDW and create all the tables and indexes.

In the security section later in this chapter, we will discuss enabling privileges for a user.

2.3.4   Data Files and Tablespaces

Once the database has been created, you can now add your own *data files* and *tablespaces*. By default, you will find a number of data files; on a Windows NT system, they will be located in *\Oracle_home\Oradata\instance name* and will comprise two control files, index area, system space, rollback, and user area. It is inside these tablespaces where information is stored in the Oracle database, and a tablespace can have one or more data files. Therefore, the tablespace is the logical name that is used within the database schema to specify where information must reside. That information is actually stored in one or more data files, and part of the tablespace definition is their physical location and size.

In our Easy Shopping Inc. example, we have decided to implement the following tablespaces:

- *Dimensions*—for all dimension data
- *Default* area which users are assigned by default
- *Summary*—for the summaries we will create
- *Purchases_month_yea*r for our partitioned fact table
- *Indx* tablespace—for indexes
- *Temp* area—for temporary space

In this example, we will create only one data file per tablespace, but, of course you can create more if required. Also, the files shown here will be very small, and in the real world, they could be extremely large.

These tablespaces and their associated data files can be created either directly from SQL or by using the Schema Manager GUI tool, which is part of Oracle Enterprise Manager, illustrated here.

When you are managing a database, using tools like Schema Manager means that you no longer have to keep querying the metadata to find out the state and information on objects in your database, because the information is already available. In Figure 2.9, we can see the easydw database. The left window is known as the *navigation* window, where we select the information to be displayed in the right window. In Figure 2.9, we have selected tablespaces, so in the right window we can see a list of tablespaces, their size, and current state.

Figure 2.9 Schema Manager

If you to prefer to create your database directly from SQL, then you can use the SQL*Plus utility. If you are unsure of the SQL required to perform a task, you can click on the *Show SQL* button in most of the GUIs, and a window appears at the bottom of the display containing the SQL. In Figure 2.10, we can see the SQL to create the dimension tablespace.

To use the Storage Manager GUI, select the option *Create Tablespace,* and Figure 2.10 appears where you specify all of the attributes of this tablespace. The first step is to enter the name of the tablespace. It is wise to choose sensible names, because you will be using these constantly throughout the schema, and it helps if they mean something to you. For example, the tablespace called DIMENSIONS will be used to hold the dimension tables, where as the purchases made in January are held in a tablespace called PURCHASES_JAN99.

Figure 2.10 Schema Manager—Create a Tablespace

To specify the data file, click on the *Add* button, and a new window appears where you can specify the physical location of the file and its size. Take care, because the initial value is displayed in kilobytes you must change the size to megabytes, or you will get a very small file!

When defining the actual data file, click on the *Extents* tab shown in Figure 2.8, which will display the page where you can set the file to autoextend. Some designers do not like files that autoextend; however, many do, because it means that a task will not fail because there is no space left in the database. Instead, the database will automatically extend itself, and you may control how large those extents are. Of course, when the disk is full, autoextend will fail.

Hint: You need to know the actual path name because there is no browse capability.

2.3.5   Creating the Fact and Dimension Tables

Now that we have a database, and the tablespaces and users are defined, we are now ready to create the fact and dimension tables. The fact and dimension tables are created as if they are any ordinary tables inside the database. Therefore, all the options that one would specify on a table, such as the initial and subsequent extent size, may be specified. Although we call them "fact" and "dimension" tables, they are no different from all of the other tables in the database.

When defining the fact table, carefully select the column data types, because selecting one that occupies too much space—when your fact table contains hundreds of millions of rows—will mean a considerable waste of disk space.

For the moment, a dimension is defined as if it were any other table in the database. In Chapter 3, we will see how to define an actual dimension object, which will be based on the table that we created here. In fact, the dimension table created at this stage is a prerequisite for creating a dimension object.

The tables can be created using the SQL CREATE TABLE command, but we will see how to create tables quickly using the Schema Manager GUI, which is part of Oracle Enterprise Manager.

When Schema Manager is stated, if you select *Create Object* and *Table* from the drop-down list and then check the box for the wizard, the screen in Figure 2.11 is the first one to appear. In Figure 2.11, you specify the name of the table, the schema in which it will reside, and the tablespace for this table. Clicking on the *Next* button will display Figure 2.12, which is where you define the columns that are to appear in the table.

This is a really nice screen for quickly creating the table. All you have to do is enter the column name, select the data type and its size, and then press the *Insert* button, and the column appears in the list on the left of the window. Define each column using this approach, and don't click on the *Next* button until you have defined *all* of the columns in the table. Doing so helps you stay on this one screen to define every column in the table.

Figure 2.11 Schema Manager—Create a Table

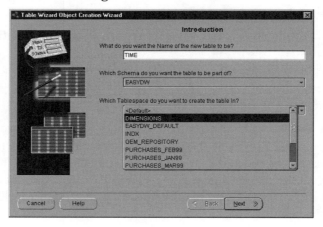

Figure 2.12 Schema Manager—Specifying the Columns in the Table

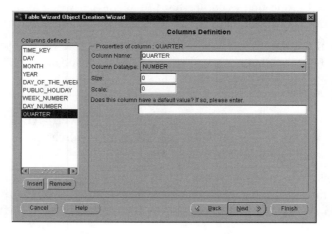

Hint: At the time of writing, this version of Schema Manager does not support partitioned tables. Therefore, initially create the table here and then manually partition it later.

If you do click on the *Next* button by mistake, you can return to this screen by clicking on the *Back* button. Once all of the columns in the table have been defined, the following screens will allow you to create the constraints.

2.3.6 Constraints

The job of the *constraint* is to ensure that all data conforms to its rules, such as, a value corresponds to a specified range of values via a CHECK constraint. If a *primary ke*y is defined, then this guarantees that the value is unique. A *foreign key* will ensure that all values correspond to one of the primary keys.

Mention constraints to a designer, and he will probably tell you that he does not want them in the database, because they are an overhead, especially when new data is being loaded. It is highly recommended that you implement at least primary and foreign key constraints, especially if you wish to use the Summary Management feature that is described in Chapter 3. One of the interesting aspects of Summary Management is the ability to rewrite a query to use a summary table. If you have defined constraints in your database, then it will be possible to do some complex forms of query rewrite.

In a data warehouse, there is often concern that, because the data can come from many sources, it may not be as "clean" as normal data, and, therefore, constraints may fail. Although this is a valid concern, clean data should always be stored in the warehouse to ensure that accurate results are returned.

Another argument put forward for not implementing constraints is that validating every record when it is first inserted into the database imposes a considerable burden on the load operation. Therefore, it takes considerably longer than via a standard load, and if the loading window is very small, then one way to reduce the time is to not have constraints.

In Oracle 8*i,* many of these concerns can be overcome thanks to some new options on the constraint:

- ENABLE NOVALIDATE
- DISABLE NOVALIDATE

If you are still concerned about the overhead of having constraints and worried that your data isn't clean enough to get past the constraint checks, you can use the ENABLE NOVALIDATE clause, which turns on a constraint, but it won't be checked. Therefore, enabling it is instant, but you should be aware that incorrect results could be returned if rows in the table have violated the constraint.

By using the ENABLE NOVALIDATE clause as illustrated below, we can turn on the constraint SYS_C001136 without having to validate all of the data.

```
SQL> ALTER TABLE todays_special_offers
  ENABLE NOVALIDATE CONSTRAINT SYS_C001136;
```

Therefore, if we know or want to assume that the data is clean, we can just turn on the constraint immediately without incurring any overhead. Using this approach, the database doesn't spend time validating the constraint against all the rows in the table, but it does mean that the designer had better be certain that the data is clean.

Likewise, before data is loaded, the constraints can be quickly disabled using the DISABLE clause as shown below.

```
SQL> ALTER TABLE todays_special_offers
    DISABLE CONSTRAINT SYS_C001136;
```

At the time of writing, Oracle Schema Manager does not support the ENABLE/DISABLE NOVALIDATE clause; therefore, you will have to enter this manually in SQL.

Hint: Every constraint in the database must be enabled or disabled manually.

There is an additional clause called RELY, which is required by the summary management feature. This clause tells the optimizer that you can rely on the accuracy of the constraint. An example of using the RELY clause is shown below on a constraint in the "todays_special_offers" table.

```
SQL> ALTER TABLE todays_special_offers
    MODIFY CONSTRAINT sys_c001137 RELY;
```

You can check the constraints that have been defined in your database using the Schema Manager. Then display the table of interest and click on the *Constraints* tab.

In Figure 2.13, we see how to create a primary key by clicking on the column in the key. Not every table will have a primary key, but some of the columns may require that they are *not null* or take a *unique* value.

Figure 2.13 Schema Manager—Specifying the Primary Key

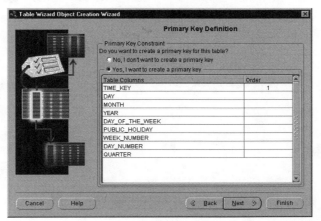

Clicking on the *Next* button in the *Create Table* wizard displays Figure 2.14. For each column in the table, click on whether it may be null or unique, and then click on the arrow button above the *Next* button to move back and forth between the columns.

Figure 2.14 Schema Manager—Null Constraint

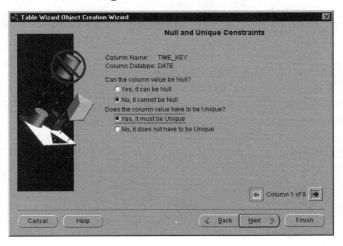

Clicking on the *Next* button again will display Figure 2.15, where you can specify check constraints. A check constraint enables you to guarantee the value that a column will take.

In our example in Figure 2.15, we have specified that the column PUBLIC_HOLIDAY may take only the values "Y" or "N." Therefore, before a value is stored in this database, a check is automatically made by the database system that the column takes one of thee values.

Figure 2.15 Schema Manager—Check Constraint

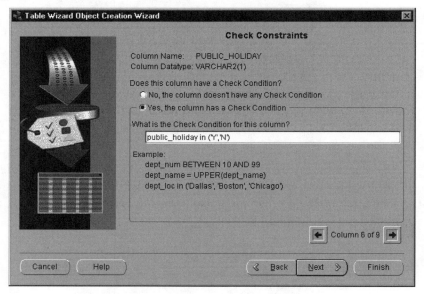

Name	Null?	Type
OWNER	NOT NULL	VARCHAR2(30)
CONSTRAINT_NAME	NOT NULL	VARCHAR2(30)
CONSTRAINT_TYPE		VARCHAR2(1)
TABLE_NAME	NOT NULL	VARCHAR2(30)
SEARCH_CONDITION		LONG
R_OWNER		VARCHAR2(30)
R_CONSTRAINT_NAME		VARCHAR2(30)
DELETE_RULE		VARCHAR2(9)
STATUS		VARCHAR2(8)
DEFERRABLE		VARCHAR2(14)
DEFERRED		VARCHAR2(9)
VALIDATED		VARCHAR2(13)

GENERATED	**VARCHAR2(14)**
BAD	**VARCHAR2(3)**
RELY	**VARCHAR2(4)**
LAST_CHANGE	**DATE**

Therefore, to see on which constraints you have used the RELY clause, use the query shown below.

```
SQL> SELECT constraint_name, rely FROM all_constraints
    WHERE OWNER = 'EASYDW';


CONSTRAINT_NAME                    RELY
------------------------------     ----
SYS_C001136
SYS_C001137                        RELY
```

Here we can see that the constraint SYS_C001137 has the RELY clause enabled, where as constraint SYS_C001136 does not. In Figure 2.16, we can see the constraints that have been defined on the table TODAYS_SPECIAL_OFFERS.

Figure 2.16 View the Constraints using Schema Manager

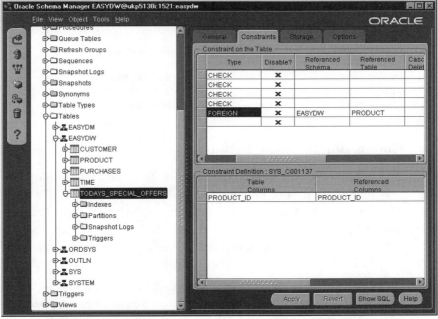

At the time of writing, you cannot see in Schema Manager whether the constraint has been enabled or disabled, but you can determine this information by querying the table ALL_CONSTRAINTS, the format of which is shown below.

Alternatively, if you wanted to see which constraints have been enabled or disabled, then use the following query.

```
SQL> DESCRIBE ALL_CONSTRAINTS

SQL> SELECT constraint_name, status FROM all_constraints
   WHERE OWNER = 'EASYDW';


CONSTRAINT_NAME                       STATUS
------------------------------        --------

SYS_C001134                           ENABLED
SYS_C001135                           ENABLED
SYS_C001136                           DISABLED
```

To see which constraints have been enabled using the NOVALIDATE clause, use the query shown below.

```
SQL> SELECT constraint_name, validated FROM all_constraints
 2   WHERE OWNER = 'EASYDW';


CONSTRAINT_NAME                      VALIDATED
------------------------------       -------------
SYS_C001134                          VALIDATED
SYS_C001135                          VALIDATED
SYS_C001136                          NOT VALIDATED
```

2.3.7   Completing the Table Definition

The definition of the table is almost complete. We have defined the columns and the constraints that are required, and we could press the *Finish* button, but that would mean that we would miss one of the very useful screens, which is shown in Figure 2.17. Here, we answer a few simple questions about how many rows are in the table and how it will change, and the wizard automatically calculates the storage options for this table.

By giving this information to the wizard, it will help determine the extent size and size of the area for the table. The extent size is important because it determines how many rows can fit in the extent. In a data warehouse, you want to have a large extent size so that you get many rows inside an extent, thus reducing the number of extents that are needed to store the data.

Figure 2.17 Schema Manager—Storage Requirements

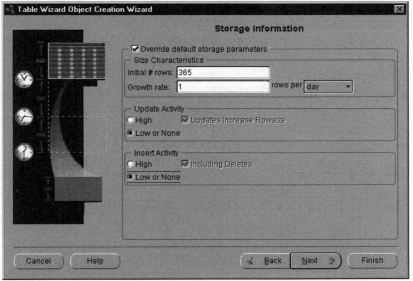

The final screen in the Create Table wizard is shown in Figure 2.18, where we can see a summary of every column in the table and the chosen options. If you are happy with the table definition, then press the *Finish* button; otherwise, press the *Back* key, and amend the entry accordingly.

When you click on the *Finish* button, the table is created, and you are now ready to create the next table. Hopefully, you will agree that this is a very easy way to create a table, and, since a data warehouse probably has a few tables, you may prefer to use this friendly approach as opposed to writing SQL commands, where you will probably make many syntax errors that you will have to correct.

2.3.8   Indexes

A data warehouse is likely to contain a number of indexes, and, just like any other database, the designer must choose the indexes that are most suitable. Oracle offers several different types of indexes, but the ones that will be of interest to the designer are:

- B*tree index
- Bitmapped index

Indexes should be selected carefully, and the various options and reasoning behind certain choices will be described in detail in Chapter 3. Please consult this section, because there you will learn whether to select a global or local index and how to partition it, if required.

Figure 2.18 Schema Manager—Reviewing the Table Definition

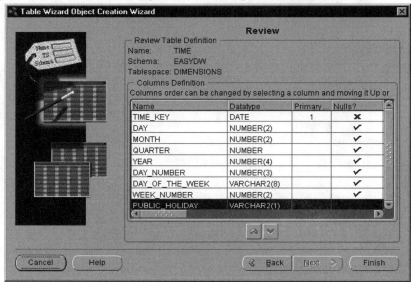

To set the scene for this section, bitmapped index is ideally suited to the data warehouse environment when you want to index a column that takes only a few values. For example, suppose we wanted to index the column PUBLIC_HOLIDAY, which has only two values "Y" or "N." A bitmapped index, which is described in more detail in Chapter 3, will store this information in an extremely compact fashion.

Although indexes can easily be dropped and created, due to the time required to create them, especially on a fact table with millions of rows, careful planning at the outset of the project will ensure that you won't have to spend a lot of time creating the index. An index can be created by using either the SQL CREATE INDEX command or the Schema Manager.

2.3.9   Partitioning

Partitioning data is a design technique that is very important in the warehouse because it provides a means of managing large amounts of data. Rather than place all of the data from a table in one tablespace, partitioning enables us to place the data in many tablespaces. To determine in which tablespace data is stored, a partition key is selected, as illustrated in Figure 2.19.

In this example, we are partitioning by month, so January's data goes in one partition, and February's in another, and so forth. You must select the partition key carefully, although a common one is by time. Therefore, you could partition data by month, then each month would reside in its own tablespace. This could then result in a manageable partition, and it all has the advantage that if you ever had to archive the data, it would be as simple as dropping a partition. Of course, don't forget to back up the partition before you drop it! This is a very quick process and doesn't invalidate any of the data that is already in the fact table.

Figure 2.19 Partitioning Data

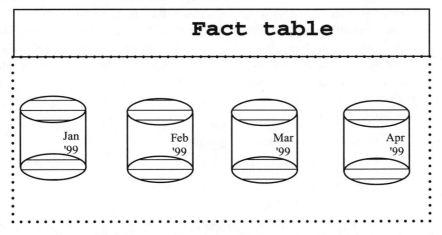

Oracle *8i* provides several different types of partitioning techniques, and, after reading the partitioning section in Chapter 3, you can pick the one that is most appropriate for your data warehouse.

2.3.10   Aggregates

We have already seen that a data warehouse or data mart can hold a huge number of records in the fact table. Even if we had the fastest machine in the world and could cache some of the data warehouse in memory, the time required to respond to queries could be days—and it would certainly be minutes or hours.

To overcome this problem, warehouse designers use the technique of creating summaries, a summary being a preaggregated table of results. For example, suppose you always query on the number of purchases of today's special offer by day. Rather than compute those results every time, a summary is created that contains the information that is required. Then whenever you make this query, instead of querying the fact table, you query the summary table instead.

Although it partially defeats the object of a warehouse where you make unknown queries to the database, it is fair to say that quite a few queries upon the warehouse are well-known. If we can improve the response time on those queries, then our users will be very grateful.

Oracle 8*i* includes a specific summary management component, which will enable you to create summary objects rather than ordinary tables then the optimizer will transparently rewrite your query to use the summary. This feature is described in detail in Chapter 3. At this stage of the design, if you can identify any queries that would lend themselves to being created as summaries, they should be recorded now for subsequent creation. Some examples of the summaries or aggregates that we might create for our easy Shopping Inc. examples are:

- Sum of sales by product by day
- Count of products sold by day
- Sum of sales by week
- Profit by product by day

The number of summaries you expect to create will determine how many tablespaces and data files should be defined for this data.

Hint: It's not necessary to create a summary for every possible combination, because we can use the dimensions and relationships to roll up the data.

2.3.11   Security

One should not forget that some data in the warehouse could be very sensitive, and, therefore, for a variety of reasons, you may not wish for all of your staff to have access to them. Oracle 8*i* provides various types of security, which prevents users from changing the objects inside the database and accessing data.

Object privileges

Object privileges can be placed on the following types of objects:

- Materialized views
- PL/SQL module
- Queues
- Sequences
- Synonyms
- Tables
- Types
- Views

You will most likely place security on tables, views, and materialized views by stating whether a user can select, insert, and update the data, along with a number of other options. If you decide to create a number of users, then always ensure that sufficient privileges have been allocated so that everyone can read the data. This can be achieved by using either the SQL statement, GRANT SELECT ON command, or the GRANT SELECT ANY TABLE command, or these privileges can be allocated directly to the user name using the Security Manager.

In Figure 2.20, we are giving the user EASYDW_DBA the rights to INSERT, SELECT, and UPDATE the CUSTOMER table in the EASYDW schema. Simply repeat this process for each user and the tables that they are allowed to access.

Figure 2.20 Using Object Security

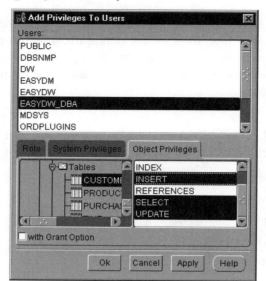

Role

Alternatively, you could create a *role*. Then you assign all of the privileges to the role, and then the role is assigned to the user. This is the preferred approach—especially if you create many users—because then you can create roles for the different job levels, and each user is granted one of those roles instead of assigning the privileges individually. By using the role approach, you reduce the likelihood of users accidentally being given access to data that they shouldn't have. It is also quicker if many users have to be defined.

In Figure 2.21, we see how to create a role using the Security Manager. Simply select *Create,* and then choose *Role* from the list. First, give your role a name, and click on the *Object Privileges* tab, and the screen shown in Figure 2.21 appears.

In this example, we first find the table, CUSTOMER, that access is to be granted to in the left window. Then in the right window, click on the privilege to be granted, and then click on the down arrow button to grant the privilege. Here we have selected four privileges, that this user is being given access to. When we have finished selecting all of the privileges, click on the *Apply* button to implement them.

Figure 2.21 Creating a Role

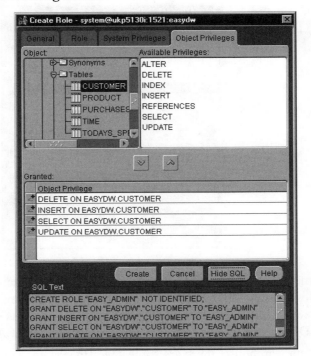

Alternatively, you could create the role by using the SQL CREATE ROLE statement, and in Figure 2.21 we can see that SQL needs to perform the equivalent operation to the Security Manager.

System Privileges

Most of the time will be spent creating roles and granting object privileges to users; however, some users will require system privileges. A system privilege is one that gives you the right to perform high level tasks such as creating or dropping a table. Since you will not want to grant this right to many users, you shouldn't have to spend too much time giving system privileges.

Figure 2.22 Granting System Privileges

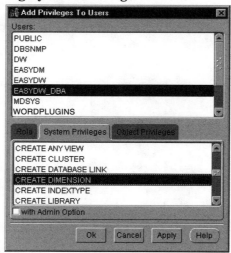

The method used to define a system privilege is the same as for an object privilege, except this time the system privileges is chosen. In Figure 2.22, we can see the screen for granting system privileges. In this example, the CREATE DIMENSION privilege is being given to the user EASYDW_DBA.

In a data warehouse, there are some specific system privileges that you may want to grant to specific users, such as CREATE DIMENSION and CREATE MATERIALIZED VIEW. In this instance, you would only be granting this privilege to users who would create dimensions and materialized views.

Later in this book, we will discuss the Summary Advisor, which will recommend which materialized views to create, drop, and retain. Unless you have the CREATE and DROP MATERIALIZED VIEW system privileges, you will not be able to perform these tasks. Therefore, depending on the users who run these tasks, you may, in a data warehouse, be granting specific warehouse system privileges to users that in a typical OLTP system would never be given those access rights.

2.3.12   Using the Parallel Option

Our database is almost complete, but there is one other important feature that is available in Oracle 8*i* that should be mentioned, and that is the *parallel* clause. A number of the statements shown here can be executed in parallel, and the use of this technique is very important in a data warehouse because it can significantly improve statement execution time. Parallel operations are available on table scans, sorts, joins, aggregates, and some table and index operations.

If you are using a symmetric multiprocessor or a massively parallel system, then serious consideration should be given to using the parallel clause. When specified, a statement, if eligible for parallel processing, will be decomposed into a number of parallel threads, and Oracle 8*i* will perform the job using parallel tasks and coordinate their running and the results. Therefore, all the user has to do is include the clause, and Oracle 8*i* does the rest.

The PARALLEL clause will expect you to specify the number of parallel processes to use. Choose this value carefully. Some testing may be required to determine the optimum value. For example, the following clause could be added to the CREATE TABLE statement for our purchases fact table:

```
PARALLEL (DEGREE 2)
```

This would mean that any operations on this table should be done using two server processes if they can be executed in parallel.

Data may also be loaded in parallel. The SQL*Loader facility, which we will discuss later, allows you to request parallel operations. Obviously, this can significantly improve the time required to store data; however, you should be aware of the possible fragmentation of your data that could occur. Therefore, it is suggested that, when data is being loaded in parallel, you specify the number of parallel operations to be equivalent to the number of data files available for that tablespace. Therefore, referring to our Easy Shopping Inc. example, if we decided to specify a value of

```
PARALLEL (DEGREE 3)
```

on our purchases table, then there should be three data files defined for every tablespace.

In each release of Oracle, you will see improvements to the commands and queries that support parallel operations; it is therefore worth verifying what is now available.

2.4 TESTING THE DESIGN

None of us would write an application and send it live without testing it first. But it is amazing how many database designs are constructed and then unleashed on unsuspecting users. Imagine the disaster and chaos that would result if airline companies never tested their planes extensively before passengers were allowed on board.

Your data warehouse is no different, especially as the business is relying on it for important information. Therefore, it is very important that all aspects of the design and processes are thoroughly tested prior to production release.

It is suggested that you initially load a small percentage of the data into the warehouse, and then test the following areas:

- Time required to load the data
- Data cleansing and transformation
- Query response times
- Summary data needs
- Time required for management tasks

If you are building a terabyte-size warehouse, then it is recommended that you repeat this process again with even more data in the warehouse, just in case there are any unexpected problems dealing with this volume of data.

Problems identified during testing are much easier to fix than trying to resolve them once the warehouse has gone live. A phased implementation to the user base is another way to test the warehouse if you don't want to wait until all of the testing is complete.

One very important point to remember is that, due to the size of the data warehouse, it will not only take much longer to load the data, but it is also unlikely that queries will complete quickly, either. Therefore, the entire testing process will take much longer than, say, a traditional OLTP database.

2.5   THE SCHEMA FOR EASY SHOPPING INC.

We have seen in this chapter how to create our database using the GUI tools, but many readers may prefer to create the database directly from SQL. The SQL to achieve this is shown below, but it assumes that the database has already been created.

The example shown here has been created for a Windows NT (NT) system, a simple edit of the file specs is all that is required for a different platform. Also note that the file sizes here are very small compared to what you would use in a production environment.

2.5.1   Setting Up the Environment

The first step is to connect to the database using a powerful user name. We have selected user *"system"* and then two rollback segments are created that are used for database recovery.

```
connect system/manager;
— create 2 rollback segments


CREATE public rollback segment r1
  tablespace rbs
  storage (initial 64k next 64k maxextents unlimited);


-- now place the rollback segment on-line
ALTER rollback segment r1 on-line;


CREATE public rollback segment r2
  tablespace rbs
  storage (initial 64k next 64k maxextents unlimited);


ALTER rollback segment r2 on-line;
```

2.5.2   Creating the Tablespaces and Data Files

The next step is to create the tablespaces where the data will reside and their associated data files.

```
— Create Tablespace for Undo Area
CREATE TABLESPACE undo
  datafile 'E:\ORACLE\ORADATA\EASYDW\easy_undo.f'
  size 8m reuse autoextend on default storage
  (initial 16k next 16k pctincrease 0 maxextents unlimited);


-- Temporary Tablespace
CREATE TABLESPACE temp
  datafile 'E:\ORACLE\ORADATA\EASYDW\easy_temp.f'
  size 10m reuse autoextend on default storage
  (initial 16k next 16k maxextents unlimited pctincrease 0)
   temporary;


-- Tablespace to store Summary data
CREATE TABLESPACE summary
  datafile 'E:\ORACLE\ORADATA\EASYDW\easy_summ.f'
  size 6m reuse autoextend on default storage
  (initial 16k next 16k pctincrease 0 maxextents unlimited);
```

```
-- Tablespace for DIMENSIONS
CREATE TABLESPACE dimensions
 datafile 'E:\EASYDW\DIMENSIONS.D' size 5m
 reuse autoextend on default storage
 (initial 16k next 16k pctincrease 0 maxextents unlimited);

-- Tablespace for the INDEXES
CREATE TABLESPACE indx
 datafile 'E:\ORACLE\ORADATA\EASYDW\indx.f'
 size 5m reuse autoextend on default storage
 (initial 16k next 16k pctincrease 0 maxextents unlimited);

-- Default Tablespace
CREATE TABLESPACE easydw_default
 datafile 'E:\ORACLE\ORADATA\EASYDW\easydw_default.f'
 size 5m reuse autoextend on default storage
 (initial 16k next 16k pctincrease 0 maxextents unlimited);
```

Once the tablespaces have been created for the dimensions, we can now create the tablespaces for the fact table, "purchases." Since we will be partitioning the data, we must now create the tablespace for each partition. There will be one partition per month for the data and another partition for the indexes. Here we will create only the January partition for the data and index; simply repeat this process for the other partitions.

```
-- create the 3 month tablespaces for the fact partitions
CREATE TABLESPACE purchases_jan99
 datafile 'E:\EASYDW\PURCHASESJAN99.f' size 5m
 reuse autoextend on default storage
 (initial 16k next 16k pctincrease 0 maxextents unlimited);

-- create the 3 month tablespaces for the fact indexes
CREATE TABLESPACE purchases_jan99_idx
 datafile 'E:\EASYDW\PURCHASESJAN99_IDX.f' size 3M
 reuse autoextend on default storage
 (initial 16k next 16k pctincrease 0 maxextents unlimited);
```

2.5.3 Creating the Tables, Constraints, and Indexes

Once the tablespaces have been defined, the EASYDW user can be created, which will create that schema where the data will be stored.

```
-- create a user called EASYDW
--  this will be the schema where the objects will reside

connect system/manager;
```

```
CREATE USER easydw identified by easydw
 default tablespace easydw_default
 temporary tablespace temp
 profile default account unlock;

GRANT unlimited tablespace to easydw ;
GRANT dba to easydw ;
```

The DBA privilege has been granted to the user so they can create and manage the tables and indexes.

Hint: Don't forget to connect as user EASYDW before creating the tables and indexes, or the tables and indexes will be defined in the wrong schema.

```
— now create the database
CONNECT easydw/easydw;

— CUSTOMER Dimension
CREATE TABLE easydw.customer
(customer_id                  varchar2(10),
 town                         varchar2(10),
 county                       varchar2(10),
 postal_code                  varchar2(10),
 dob                          date,
 country                      varchar2(20),
 occupation                   varchar2(10))
pctfree 0 pctused 99 tablespace dimensions
storage (initial 16k next 16k pctincrease 0) ;

CREATE INDEX easydw.customer_pk_index ON customer
 (customer_id)
 pctfree 5
 tablespace indx
 storage (initial 16k next 16k pctincrease 0) ;
ALTER TABLE customer
 ADD CONSTRAINT pk_customer PRIMARY KEY (customer_id);
```

We have defined the constraint here by adding it later. It could also be created within the CREATE TABLE definition, but if this approach is used, then you cannot control the name of the index it creates by default to ensure fast validation of the primary key. Therefore, we create the index first, and when the constraint is defined, it will use this index rather than create its own.

```
— PRODUCT Dimension
CREATE TABLE easydw.product
(product_id                        varchar2(8),
 product_name                      varchar2(30),
 category                          varchar2(4),
 cost_price                        number (6,2)
   constraint cost_price_not_null NOT NULL,
 sell_price                        number (6,2)
   constraint sell_price_not_null NOT NULL,
 weight                            number (6,2),
 shipping_charge                   number (5,2)
   constraint shipping_charge_not_null NOT NULL,
 manufacturer                      varchar2(20),
 supplier                          varchar2(10))
 pctfree 0 pctused 99
tablespace dimensions
storage (initial 16k next 16k pctincrease 0) ;


CREATE INDEX easydw.product_pk_index ON customer
 (product _id)
 pctfree 5 tablespace indx
 storage (initial 16k next 16k pctincrease 0) ;


ALTER TABLE product
 ADD CONSTRAINT pk_product PRIMARY KEY (product_id);
```

Next the TIME table is created. In this table, we have included a CHECK
constraint to ensure that the column "public_holiday" can take only the
values "Y" or "N."

```
— TIME Dimension
CREATE TABLE easydw.time
(time_key                          date,
 day                               number (2,0),
 month                             number (2,0),
 quarter                           number (2,0),
 year                              number (4,0),
 day_number                        number (3,0),
 day_of_the_week                   varchar2(8),
 week_number                       number (2,0),
 public_holiday                    varchar2(1)
   constraint public_holiday
   CHECK (public_holiday IN ('Y','N'))  )
pctfree 0 pctused 99
tablespace dimensions
storage (initial 16k next 16k pctincrease 0) ;
```

```
CREATE INDEX easydw.time_pk_index ON time
 (time_key)
 pctfree 5 tablespace indx
 storage (initial 16k next 16k pctincrease 0) ;


ALTER TABLE time
 ADD CONSTRAINT pk_time PRIMARY KEY (time_key);


— TODAYS_SPECIAL_OFFERS Dimension

CREATE TABLE easydw.todays_special_offers
(product_id                         varchar2(8),
 offer_date                         date,
 special_price                      number (6,2),
 offer_price                        number (6,2))
pctfree 0 pctused 99
tablespace dimensions
storage (initial 16k next 16k pctincrease 0) ;


CREATE INDEX easydw.tso_pk_index ON todays_special_offers
 (offer_date, product_id)
 pctfree 5 tablespace indx
 storage (initial 16k next 16k pctincrease 0) ;
```

For the TODAYS_SPECIAL_OFFERS table, we have defined the primary key to include two columns rather than a single column.

```
ALTER TABLE todays_special_offers
 ADD CONSTRAINT pk_specials PRIMARY KEY
        (offer_date,product_id );
```

Now we come to creating the all-important fact table, which is called PURCHASES. This table definition is quite complex because it includes FOREIGN KEYS to several tables that are identified by the REFERENCES clause. For the column product_id, two constraints have been defined on the table, a NOT NULL and a FOREIGN KEY constraint. Provided each constraint is given a unique name, then is allowed on a column in a table.

Here we have also illustrated how to partition the table, which will be discussed in detail in Chapter 3.

```
— Fact Table PURCHASES
CREATE TABLE easydw.purchases
(product_id                                 varchar2(8)
 constraint not_null_product_id   NOT NULL
```

```
     constraint fk_product_id REFERENCES product(product_id),
     time_key                                      date
     constraint not_null_time  NOT NULL
     constraint fk_time REFERENCES time(time_key),
     customer_id                              varchar2(10)
     constraint not_null_customer_id  NOT NULL
     constraint fk_customer_id REFERENCES
            customer(customer_id),
   purchase_date                           date,
   purchase_time                           number(4,0),
   purchase_price                      number(6,2),
   shipping_charge                       number(5,2),
   today_special_offer               varchar2(1)
    constraint special_offer
    CHECK (today_special_offer IN ('Y','N'))   )
PARTITION by RANGE (time_key )
 (
  parition purchases_jan99
  values less than (TO_DATE('31-01-1999', 'DD-MM-YYYY'))
   pctfree 0 pctused 99
   storage (initial 64k next 16k pctincrease 0)
   tablespace purchases_jan99 ,
  partition purchases_feb99
   values less than (TO_DATE('28-02-1999', 'DD-MM-YYYY'))
   pctfree 0 pctused 99
   storage (initial 64k next 16k pctincrease 0)
   tablespace purchases_feb99 ,

  partition purchases_mar99
   values less than (TO_DATE('31-03-1999', 'DD-MM-YYYY'))
   pctfree 0 pctused 99
   storage (initial 64k next 16k pctincrease 0)
   tablespace purchases_mar99 );
```

In this example, we have created the indexes immediately after the table definition. In a real data warehouse, the number of indexes created prior to loading the data is kept to an absolute minimum to ensure that the loading time is as fast as possible. Therefore, indexes exist usually only to check constraints.

```
— Now create the indexes

— Partition on the Time Key  Local prefixed index
CREATE BITMAP INDEX easydw.purchase_time_index
  ON purchases  (time_key )
local
 (partition indexJan99 tablespace purchases_jan99_idx,
 partition indexFeb99 tablespace purchases_feb99_idx,
 partition indexMar99 tablespace purchases_mar99 );
```

```
CREATE BITMAP INDEX easydw.purchase_product_index
  ON purchases (product_id )
 local
 pctfree 5  tablespace indx
 storage (initial 64k next 64k pctincrease 0) ;

CREATE INDEX easydw.purchase_customer_index
  ON purchases (customer_id )
 local
 pctfree 5  tablespace indx
 storage (initial 64k next 64k pctincrease 0) ;

CREATE BITMAP INDEX easydw.purchase_special_index
  ON purchases (today_special_offer )
 local
 pctfree 5  tablespace indx
 storage (initial 64k next 64k pctincrease 0) ;
```

2.5.4   Defining Security

The next step is to grant some privileges to our user, EASYDW. We will start with the following ones, which will allow us to use summary management, and, as we progress through this book, we will discuss other privileges that should be granted to users.

```
connect system/manager;


— Add privileges
GRANT select any table to easydw;
GRANT execute any procedure to easydw;


— Add privileges for summary management
GRANT create any dimension to easydw;
GRANT alter any dimension to easydw;
GRANT drop  any dimension to easydw;
GRANT create any materialized view to easydw;
GRANT alter any materialized view to easydw;
GRANT drop  any materialized view to easydw;
GRANT query rewrite to easydw;
GRANT global query rewrite to easydw;
```

You will have to repeat these steps for every user that has been created and the privileges granted will, of course, vary by user.

2.5.5   **Final Steps**

The final step is actually not completed now, but after the data is loaded. However, it is included here to remind you not to forget this important step, which is to analyze the table and indexes.

The purpose of the ANALYZE command is to gather statistics that are used by the optimizer. Without these statistics, features like Summary Management will be unavailable. The ANALYZE command will be explained further in Chapter 7.

```
— Now Analyze the Tables and Indexes
ANALYZE TABLE customer COMPUTE STATISTICS;
ANALYZE TABLE todays_special_offer COMPUTE STATISTICS;
ANALYZE TABLE product COMPUTE STATISTICS;
ANALYZE TABLE time COMPUTE STATISTICS;
ANALYZE TABLE purchases COMPUTE STATISTICS;

ANALYZE INDEX purchase_customer_index COMPUTE STATISTICS;
```

Our database is now complete. We have a basic framework, and now we will learn in the next chapter how to enhance our basic database design to include and use the sophisticated features that are available in Oracle 8*i*.

3 Data Warehouse Features

3.1 OPTIMIZATIONS FOR DATA WAREHOUSING

As data warehouses continue to grow in size, it's not uncommon to find a fact table that is very large—between 25 and 100 gigabytes in size. Management of very large tables in very large databases in a highly available 24 x 7 environment requires the ability to work on parts of the table or database at a time without impacting other parts of the database. The ability to load new data, reorganize data, back up, and recover after failures on pieces of the database is critical. A good physical database design is essential to the success of the warehouse. Ensuring good response times for user queries requires careful selection of indexes and creation of summaries.

Performance optimizations for OLTP systems are well-understood, and the majority of relational database management systems use similar techniques for achieving good performance. It has just been in the past few years that database vendors have added functionality to improve performance of decision support and data warehousing.

In this chapter, we'll look at several features in Oracle 8*i* specifically designed to improve performance and manageability for the data warehouse.

3.2 INDEXING

Improving performance for query processing is key to an efficiently run data warehouse. One of the techniques to achieve this goal is to create indexes on many columns and combinations of columns. If a user was looking for the location of all stores in the Northeast region, an index built on the column "region," could be used to locate just those rows in the Northeast rather than reading every row in the table.

As a rule, update activity, other than for loading new data, is minimal, so a warehouse will have many more indexes than an OLTP system. However, you want to try to keep indexing on the fact table to a minimum. The space in a warehouse needed for indexes is often significantly larger than the space needed to store the data. As a rule of thumb, try to aim for indexes on the fact table occupying about 50 percent of the space used by the fact table and 100 percent more space for indexing the dimension tables.

Deciding which indexes to create is an important part of the physical design. Indexes should be built on columns that are often part of the *selection criteria* of a query. Columns that are frequently referenced in the SQL WHERE clause are good candidates for indexing. In the SQL statement below, "region" would be a potential column to index.

```
SELECT store, location FROM stores WHERE region = 'Northeast';
```

The index is built on one or more columns, called *keys*. For each key value, the index contains a pointer, in the form of a rowid, to the location of the rows with that key value.

Whenever a row is inserted, deleted, or the value of the key column changes, the index is automatically maintained. For example, if a new row is inserted, the index is automatically updated to point to the new row. Oracle has two types of indexes: b*trees and bitmaps.

3.2.1   B*Tree Indexes

B*tree indexes are hierarchical structures that allow rapid searching in order to obtain the address of a row in a table with a particular value. There are two varieties of b*tree indexes:

- Unique
- Non-unique

A *unique index* ensures that each row has a distinct value for its key. No duplicates are allowed. A unique index is automatically created when a PRIMARY KEY or UNIQUE constraint is enabled on a table.

B*tree indexes may also be non-unique. Non-unique indexes improve query performance when a small number of rows are selected.

When multiple columns are used together in the WHERE clause, you can build an index on that group of columns. Indexes made up of multiple columns are called *composite*, *multi-key*, or *concatenated* indexes. For example, city and state are both needed to differentiate Portland, Maine, from Portland, Oregon. The column that is used most frequently by itself should be specified as the first column in the index. In the example, *state* should be the leading column, since we can anticipate queries on *state* alone or *city* and *state* used together.

Hint: Create a multi-key b*tree index composed of all keys in the fact table that correspond to the primary key of each dimension table.

Whenever a row is inserted, deleted, or the value of the key column changes, the index is automatically maintained. If a new row is inserted, the index is automatically updated to point to the new row. There is typically one I/O required to retrieve each level of an index. As new index nodes are created, the b*tree is automatically rebalanced to ensure equivalent search times using any branch of the index. When loading a large number of rows, it is sometimes faster to drop the index, load the table, and then re-create the index.

Building a b*tree index on a column that has only a few distinct values provides little if any performance benefit. Since there are only two possible values for the column "sex," finding all the males may result in reading all the data blocks, since multiple records are typically stored in one block. A full table scan may be more efficient. This is where bitmap indexes are useful.

3.2.2   Bitmap Indexes

Bitmap indexes were designed to improve query performance in the data warehouse and help with queries such as, "How many women who live in California buy tents?"

They improve performance for tables when there are a large number of rows, with a small number of distinct values for any particular column. This type of column is called a column with low cardinality. A bitmap is built for each distinct value in a column. Each bitmap contains a single bit to represent each row in the table. This bit indicates the presence or absence of that row in the set. Figure 3.1 shows a bitmap index for the "sex" column. Two bitmaps are created, one for the males and one for the females. In the male bitmap, all rows with male customers would have their bit set to "1." All female customers would have their bit set to "0."

Figure 3.1 Sex Bitmap Index

Row	Sex	Male Bitmap	Female Bitmap
1	M	1	0
2	F	0	1
3	M	1	0
4	M	1	0
5	M	1	0
6	F	0	1
7	M	1	0
8	M	1	0
9	F	0	1
10	M	1	0

If a query refers to only one bitmapped index column in the WHERE clause, the optimizer may decide it is more efficient to use a full table scan. The major performance improvements of bitmapped indexes are seen when multiple columns with bitmapped indexes are specified in the WHERE clause.

To answer queries such as, "How many women bought a tent?", multiple bitmaps can be efficiently combined using "and" and "or" set operators. Given the sex bitmap defined in Figure 3.1 and the product bitmap defined in Figure 3.2, the bitmaps can be combined together to quickly determine the answer.

When new rows are added to a table the existing bitmaps don't change; the values of the newly added rows are appended to the end of the existing bitmap.

Hint: Create a bitmap index for each foreign key column in the fact table. This is useful for star query join processing.

3.3   DATA PARTITIONING

Whenever any task seems daunting, breaking it up into smaller tasks often makes it easier to accomplish. Imagine packing your house, and getting ready to move. Dividing it up room by room, makes it easier. If each member of the family packs a room at the same time, you can get the entire house packed faster. This is the idea behind partitioning and parallelism. Very large tables and indexes can be *partitioned* into smaller, more manageable partitions. If you have a multi-processor system, each part can be worked on in parallel.

Figure 3.2   Product Bitmap Index

Row	Product	Tent Bitmap	Camera Bitmap	Stove Bitmap	Book Bitmap
1	Tent	1	0	0	0
2	Camera	0	1	0	0
3	Tent	1	0	0	0
4	Tent	1	0	0	0
5	Tent	1	0	0	0
6	Tent	1	0	0	0
7	Camera	0	1	0	0
8	Book	0	0	0	1
9	Camera	0	1	0	0
10	Stove	0	0	1	0

To determine "How many females bought a tent?" the two bitmaps can be quickly "and"ed or "or"ed together, as shown below in Figure 3.3.

Figure 3.3   Using Bitmaps—'How many females bought a tent?'

Row	Female Bitmap		Tent Bitmap	Result	
1	0		1	0	
2	1		0	0	
3	0		1	0	
4	0	AND	1	0	
5	0		1	0	
6	1		1	1	*One female bought a tent!
7	0		0	0	
8	0		0	0	
9	1		0	0	
10	0		0	0	

Bitmap indexes are compressed and, therefore, require less storage space than an equivalent b*tree; however, maintenance of a bitmap index after inserting, updating, or deleting rows is more costly than a B*tree index because it requires uncompressing and recompresssing the bitmaps as data rows are modified. If a large number of rows need to be modified, it may be faster to drop the index before performing table maintenance and then rebuild it.

It is assumed data will be bulk loaded into the warehouse and that individual rows will be updated only on rare occasions, maintaining a bitmap index after a bulk load via direct path load is optimized. When new rows are added to a table, the existing bitmaps don't change. The values of the newly added rows are appended to the end of the existng bitmap.

An example of creating a bitmap index is shown below for our Easy Shopping example, where one is created on the purchases table on product_id.

```
CREATE BITMAP INDEX easydw.purchase_product_index
    ON purchases (product_id )
  local
  pctfree 5    tablespace indx
  storage (initial 64k next 64k pctincrease 0) ;
```

Alternatively, you can create a bitmap index in Schema Manager, as shown in Figure 3.4, where an index is being built on the customer_id column from the purchases table. In order to create a bitmap index rather than a b*tree, check the bitmap box. You can also add storage parameters and see the SQL generated for the index creation.

Figure 3.4   Creating a Bitmap Index

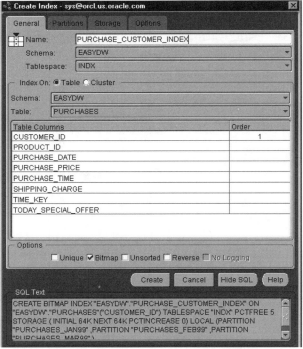

3.3.1   Data Partitioning

Partitioning the data makes it possible for data management operations to be performed in parallel at the partition level. Many operations, such as loading data, building indexes, enforcing constraints, gathering optimizer statistics, purging data, and backup and recovery can be done at the granularity of a partition. Reorganization tasks, such as moving partitions and splitting partitions, can be performed on one partition at a time.

Partitions are also useful in the data warehouse to improve the performance of user's queries. When the data is partitioned by a range of values, as explained below, the optimizer knows which partition to look in for any given query, and doesn't bother searching any partitions outside that range. *Partition elimination*, is used to avoid searching the entire table. If the warehouse was partitioned by month, and a query asked for sales from December 1998, the optimizer would know which partition the data was stored in, and would eliminate partitions containing other months from its search.

It is important to partition the data by a column that does not change, such as the purchase date. If partitioning was done by product_id and the business changed its product encoding scheme, updating the partitioning column would require moving data to a different partition.

In data warehouses, it is common to partition by time, as we have done in the example above. This allows us to perform "rolling window operations." If our warehouse contained one year's worth of data, at the end of April 1999, we could add a new partition with that month's data, and delete April 1998's data. In Chapter 4 we will look at loading data into a new partition.

Partitioning improves the availability of the data warehouse. By placing each partition on its own disk, if one disk fails and is no longer accessible, only the data in that partition is unavailable, not the entire table. Maintenance operations can be performed on one partition, while users continue to access data from the other partitions in the table, improving the overall availability of the warehouse.

Each partition should be stored in a separate tablespace, this could also include the subpartitions, and each tablespace should be stored on one or more separate storage devices. On larger systems, the I/O should also be spread across different controllers and channels. By spreading the data across several different physical devices, you balance the I/O and improve query performance, availability, and manageability.

There are three ways to partition your data:

- by *range*
- via a *hash* function
- composite

It is imperative that, irrespective of the partitioning strategy chosen, you do not select a column that is volatile because then you would have to move the data from one partition to another. This is can be an extremely time consuming exercise.

Range Partitioning

Range partitioning allows you to define non-overlapping ranges of data. Each row is placed in the appropriate partition based on the value of a particular column, called the *partition key*.

In the EASYDW warehouse, each month's purchases are stored in their own partition. The easydw.purchases fact table shown below is partitioned by range, using the time_key as the partition key. Each partition is stored in its own tablespace,which are spread across multiple devices as illustrated in Figure 3.5, and here is the SQL that would create this partitioned table.

Figure 3.5 Range Partitioning

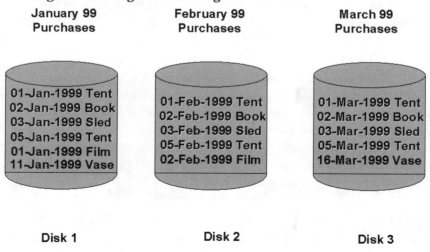

```
CREATE TABLE easydw.purchases
(product_id                      varchar2(8)
 constraint not_null_product_id NOT NULL
 constraint fk_product_id REFERENCES product(product_id),
 time_key                        date
 constraint not_null_time NOT NULL
 constraint fk_time REFERENCES time(time_key),
 customer_id                     varchar2(10)
 constraint not_null_customer_id NOT NULL
 constraint fk_customer_id REFERENCES customer(customer_id),
 purchase_date                   date,
 purchase_time                   number(4,0),
 purchase_price                    number(6,2),
 shipping_charge                 number(5,2),
 today_special_offer     varchar2(1)
 constraint special_offer
 CHECK (today_special_offer IN ('Y','N')) )
PARTITION by RANGE (time_key )
 (
 partition purchases_jan99
  values less than (TO_DATE('31-01-1999', 'DD-MM-YYYY'))
  pctfree 0 pctused 99
  storage (initial 64k next 64k pctincrease 0)
  tablespace purchases_jan99 ,
 partition purchases_feb99
  values less than (TO_DATE('28-02-1999', 'DD-MM-YYYY'))
  pctfree 0 pctused 99
  storage (initial 64k next 64k pctincrease 0)
  tablespace purchases_feb99 ,
 partition purchases_mar99
  values less than (TO_DATE('31-03-1999', 'DD-MM-YYYY'))
  pctfree 0 pctused 99
  storage (initial 64k next 64k pctincrease 0)
  tablespace purchases_mar99 );
```

Hash Partitioning

Depending on the data distribution, it is possible to end up with a situation in which the data is not evenly divided up among the partitions. Some partitions may be very large, and others small. If the data was partitioned by product purchased, and we sold a large number of tents, but very few cameras, this would result in partitions that are very different in size. When the data is skewed in this way often "hot spots" form where there is contention for resources in for one area.

Hash partitioning minimizes the chance of this type of data skew, by applying a hashing function to one of the columns in the table, the hash key. The resulting output value is used to determine which partition to store the row in. Hash partitioning is good for finding an individual row, but cannot be used by the optimizer to perform partition elimination.

Figure 3.6 Hash Partitioning

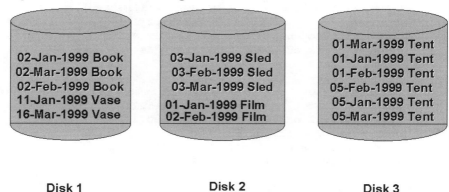

| Disk 1 | Disk 2 | Disk 3 |

Figure 3.6 shows the purchases table partitioned via the hash key, product_id. Hashing scatters the data among the partitions; since several values will hash to the same partition the data skew may be evened out. This type of partitioning facilitates queries based on product, such as looking for all "Tents." However, all partitions would need to be searched if we were looking for sales of all tents for the month of January.

Below we illustrate the SQL required to create a hash partition. In general, only using hash partitioning may not be the best method to use on a fact table.

```
CREATE TABLE easydw.purchases
 (product_id                 varchar2(8)
 constraint not_null_product_id NOT NULL
 constraint fk_product_id REFERENCES product(product_id),
 time_key                    date
 constraint not_null_time NOT NULL
 constraint fk_time REFERENCES time(time_key),
 customer_id                 varchar2(10)
 constraint not_null_customer_id NOT NULL
 constraint fk_customer_id REFERENCES
  customer(customer_id),
 purchase_date               date,
 purchase_time               number(4,0),
 purchase_price                 number(6,2),
 shipping_charge             number(5,2),
```

```
today_special_offer            varchar2(1)
constraint special_offer
CHECK (today_special_offer IN ('Y','N')) )
PARTITION BY HASH(product_id)
PARTITIONS 3;
```

Composite Partitioning

Composite partitioning, which combines the benefits of range and hash partitioning, was introduced in Oracle 8*i*. The data is first partitioned by range and then further subdivided into subpartitions by using a hash function. When partitioning by date, the last partition is often a "hot spot." By further subpartitioning, Oracle 8*i* uses a hash function, and I/O contention is reduced because access is divided among the subpartitions.

All partitions of a table or index have the same logical attributes, but can have different physical attributes. For example, all partitions in a table have the same column and constraint definitions, but they can have different storage attributes and physical placement. Subpartitions of a single partition cannot have different physical attributes. This allows you to move older, less frequently accessed data to a slower type of medium.

In Figure 3.7 The data is first partitioned by the month, then further partitioned by the product, allowing you to spread a very large fact table across more physical devices. The optimizer can quickly determine which partitions to search when looking for January data. Looking for all sales of a particular product requires scanning all partitions and subpartitions.

Figure 3.7 Composite Partitioning

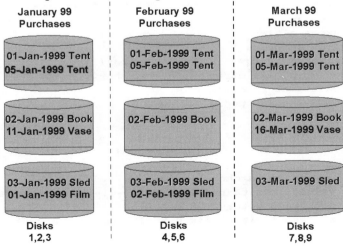

Below we can see an example of how to create a composite partition using SQL. Each partition has three subpartitions. Each subpartition has been stored in its own tablespace. This allows you to spread the subpartitions across multiple devices.

```
-- create the 3 month subpartitions for the fact partitions
-- only some of the partitions required are shown here

create tablespace purchases_jan99_2
 datafile 'd:\ora815\oradata\orcl\PURCHASESJAN992.f'
  size 5m reuse autoextend on default storage
  (initial 16k next 16k pctincrease 0 maxextents unlimited);

create tablespace purchases_jan99_3
 datafile 'd:\ora815\oradata\orcl\PURCHASESJAN993.f'
  size 5m reuse autoextend on default storage
  (initial 16k next 16k pctincrease 0 maxextents unlimited);

-- create the table and all of its partitions

CREATE TABLE easydw.purchases
 (product_id                 varchar2(8)
 constraint not_null_product_id NOT NULL
 constraint fk_product_id
  REFERENCES product(product_id),
 time_key                          date
 constraint not_null_time NOT NULL
 constraint fk_time REFERENCES time(time_key),
 customer_id                varchar2(10)
 constraint not_null_customer_id NOT NULL
 constraint fk_customer_id REFERENCES customer(customer_id),
 purchase_date              date,
 purchase_time              number(4,0),
 purchase_price                number(6,2),
 shipping_charge            number(5,2),
 today_special_offer        varchar2(1)
 constraint special_offer
 CHECK (today_special_offer IN ('Y','N')) )

PARTITION by RANGE (time_key )
 SUBPARTITION BY HASH(product_id)
 SUBPARTITIONS 3
  (partition purchases_jan99
   values less than (TO_DATE('31-01-1999', 'DD-MM-YYYY'))
   pctfree 0 pctused 99
   storage (initial 64k next 16k pctincrease 0)
        STORE IN
```

```
 (purchases_jan99, purchases_jan99_2, purchases_jan99_3),

  partition purchases_feb99
   values less than (TO_DATE('28-02-1999', 'DD-MM-YYYY'))
   pctfree 0 pctused 99
   storage (initial 64k next 16k pctincrease 0)
        STORE IN
  (purchases_feb99, purchases_feb99_2, purchases_feb99_3),

  partition purchases_mar99
   values less than (TO_DATE('31-03-1999', 'DD-MM-YYYY'))
   pctfree 0 pctused 99
   storage (initial 64k next 16k pctincrease 0)
        STORE IN
(purchases_mar99, purchases_mar99_2, purchases_mar99_3));

-- next create the indexes
CREATE INDEX easydw.purchase_product_index ON purchases
 (product_id )
 local
 (partition indexJan99 tablespace purchases_jan99_idx,
 partition indexFeb99 tablespace purchases_feb99_idx,
 partition indexMar99 tablespace purchases_mar99 );

create tablespace indx1
 datafile 'd:\ora815\oradata\orcl\indx1.f'
 size 5m reuse autoextend on
 default storage
(initial 16k next 16k pctincrease 0 maxextents unlimited);

create tablespace indx2
 datafile 'd:\ora815\oradata\orcl\indx2.f'
 size 5m reuse autoextend on
 default storage
(initial 16k next 16k pctincrease 0 maxextents unlimited);

create index easydw.global_product_index on purchases
(product_id)
global PARTITION BY RANGE (product_id)
 (PARTITION VALUES LESS THAN ('N') TABLESPACE indx1,
 PARTITION VALUES LESS THAN (MAXVALUE) TABLESPACE
   indx2);
```

3.3.2   Partitioned Indexes

Both b*tree and bitmap indexes can also be partitioned. They may be partitioned the same way that the table is partitioned or by different criteria. A b*tree index may be partitioned even if the underlying table is not. Partitioned indexes may be local or global.

In a *local* index, all the keys in an index partition refer to rows in only one table partition. A local index is equipartitioned with the table, and inherits its partitioning criteria from the table. It has the same number of partitions, subpartitions and partition bounds. When partitions are added, dropped, split, or merged in the underlying table, the index partitions are modified to correspond.

In a *global* index, the keys in an index partition can refer to rows in more than one table partition or subpartition. There are two types of local partitioned index:

- prefixed
- nonprefixed

If the first column or group of columns of the index are the same columns used to partition the index, it is called a *prefixed* index. If they are not the same, the index is *nonprefixed*.

Prefixed Local Indexes

If the index is partitioned by the first column, or group of columns, it is called a *prefixed local index*.

In our example, both the purchases table and the index, easydw.purchase_time_index are partitioned via the time_key. Figure 3.8 shows a bitmap index based on the time_key, which is the date of the purchase, for the purchases table. The index is built on the same column, time_key, that the index is partitioned by.

Figure 3.8 Local Prefixed Index Partitioned by Time_key

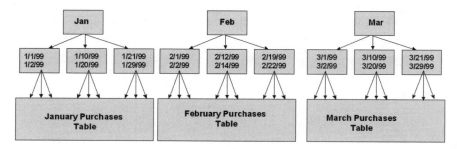

Here is the SQL required to create this index.

```
CREATE bitmap INDEX easydw.purchase_time_index
 ON purchases (time_key )
local
 (partition indexJan99 tablespace purchases_jan99_idx,
 partition indexFeb99 tablespace purchases_feb99_idx,
 partition indexMar99 tablespace purchases_mar99 );
```

NonPrefixed Local Indexes

We want our indexes and tables to be partitioned by date, so it's easy to add a new month's data and build data for that month. In addition to the index on date, we need to create indexes on other columns.

In addition to retrieving sales by month, we also want to know about sales by product. Therefore, we want to build an index on the product_id as shown here.

```
CREATE INDEX easydw.purchase_product_index ON purchases
 (product_id )
local
 (partition indexJan99 tablespace purchases_jan99_idx,
 partition indexFeb99 tablespace purchases_feb99_idx,
 partition indexMar99 tablespace purchases_mar99 );
```

Local indexes built on the foreign keys of the fact table that don't include the first column, are called *nonprefixed local indexes.* When searching for sales of tents, since they have been sold in each month, the optimizer must search for the data for all months, and is not able to perform partition elimination. Figure 3.9 shows a nonprefixed local index built on product_id.

Figure 3.9 Local Nonprefixed Index on Product_id

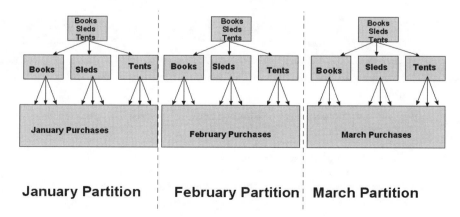

January Partition   **February Partition**   **March Partition**

Global Indexes

A *global partitioned index* can be viewed conceptually as a single B*tree containing entries for all rows in all partitions. Each index partition may contain keys that refer to many different partitions or subpartitions in the table. A global index may be partitioned by range. Bitmap indexes may not be global indexes. Only prefixed global indexes are supported.

Figure 3.10 shows an alternate way we could have built the product index, as a global index. Here we have built an index whereby the table is partitioned by month, the index is partitioned by product, and the leading edge of the index is product.

Looking at the complexity of this simple diagram, you can guess why global indexes are less efficient than local one's. In addition, when the data in an underlying table partition is moved or removed (SPLIT, MOVE, DROP, or TRUNCATE), all partitions of a global index are affected. A global index does not inherit the underlying table partitioning, thus it is not as easy to maintain.

Figure 3.10 Global Index

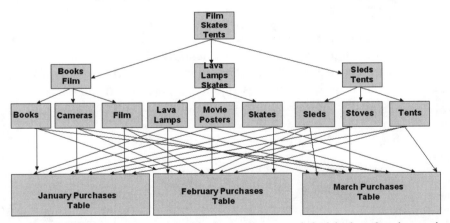

Below we can see an example of how to create a global index that is partitioned by range.

```
CREATE INDEX easydw.global_product_index on purchases
  (product_id)
  global
  partition by range (product_id)
  (partition values less than ('n') tablespace indx1 ,
  partition values less than (maxvalue) tablespace indx2);
```

To summarize, local prefix indexes are the most efficient type of indexes for query performance, since the optimizer can use partition elimination to avoid looking in unnecessary partitions. In our examples, when queries look for data by a particular month, the optimizer can quickly determine which indexes to look at when there are local indexes defined. Local indexes also facilitate rolling window operations. Avoid using global indexes if possible, since additional maintenance is required and bitmap indexes cannot be global.

Hint: Partition your fact table by date if possible. Load data into a new partition. Use local indexes, as opposed to global ones. Local indexes support rolling window operations, purging of old data, and adding new data in historical tables. Use composite partitioning to eliminate "hot spots."

3.3.3   Raid Technology

An alternative technique for spreading the I/O requests across multiple devices is by using RAID storage technology, redundant arrays of inexpensive disks. By using multiple disks together, performance and reliability can be improved. Rather than storing all data in one file on a single disk, it is striped across multiple disks, reducing contention for disk arms. Raid technologies can be used with all the data warehousing features discussed in this book.

However, although the I/O is distributed across the storage devices, it does not help you perform partition maintenance.

3.4   SUMMARY MANAGEMENT

One of the techniques many people use in data warehouses today to improve performance is to create summary or aggregate tables. If multiple users are interested in the total sales of each product for each month, the data would be selected, joined, sorted, and aggregated over and over again for each user. Rather than wasting resources re-executing the same query repeatedly, a summary table could be created, and the result saved.

3.4.1   **Before Oracle 8*i***

Figure 3.11 shows a summary containing the total number of items sold for each month of the year. Summary tables are usually much smaller than the tables containing the detail data. In this example, 17 rows of detailed sales transaction data are summarized into nine rows. Depending on the data, a greater reduction in size is possible and can often be quite significant.

Once a summary has been created, the result could be obtained from the summary when a user asks for the total sales of each product for each month. Other queries could also use the summary table. If we were interested in the total sales of each product for each year, the result can be obtained by adding the months for that year together since months roll up into years.

As new detail data is loaded into the warehouse, the summaries become stale and are no longer up to date. Figure 3.12 shows a stale summary. New detail data has been loaded into the warehouse, but the summary has not yet been refreshed. One technique used to refresh a summary is to completely re-create it. A faster type of refresh is possible for some types of summaries. In our example, it is possible to add new sales transactions incrementally into the existing summary to bring it up to date. Prior to Oracle 8*i*, procedures needed to be developed manually to refresh the summaries. Optimizations to incrementally refresh the summaries require writing custom programs.

Figure 3.11 Summary Table

Detail Sales Transactions		
Date	**Customer**	**Product**
1/5/98	Smith	Book
1/6/98	Jones	Tent
2/5/98	Smith	Tent
2/6/98	Miller	Book
3/5/98	Smith	Stove
3/5/98	Smith	Stove
3/5/98	Jones	Tent
1/5/99	Smith	Tent
1/5/99	Smith	Tent
1/5/99	Smith	Stove
2/5/99	Miller	Book
2/5/99	Miller	Book
2/5/99	Smith	Book
3/5/99	Smith	Stove
3/5/99	Jones	Tent
3/5/99	Jones	Tent
3/5/99	Smith	Tent

Total Sales by product by month		
Month	**Product**	**Qty Sold**
1/98	Book	1
2/98	Tent	1
3/98	Stove	2
3/98	Tent	1
1/99	Tent	2
1/99	Stove	1
2/99	Book	3
3/99	Stove	1
3/99	Tents	3

Choosing which summaries to create requires an understanding of the workload what types of questions users are asking, and how often the same types of information are being requested. The number of possible summary tables that could be created are very large. Since summaries consume disk space and take time to refresh, it is important to select the smallest number of summaries that produce the most performance benefits.

Once summary tables are created, programs must be modified to reference the summaries. The users need to be informed of their existence and trained on which summary tables to use for each particular query. Thus, while summary tables improve query performance, problems may occur if not carefully managed. The following questions must be addressed:

(1) What is the best set of summaries to create?

(2) How will the users know what summaries exist and when to use them? If summaries are later determined not to be that useful and are dropped, users also need to know about this.

(3) As the detail data changes, how will the summaries be kept up to date?

Figure 3.12 Stale Summary

Detail Sales Transactions		
Date	**Customer**	**Product**
1/5/98	Smith	Book
1/6/98	Jones	Tent
2/5/98	Smith	Tent
2/6/98	Miller	Book
3/5/98	Smith	Stove
3/5/98	Smith	Stove
3/5/98	Jones	Tent
1/5/99	Smith	Tent
1/5/99	Smith	Tent
1/5/99	Smith	Stove
2/5/99	Miller	Book
2/5/99	Miller	Book
2/5/99	Smith	Book
3/5/99	Smith	Stove
3/5/99	Jones	Tent
3/5/99	Jones	Tent
3/5/99	Smith	Tent
3/5/99	Smith	Stove
2/5/99	Jones	Book
1/5/99	Jones	Tent
3/5/99	Smith	Book

Total Sales by product by month		
Month	**Product**	**Qty Sold**
1/98	Book	1
2/98	Tent	1
3/98	Stove	2
3/98	Tent	1
1/99	Tent	2
1/99	Stove	1
2/99	Book	3
3/99	Stove	1
3/99	Tents	3

← **New Data in Detail Table, not yet in summary**

Some query tools eliminate the need for users to be aware of what summaries exist by using a technique called *aggregate navigation*. The user references the detail tables in his query, and the tool automatically redirects the query to use the summary tables whenever possible. Aggregate navigation is available in Oracle Discoverer 3.0 and in other tools such as Microstrategy's DSS Agent and Information Advantage's Decision Suite.

3.4.2   **Summary Management with Oracle 8*i***

Summary management, a new feature in the Oracle 8*i* Enterprise Edition, addresses these problems and makes the management of summaries easier because it comprises the following components:

- A special object called a *materialized view,* which holds the summary
- *Dimensions* to describe the hierarchy
- A *summary advisor,* to determine what summaries to create
- A *query rewrite,* which transparently rewrites SQL queries to use summary tables
- A complete and fast *incremental refresh* mechanism

A significant benefit when using summary management is that the end users and database applications no longer need to be aware of the existence of the summaries. Aggregate navigation in the Oracle server makes query rewrite available to all SQL applications and tools. Both complete and fast *refresh procedures* are supplied to update the summary tables after new detail data is loaded into the warehouse, eliminating the need to write complex incremental refresh programs by hand.

Creating the Hierarchies and Dimensions

In a relational database, tables are related to each other by storing a common column in each table. The tables are joined together via the common column, or join key, when querying the database. With Oracle 8*i*, in addition to defining relationships among tables, you can also describe the relationships between the columns within one or more tables by creating a new schema object, called a *dimension*.

Telling Oracle about the relationships among the data makes it possible for the advisor to recommend the best set of summaries to create, for the optimizer to rewrite more queries to use the summaries, and for the OLAP tools to perform rollup and drill-down operations. There are several types of relationships you can define:

(1) **The relationship between the fact and dimension tables.** This lets Oracle know that the two tables will be joined together. The relationship between two tables is defined by creating a *referential integrity constraint* using primary key, not null, and references or foreign key constraints.

(2) **The hierarchical relationships among the data within the dimension tables.** This lets Oracle know what data can be *rolled up* to higher levels within the hierarchy for summarization and how to *drill down* to a lower level in the hierarchy to see more detail. Hierarchical relationships are described using HIERARCHY clauses in the Oracle 8i CREATE DIMENSION statement.

(3) **Functional dependencies or one-to-one relationships between two columns in a dimension table.** This is useful for looking up one value based on another value in the table. For example, given a date, we can determine the day of the week. Given a month number, we can determine the month name. Given a postal code, we can determine the town. One-to-one relationships are defined using the ATTRIBUTE clause in the Oracle 8*i* CREATE DIMENSION statement.

Using Referential Integrity Constraints to Define Relationships

In OLTP systems, constraints are used to enforce data integrity. In a data warehouse, constraints can be used to define the relationship between the fact and dimension tables.

A primary key constraint should be defined for the unique key column on each dimension table. A foreign key constraint and a NOT NULL constraint should be defined on each corresponding key in the fact table.

In the Easy Shopping example, primary keys have been defined for each dimension: customer, product, time, and todays_special_offers.

```
ALTER TABLE customer
 ADD CONSTRAINT pk_customer PRIMARY KEY (customer_id);

ALTER TABLE product
 ADD CONSTRAINT pk_product PRIMARY KEY (product_id);
ALTER TABLE time
 ADD CONSTRAINT pk_time PRIMARY KEY (time_key);

ALTER TABLE todays_special_offers
 ADD CONSTRAINT pk_specials
 PRIMARY KEY (offer_date,product_id );
```

Foreign key constraints, specified by the REFERENCES clause, and not null constraints are defined for each of the corresponding columns in the fact table, product_id, time_key, and customer_id.

```
CREATE TABLE easydw.purchases
  (product_id                  varchar2(8)
constraint not_null_product_id NOT NULL
constraint fk_product_id
REFERENCES product(product_id),
time_key                        date
constraint not_null_time NOT NULL
constraint fk_time REFERENCES time(time_key),
customer_id                  varchar2(10)
constraint not_null_customer_id NOT NULL
constraint fk_customer_id
  REFERENCES customer(customer_id),

(the rest of the table definition has been omitted):
```

As described in Chapter 2, when a constraint is enabled, you can choose to have Oracle validate the integrity of the data. If it has already been checked either at the operational system or during the ETT process prior to loading the data, use the NOVALIDATE clause to save Oracle from revalidating it.

```
ALTER TABLE todays_special_offers
  ENABLE NOVALIDATE CONSTRAINT sys_coo1136;
```

In addition, the RELY clause should be used if using summary management to tell Oracle that it can rely upon the constraints being correct. It allows the Database Administrator (DBA) to say "Trust me. I've already checked the data validity; you don't have to do it again."

```
ALTER TABLE todays_special_offers
  MODIFY CONSTRAINT sys_coo1136 RELY;
```

3.4.3   Creating a Dimension

Once the tables that contain the dimension data are created, you can create the DIMENSION object, using the CREATE DIMENSION statement. It helps to draw a bubble diagram showing the hierarchical relationships among the columns prior to defining a dimension.

Figure 3.13 shows a bubble diagram for the geography dimension. Postal codes roll up into towns, which roll up into counties, which, in turn, roll up into countries.

To convert the bubble diagram in Figure 3.13 into a dimension definition, each bubble in the diagram becomes a LEVEL in the hierarchy, as shown in the CREATE DIMENSION statement below.

```
CREATE DIMENSION geography_dim

LEVEL postal_code IS customer.postal_code
LEVEL town IS customer.town
LEVEL county IS customer.county
LEVEL country IS customer.country

HIERARCHY loc_rollup (
postal_code     CHILD OF
town            CHILD OF
county          CHILD OF
country );
```

Figure 3.13 Bubble Diagram for the Geography Dimension

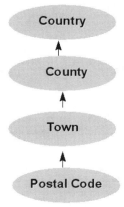

The relationships between the levels are described with the HIERARCHY clause. The bubbles with arrows coming out of them in the diagram are described with the CHILD OF clause.

In our example, postal code (or zip code in the U.S.) rolls up into town; therefore, postal_code is a CHILD OF town. Town rolls up into county; therefore, town is a CHILD OF county. County rolls up into country, so county is a CHILD OF country.

For any child in a hierarchy, there must be one and only one parent. This is true in the geography dimension as well. Postal code "02134" is in Boston, which is in Suffolk County, in the United States. Since a postal code is unique to any given town, it satisfies this rule. "02134" refers to addresses in Boston only. It can't also be used to refer to addresses in San Francisco.

Defining a Dimension with Multiple Hierarchies

Sometimes the same data can be rolled up in different ways. In the EASYDW business, as in many businesses, we use both a Julian calendar and a fiscal calendar. In the Julian calendar, days roll up into months, which roll up into years. In the fiscal calendar, days roll up into weeks, which roll up into fiscal quarters. This can be represented by defining multiple hierarchies within the dimension.

Figure 3.14 Bubble Diagram for the Time Dimension

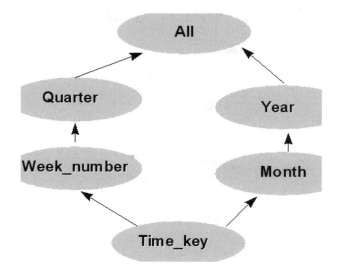

Figure 3.14 shows the bubble diagram for the time dimension. It contains two hierarchies, describing the different ways the time_key can be rolled up. From a given date, one hierarchy tells us which week and fiscal quarter this date is in; the other, the Julian month and year. At the top of every bubble diagram is the special level ALL. All levels of a hierarchy can be rolled up to ALL.

Below we can see an example of a multiple hierarchy dimension.

```
CREATE DIMENSION time
LEVEL time_key IS time.time_key
LEVEL month  IS time.month
LEVEL quarter IS time.quarter
LEVEL year  IS time.year
LEVEL week_number IS time.week_number
```

```
HIERARCHY julian_rollup (
time_key CHILD OF
month   CHILD OF
year)

HIERARCHY fiscal_rollup (
 time_key CHILD OF
 week_number CHILD OF
 quarter  );
```

For each child in a hierarchy, there is only one parent. Given a date, such as "21-Mar-1999," it is Sunday, March 21, 1999. It falls into one and only one fiscal week_number. There are two hierarchy statements describing each parent–child relationship. Each arrow coming out of a bubble is described in a CHILD OF clause. Since there are two arrows coming out of the "time_key," there are two "CHILD OF" statements, one in each hierarchy.

Defining a Dimension with Attributes

Sometimes we are interested in querying the data by columns that are not part of the hierarchy but that are related to the columns in the hierarchy in that they are functionally dependent on the column. (You may have learned about functional dependencies if you learned normalization techniques to design a database.) Often users do not know the unique identifier for a record, but know the name. For example, a customer may not know the product_id, but does know the product_name of what he's interested in purchasing.

When dimensions are defined, the ATTRIBUTE clause is used to define any functional dependencies or 1:1 relationships between the dimension columns and other columns in the table. In this case, product_id DETERMINES product_name. The ATTRIBUTE clause should be used only when there is a 1:1 relationship between the two columns. Given a product_id, there is only one product_name. Here we see the definition of a dimension with the attribute clause.

```
CREATE DIMENSION product_dim
LEVEL product_id IS product.product_id
LEVEL category  IS product.category
HIERARCHY merchandise_rollup (
product_id   CHILD OF
category             )
ATTRIBUTE product_id DETERMINES product_name;
```

Defining a Dimension with Normalized Tables

If you have a snowflake or other normalized schema, you can create dimension objects where the columns in the levels of the hierarchy come from different tables. In the example in Figure 3.15, there is a separate table for week, month, quarter, and year. The table name and column name for each item is specified in the LEVEL clause in the form of tablename.columnname. For example, week.week_number is the column "week_number" in the table "week." The JOIN KEY specifies how the tables that make up the levels in the hierarchy are joined together.

Below is an example of how to create a normalized dimension in SQL.

```
CREATE DIMENSION time
LEVEL time_key IS time.time_key
LEVEL month IS month.month
LEVEL quarter IS quarter.quarter
LEVEL year IS year.year
LEVEL week IS week.week_number
HIERARCHY julian_rollup (
  time_key CHILD OF
  month CHILD OF
  year
JOIN KEY time.month REFERENCES month
JOIN KEY month.year REFERENCES year)
HIERARCHY fiscal_rollup(
  time_key CHILD OF
  week CHILD OF
  quarter
JOIN KEY time.week_number REFERENCES week
JOIN KEY week.quarter REFERENCES quarter);
```

Figure 3.15 A Normalized Dimension

3.4.4   Creating the Summaries

Summaries are created in a new type of Oracle 8*i* object called a *materialized view*. A view provides a mechanism to look at data in another way. By materializing the view, you save the results. Materialized views can be used to save the result of any query, not just a summary. In this book we will use summaries and materialized views interchangeably. To create a materialized view, use the CREATE MATERIALIZED VIEW command.

The statement below creates a materialized view that contains the total sales of each product for each month, and stores the results in a materialized view named total_products_by_month. Each clause will be explained briefly, and then expanded upon later. The materialized view definition contains the following parts:

- A description of how to physically store the materialized view
- When to create it—now or later. Or, you may already have a summary table that you'd like to use as a materialized view. This makes management of existing summaries possible
- How to refresh it when data in the underlying detail tables have changed —by completely rebuilding it, or by a fast incremental merge of the changes
- When to refresh it—at the end of a transaction or at a later time
- Whether you want to use it for query rewrite
- A SELECT statement, which describes the contents of the materialized view

```
CREATE MATERIALIZED VIEW product_sales_by_month
 PCTFREE 0 TABLESPACE summary
 STORAGE (initial 64k next 64k pctincrease 0)
 BUILD IMMEDIATE
 REFRESH FORCE
 ON DEMAND
 ENABLE QUERY REWRITE
  AS
   SELECT t.month, t.year, p.product_id,
 SUM (purchase_price) as sum_of_sales,
 COUNT (purchase_price) as total_sales
 FROM time t, product p, purchases ps
 WHERE t.time_key = ps.purchase_date AND
 ps.product_id = p.product_id
 GROUP BY t.month, t.year, p.product_id;
```

The Physical Storage for the Materialized View

The materialized view has a storage specification so that you can specify in which tablespace it is to be stored, its initial allocation, and the size of its extents. You can also include the partition clause so that the contents of the materialized view can be stored across multiple tablespaces. Large materialized that views containing summary information should be partitioned in the same way that their underlying detail fact tables are partitioned, whenever possible.

In our example the materialized view is being placed in the tablespace called summary, the first extent will be 64k, and all subsequent extents will be 64k.

When Should the Materialized View be Created?

The materialized view definition describes when you would like the materialized view to be created—now or later. If you specify BUILD IMMEDIATE, as in the example, the materialized view is populated immediately. If you specify BUILD DEFERRED, then the materialized view will be populated later, when you execute the REFRESH operation.

How Should the Materialized View be Refreshed?

As new detail data is periodically loaded into the data warehouse, the materialized views have to be *refreshed* to reflect the changes. Four refresh options are available:

- Complete
- Fast
- Force
- Never

The materialized views can be completely rebuilt by specifying REFRESH COMPLETE. Or, they can be incrementally updated by specifying the REFRESH FAST option. It is usually faster to perform a fast refresh than a complete refresh; however, it is not always possible for Oracle to do a FAST refresh.

The example shown here, uses REFRESH FORCE, which says by default to perform a FAST incremental refresh whenever possible, and to only do a COMPLETE refresh if necessary.

It is important to consider how the underlying detail data will change. Will you perform bulk operations, such as loading next month's data into the warehouse, or do you need to modify the rows one at a time, perhaps running compensating transactions to correct errors, after the data has been loaded?

At the time of writing, materialized views with joins and aggregates can only be refreshed "*fast*" when new data is added using direct path mode. Any changes using SQL update, delete, or insert will require a full refresh.

In Oracle 8*i* the direct path option is available in SQL*Loader and the SQL INSERT AS SELECT with the APPEND or PARALLEL hints. Many ETT tools, including the Oracle Datamart Builder have a direct path option for loading the data as well.

An example of an insert statement with the append hint is shown below.

```
SQL> INSERT /*+ APPEND */ INTO easydw.purchases
 SELECT * FROM oltp.apr_orders
```

When Should the Materialized View be Refreshed?

As the underlying detail data changes, the summaries that are based on those detail tables become stale, and no longer reflect the results of summarizing all the detail data. You can choose to refresh the summaries ON DEMAND or ON COMMIT.

ON DEMAND allows you to control when the materialized view will be refreshed, which means that you must manually request that it be refreshed. There are many uses of ON DEMAND.

Detailed sales transactions may be loaded nightly, and the weekly sales summary may be refreshed once a week at midnight Saturday. You can set up your procedures to refresh the weekly sales summary at the appropriate time.

In many types of analysis, such as trend analysis, the summary, is "close enough." There is no need for the summary to exactly match the detail data to be "right." To optimize query performance in the day, you may choose to delay refreshing materialized views until the evening

Refreshing of materialized views may be part of the batch load operation. After new data is loaded in the ETT process, the materialized views may be refreshed.

If your business is such that it requires the materialized view be kept up to date with the detail data at the transaction level, the materialized view can be refreshed at the end of each transaction, by specifying the ON COMMIT option. This option is available when updating the detail data a row at a time using SQL, and requires the creation of a materialized view log on the detail table. However, there are currently restrictions on the types of materialized views that you can create using the ON COMMIT clause.

Enabling the Materialized View for Query Rewrite

In most cases you will want queries to be rewritten to use your materialized views. Whenever a materialized view is defined, if you wish it to be eligible for query rewrite, then include the clause ENABLE QUERY REWRITE, as shown in the example.

If you don't want a materialized view to be used for query rewrite, you can DISABLE QUERY REWRITE. If you already have summary tables and you would like Oracle 8i to incrementally refresh them, but not to make them eligible for query rewrite, disable query rewrite in the materialized view definition.

In addition to specifying if a materialized view is eligible for rewrite, you must consider several other. These will be discussed in the rewrite section later in this chapter.

Specifying the Contents of the Materialized View

The materialized view definition contains a SELECT statement that describes the contents. If you are using a materialized view to create a summary it will contain:

(1) A WHERE clause that joins the fact table and one or more dimension tables. In this example, the fact table purchases is joined with the dimension tables time and products.

(2) One or more aggregate operators. In this case COUNT is used to obtain the total sales. Operators that can be included are SUM, MIN, MAX, AVG, COUNT(*), COUNT(x), COUNT(DISTINCT x), VARIANCE, and STDDEV.

(3) A group by clause. In this case we are counting the total items sold by the columns year, month and product_name.

Using Summary Management with Existing Summary Tables

If you already have a data warehouse with summaries stored in user tables, and do not want to completely recreate them, summary management in Oracle 8i can still be used to perform query rewrite.

To register your summary table with summary management, create a materialized view, and use the ON PREBUILT TABLE clause to let Oracle know you have already created the summary. The metadata needed for rewrite and dependency management will be created for your preexisting summary, if you ENABLE QUERY REWRITE. For example, you may already have a table named monthly_customer_sales, which summarizes the amount of money each customer spent each month. If you'd like to use the table as a summary, and make it eligible for query rewrite, create a materialized view definition describing the table, and enable it for query rewrite.

You must check that the summary correctly represents a summarization of the detail data, and set the QUERY_REWRITE_INTEGRITY level to TRUSTED or STALE_TOLERATED for rewrite to occur. "TRUSTED" says "trust me, I've ensured the data is correct" and "STALE_TOLERATED" tells the optimizer to use the summary, irrespective of whether the data inside it is considered to be fresh. This can be achieved by setting an initialization parameter, or using the ALTER SYSTEM or ALTER SESSION command.

In the example below, we create a table for illustration purposes, followed by the materialized view, using the create table as select clause. In your case, you would already have the monthly_customer_sales built and populated, so that step would not be necessary. When creating the materialized view on a prebuilt table, the name of the table and materialized view are the same. The contents of the table are described with the select clause in the materialized view.

```
CREATE TABLE monthly_customer_sales
 AS
 SELECT t.year, t.month, c.customer_id,
 SUM(f.purchase_price) as dollar_sales
 FROM time t, purchases f, customer c
 WHERE f.time_key = t.time_key AND
 f.customer_id = c.customer_id
 GROUP BY t.year, t.month, c.customer_id;

CREATE MATERIALIZED VIEW monthly_customer_sales
 ON PREBUILT TABLE
 ENABLE QUERY REWRITE
 AS
 SELECT t.year, t.month, c.customer_id,
   SUM(f.purchase_price) AS dollar_sales
 FROM time t, purchases f, customer c
 WHERE f.time_key = t.time_key AND
        f.customer_id = c.customer_id
   GROUP BY t.year, t.month, c.customer_id;
```

3.4.5   Refreshing the Summaries

When defining the materialized view, if you chose to refresh ON DEMAND, then you can refresh your materialized view by calling one of the procedures in the DBMS_MVIEW package which is supplied by Oracle.

If you want to refresh all summaries, which is often done after bulk loading new detail data, you can use the DBMS_MVIEW_REFRESH_ALL PL/SQL procedure.

If you have materialized views that are refreshed at different times, for example, some weekly, and others monthly, you can specify a list of summaries to refresh using the DBMS_MVIEW.REFRESH procedure.

If you want to refresh all materialized views that are based on a particular detail table that has changed, use the DBMS_MVIEW.REFRESH_DEPENDENT procedure, specifying the detail table.

In Chapter 4, we'll take a look at executing the refresh procedures after loading your data warehouse.

3.4.6   Security of Materialized Views

Some information in the data warehouse may have restricted access, and it is important to ensure that the appropriate security policies are implemented regarding access to materialized views. You may want to allow users access to a summary, but not allow them to see the underlying detail data. For example, you may allow a user to see the average salary by department, but not to see individual employees' salaries.

On the other hand, you want to ensure that materialized views and query rewrite are not used as a mechanism for bypassing security. A number of new privileges have been added to Oracle 8*i* to enforce these types of security.

To *create a materialized view*, a user must have the CREATE MATERIALIZED VIEW privilege. To create a materialized view that references a table in another schema, the privilege CREATE ANY MATERIALIZED VIEW is needed. The owner of the schema must have CREATE ANY TABLE privilege.

To *create a dimension object*, the CREATE DIMENSION privilege is needed.

Hint: To allow a query to be rewritten to *use a materialized view*, the privilege QUERY REWRITE should be granted, or if the materialized view references tables not in your schema, then GLOBAL QUERY REWRITE must be granted.

To refresh a materialized view in another schema, ALTER ANY materialized view privilege is required.

In our example, the user EASYDW is granted the appropriate privileges to create materialized views and dimensions, and to allow these to be used for query rewrite.

```
— Add privileges
GRANT select any table to easydw;
GRANT execute any procedure to easydw;

— Add privileges for summary management
GRANT create any dimension to easydw;
GRANT alter any dimension to easydw;
GRANT drop any dimension to easydw;
GRANT query rewrite to easydw;
GRANT global query rewrite to easydw;

GRANT select on total_products_by_month to public;
GRANT insert on total_products_by month to public;
```

3.4.7   Indexing the Materialized View

You can build indexes on your materialized view to improve the performance of your queries. Indexes are also important in improving the performance of FAST incremental refresh.

To improve query performance, choose which indexes to create on the materialized view the same way you would choose them for any table. Build indexes on individual columns or groups of columns, which are often specified in the WHERE clause. Individual bitmap indexes are useful for the columns with low cardinality, as described previously.

In incrementally refreshing the materialized views using fast refresh, the row in the materialized view is matched with the row in the detail table, so performance is best when there is a concatenated b*tree index that contains all the key columns in the materialized view.

Hint: Create a concatenated b*tree index on all of the columns in the group by clause in the materialized view to improve performance of Fast refresh

In the example below, an index is created for the product_sales_by_month summary shown earlier in this chapter. A concatenated index is created using the year, month, and product_id columns.

```
CREATE INDEX easydw.products_by_month_concat_index
ON product_sales_by_month
 (year,month, product_id)
 pctfree 5
tablespace indx
storage (initial 64k next 64k pctincrease 0) ;
```

Hint: Create single-column bitmap indexes on each key in the materialized view to improve query performance.

```
CREATE bitmap INDEX easydw.total_products_by_month_index
ON product_sales_by_month (year, month);

CREATE bitmap INDEX easydw.total_products_by_id_index
ON product_sales_by_month (product_id);
```

3.4.8   Running the Advisor

To help you select which materialized views would improve performance most for your warehouse, use the materialized view analysis and advisory functions in the DBMS_OLAP package. RECOMMEND_MV advises you on what summaries to create, and whether you should keep or drop summaries you already have.

The more information you give the advisor, the better its recommendations. At the minimum, it requires referential integrity constraints between the fact and dimension tables, the definition of a dimension object, and optimizer statistics. Since summaries occupy disk space, and take time to refresh to keep them synchronized with the detail data, you want to create a few materialized views that are able to be used to rewrite many queries. In order to run the advisor take the following steps:

Step 1

Create your dimensions and constraints. By understanding the hierarchical rollup relationships the advisor is able to determine that since fiscal weeks roll up into fiscal quarters, a summary of the sales by week could be used to rewrite queries interested in both week and quarter.

Step 2

Gather optimizer statistics. In making its recommendations, the advisor looks at the size of the fact and dimension tables, and number of distinct column values in each level of the hierarchy of a dimension.

Gather cardinalities for each fact table and dimension table, and gather the distinct cardinalities of every dimension LEVEL column, JOIN KEY column, and fact table key column.

Both after the initial load, and again each time you add more data into your data warehouse, you must gather optimizer statistics, using the DBMS_STATS package or the ANALYZE TABLE statement. Because extreme statistical accuracy is not required, statistics can be estimated.

Step 3

Actual workload statistics can be used by the advisor to get a more accurate prediction of the best summaries to create. Use the OEM Performance Pack to gather the workload statistics. Using the Oracle Trace Manager application, select the *Materialized View Workload* event set option

By analyzing the workload, looking at things such as which tables and columns are accessed, how often they are accessed, which tables are joined together, and how data is summarized, the advisor can predict an optimal set of materialized views to create. This step is optional.

Step 4

Run the advisor. In Chapter 7, we will look at using the advisor to determine what summaries you should create, and how effective your existing summaries are.

3.4.9   Query Rewrite

The optimizer determines whether the result of any query can be obtained from the summary or if it needs to use the detail tables. We'll look at some examples to show what types of queries can be rewritten. These examples use the product sales by month summary previously illustrated in Figure 3.7.

If we wanted to know the top five best-selling items in the last three months, we could get the result from either the detail table or the summary. Since the summary contains fewer rows, the optimizer would choose it.

If we wanted to know the total products sold for the year, since we defined a hierarchy where months roll up into years, the optimizer could obtain the result from the summary.

If we wanted to send mail about a special offer to all our customers that have not purchased anything in the last three months, we would need to use the detail tables since the summary contains only the total sales by product and has no information about individual purchases by customers.

If we wanted to compare sales on public holidays with non-holidays, we would need to use the detail tables, as there are no dates in the summaries.

Fortunately, with Oracle 8*i*, you don't need to do this type of analysis and direct the queries to the appropriate table; the optimizer will do it for us. All you have to do is define the data relationships by creating referential integrity constraints and dimension objects. The more information you give the optimizer, the more queries it can rewrite, and the greater the performance benefit you will get from your materialized views.

At the time of writing, the optimizer can rewrite queries to use materialized views for SELECT, CREATE TABLE...AS SELECT, or INSERT INTO ... SELECT statements. Subqueries containing the set operators UNION, UNION ALL, INTERSECT, and MINUS can also be rewritten.

The Oracle optimizer uses two different methods to determine when a materialized view can be used to rewrite a query. If the SQL query is the exact same as the SQL text of the materialized view definition the query can be rewritten to use that materialized view.

If the SQL text does not match, the optimizer compares join conditions, data columns, grouping columns, and aggregate functions between the query and a materialized view.

Oracle 8*i* can rewrite several types of queries. We'll take a look at some examples illustrating the main types of queries that can be rewritten. For reference purposes, we'll show the summary and dimension definitions used in these examples again.

```
CREATE DIMENSION time
LEVEL time_key      is time.time_key
LEVEL month         is time.month
LEVEL quarter       is time.quarter
```

```
LEVEL year              is time.year
LEVEL week_number       is time.week_number
HIERARCHY fiscal_rollup (
time_key                CHILD OF
week_number             CHILD OF
quarter )
HIERARCHY julian_rollup(
time_key                CHILD OF
month                   CHILD OF
year);

CREATE DIMENSION product_dim
LEVEL product_id        is product.product_id
LEVEL category          is product.category
HIERARCHY merchandise_rollup(
product_id CHILD OF category)
ATTRIBUTE product_id DETERMINES product_name;

CREATE MATERIALIZED VIEW product_sales_by_month
 PCTFREE 0 TABLESPACE summary
 STORAGE (initial 64k next 64k pctincrease 0)
 BUILD IMMEDIATE
 REFRESH FORCE
 ON DEMAND
 ENABLE QUERY REWRITE
 AS
 SELECT t.month, t.year, p.product_id,
  SUM(purchase_price) as sum_of_sales,
  COUNT (purchase_price) as total_sales
   FROM time t, product p, purchases ps
   WHERE t.time_key = ps.purchase_date AND
         ps.product_id = p.product_id
   GROUP BY t.month, t.year, p.product_id;
```

To determine if the query was rewritten, use EXPLAIN PLAN to look at the optimizer strategy. The examples below were generated using SQL*PLUS. The SET AUTOTRACE statement is used to trace the optimizer strategy. For queries to be rewritten, the QUERY_REWRITE_ENABLED parameter must be set to true. In this example, it is done using the ALTER SESSION command.

```
SQL> SET AUTOTRACE ON EXPLAIN;

— enable query rewrite
SQL> ALTER SESSION SET QUERY_REWRITE_ENABLED=TRUE;
Session altered.
```

SQL Text Match

The optimizer is able to rewrite queries *when the text of the SQL query matches the text of the SQL query* in the materialized view definition. A portion of the output is displayed. The explain plan text shows that the optimizer chose to access the table via a full table scan on the materialized view, product_sales_by_month

```
SQL> — exact text match
SQL> SELECT t.month, t.year, p.product_id,
 SUM (purchase_price) as sum_of_sales,
 COUNT (purchase_price) as total_sales
 FROM time t, product p, purchases ps
 WHERE t.time_key = ps.purchase_date AND
 ps.product_id = p.product_id
 GROUP BY t.month, t.year, p.product_id;
```

MONTH	YEAR	PRODUCT_ ID	SUM_OF_SALES	TOTAL_SALES
1	1999	SP1000	6185.16	92
1	1999	SP1001	3445.2	96
1	1999	SP1010	4405.88	92
1	1999	SP1011	4405.88	92
1	1999	SP1012	4405.88	92

```
              :
              :
```

162 rows selected.

```
Execution Plan
```
___

```
0         SELECT STATEMENT Optimizer=CHOOSE (Cost=1 Card=162
          Bytes=4050)

1 0 TABLE ACCESS (FULL) OF 'PRODUCT_SALES_BY_MONTH'
          (Cost=1 Card=162 Bytes=4050)
```

___

Hint: If your query does not rewrite, then set the parameter QUERY-REWRITE_INTEGRITY=STALE_TOLERATED, and try again. If it still fails to rewrite, then check other settings.

___

Roll Up to a Higher Level in the Hierarchy

A materialized view can be used to roll up aggregates to higher levels in the hierarchy of a dimension.In the query below, we want to know the total sales by product by year. Since we have a summary of the total sales by product by month and months can be rolled up into years, as specified in the Julian_rollup hierarchy in the time dimension, the optimizer will rewrite the query to use the product_sales_by_month materialized view.

```
SQL> — rollup to higher LEVEL in the HIERARCHY
SQL>
SQL> SELECT t.year, p.product_id,
   COUNT (purchase_price) as total_sales
 2 FROM time t, product p, purchases ps
 3 WHERE t.time_key = ps.purchase_date AND
 4 ps.product_id = p.product_id
 5 GROUP BY t.year, p.product_id;
```

YEAR	PRODUCT_ID	TOTAL_SALES
1999	SP1000	92
1999	SP1001	96
1999	SP1010	92
1999	SP1011	92
:		
:		

162 rows selected.

```
Execution Plan
_____

 0 SELECT STATEMENT Optimizer=CHOOSE (Cost=3
         Card=115 Bytes=2875)
 1 0 SORT (GROUP BY) (Cost=3 Card=115 Bytes=2875)
 2 1 TABLE ACCESS (FULL) OF 'PRODUCT_SALES_BY_MONTH'
   (Cost=1 Card=162 Bytes=4050)
```

Data Sufficiency

In the following example, we want to know the total_sales by product_name by month. The materialized view contains the product_id, but not the product_name. If all the columns are not available in the materialized view, it still may be possible to use the materialized view and join back to another table to get the rest of the columns if one column is functionally dependent on the other.

The product_id can be used to look up the product_name from the product dimension table because an attribute clause defines the functional dependency. (ATTRIBUTE product_id DETERMINES product_name). Looking at the strategy, the optimizer used a hash join to join the product_sales_by_month materialized view back to the product table to look up the product_name.

```
SQL> — joinback (data sufficiency check)
SQL>
SQL> SELECT t.month, t.year, p.product_name,
   COUNT(purchase_price) as total_sales
 2 FROM time t, product p, purchases ps
 3 WHERE t.time_key = ps.purchase_date AND
 4 ps.product_id = p.product_id
 5 GROUP BY t.month, t.year, p.product_name;
```

MONTH	YEAR	PRODUCT_NAME	TOTAL_SALES
1	1999	APS Camera	96
1	1999	CD LX1	92
1	1999	CD LX2	92
1	1999	CD LX3	92
1	1999	CD LX4	92

157 rows selected.

Execution Plan
```
 0 SELECT STATEMENT Optimizer=CHOOSE
  (Cost=6 Card=79 Bytes=5135)
 1 0 SORT (GROUP BY) (Cost=6 Card=79 Bytes=5135)
 2 1 HASH JOIN (Cost=3 Card=162 Bytes=10530)
 3 2 TABLE ACCESS (FULL) OF 'PRODUCT_SALES_BY_MONTH'
  (Cost=1 Card=162 Bytes=4050)
 4 2 TABLE ACCESS (FULL) OF 'PRODUCT'
        (Cost=1 Card=162 Bytes=6480)
```

Aggregate Computability

In the following query, we want to know the average purchase price of each item by month and year. Since the average can be computed by dividing the sum by the count of the purchase_price, the query is rewritten to use the product_sales_by_month table.

```
SQL>
SQL> — aggregate computability
SQL>
SQL> SELECT t.month, t.year, p.product_id,
 AVG(purchase_price) as ave_sales
 2 FROM time t, product p, purchases ps
 3 WHERE t.time_key = ps.purchase_date AND
 4 ps.product_id = p.product_id
 5 GROUP BY t.month, t.year, p.product_id;
```

MONTH	YEAR	PRODUCT _	AVE_SALES
1	1999	SP1000	67.23
1	1999	SP1001	35.88
1	1999	SP1010	47.89
1	1999	SP1011	47.89
1	1999	SP1012	47.89
	:		
	:		

162 rows selected.

Execution Plan

```
0 SELECT STATEMENT Optimizer=CHOOSE
            (Cost=1 Card=162 Bytes=4050)
1 0 TABLE ACCESS (FULL) OF `PRODUCT_SALES_BY_MONTH'
            (Cost=1 Card=162 Bytes=4050)
```

Query Rewrite When the Data is Stale

Most of the time, you would like the optimizer to get the result the fastest way possible, rewriting your queries to use materialized views. However, if your summaries have become stale and no longer represent the summarization of all your detail data, you may prefer to get the results from the detail tables until you can perform your next refresh. You must decide when query rewrite is appropriate for your application. It may be appropriate to use the summary when the fact table is stale, but not when a dimension is updated.

If the results obtained from a summary are "good enough" for your application, you may still want to use the materialized view even if it's stale. To determine the month-over-month growth rate of our on-line sales, we don't need every single sales transaction in our summary. If most of them were there, we could still get an answer that was close enough. Or, if the application knows that the updates are beyond the scope of the query (i.e. data for the next month) you still may want to use the summary.

To tell the optimizer you'd like to use the summary—even if it's stale—set the QUERY_REWRITE_INTEGRITY parameter to STALE_TOLERATED.

If your application requires the exact same result be obtained from using the materialized view as from using the detail tables, set QUERY_REWRITE_INTEGRITY to ENFORCED. This is also the default.

A checklist for when a query will be rewritten to use a materialized view is given:

- **When query rewrite is enabled for the materialized view.** This can be done when you create the materialized view, as shown previously in Figure 3.12. You can also ALTER the materialized view to enable query rewrite.

- **When query rewrite is enabled for the session.** This can be done by setting the QUERY_REWRITE_ENABLED initialization parameter to TRUE or by using the ALTER SESSION command.

- **When using cost-based optimization.** While it is normally faster to obtain the results from a summary, it is possible there are times when it is faster to retrieve the results from the detail table. The optimizer uses the statistics to determine the cost of each possible solution and pick the one with the lowest cost. Therefore, you need to collect statistics both on the detail tables involved in the query and on the materialized views using the ANALYZE statement or the DBMS_STATISTICS package. Set the initialization parameter, OPTIMIZER_MODE, to "CHOOSE" to allow the optimizer to choose cost-based optimization.

- **When the rewrite integrity level allows the use of the materialized view.** If a materialized view is stale and query rewrite integrity is set to ENFORCED, then the materialized view will not be used.

- **When using Oracle 8*i*, or later versions, let Oracle know you are using the correct version of the software by setting the initialization parameter, COMPATIBLE = 8.1.0 (or greater).**

In the example, we will insert four new rows into the purchases fact table. The product_sales_by_month summary is now stale. All the data in the detail table is not reflected in the summary.

```
SQL> INSERT INTO purchases VALUES ( 'SP1061','1-FEB-1999',
  'AB123456','1-FEB-1999', 0024,28.01, 4.50, 'Y');

SQL> INSERT INTO purchases VALUES ( 'SP1062','1-FEB-1999',
  'AB123457','1-FEB-1999', 1024,28.01, 4.50, 'Y');

SQL> INSERT INTO purchases VALUES ( 'SP1063','2-FEB-1999',
  'AB123457','2-FEB-1999', 0024,28.01, 4.50, 'N');

SQL> INSERT INTO purchases VALUES ( 'SP1064','2-FEB-1999',
  'AB123457','2-FEB-1999', 1024,28.01, 4.50, 'N');
SQL> COMMIT;
```

If you do not want to use the summaries when they have become stale, set the QUERY_REWRITE_INTEGRITY TO ENFORCED. This will cause the optimizer to use the base detail tables rather than the materialized view. The new rows for February appear in the output, making the total rows 166. Many rows have been deleted from the text of the query output.

```
SQL> ALTER SESSION SET QUERY_REWRITE_INTEGRITY=ENFORCED;
Session altered.

SQL> SELECT t.month, t.year, p.product_id,
    SUM(purchase_price) as sum_of_sales,
    COUNT (purchase_price) as total_sales
 2 FROM time t, product p, purchases ps
 3 WHERE t.time_key = ps.purchase_date AND
 4 ps.product_id = p.product_id
 5 GROUP BY t.month, t.year, p.product_id;
```

MONTH	YEAR	PRODUCT_ID	SUM_OF_SALES	TOTAL_SALES
1	1999	SP1000	6185.16	92
1	1999	SP1001	3445.2	96
1	1999	SP1010	4405.88	92
1	1999	SP1011	4405.88	92
:				
2	1999	SP1061	28.01	1
2	1999	SP1062	28.01	1
2	1999	SP1063	28.01	1
2	1999	SP1064	28.01	1

166 rows selected.

```
Execution Plan
---------------------------

 0 SELECT STATEMENT Optimizer=CHOOSE
               (Cost=717 Card=243 Bytes=23814)
 1 0 SORT (GROUP BY) (Cost=717 Card=243 Bytes=23814)
 2 1 NESTED LOOPS (Cost=28 Card=15004 Bytes=1470392)
 3 2 HASH JOIN (Cost=28 Card=15004 Bytes=1200320)
 4 3   TABLE ACCESS (FULL) OF 'TIME'
               (Cost=1 Card=6 Bytes=234)
 5 3   PARTITION RANGE (ALL)
 6 5   TABLE ACCESS (FULL) OF 'PURCHASES'
               (Cost=16 Card=1 5004 Bytes=615164)
 7 2 INDEX (RANGE SCAN) OF 'PRODUCT_PK_INDEX' (NON-UNIQUE)
```

If the result obtained from using the summary is "good enough" for your application, and you can tolerate stale data, then set the QUERY_REWRITE_INTEGRITY TO STALE_TOLERATED. Note that the summary is now used and that the new rows that were inserted are not reflected in the total!

```
SQL> ALTER SESSION SET QUERY_REWRITE_INTEGRITY=STALE_TOLERATED;

Session altered.

SQL> SELECT t.month, t.year, p.product_id,
        SUM(purchase_price) as sum_of_sales,
        COUNT (purchase_price) as total_sales
  2 FROM time t, product p, purchases ps
  3 WHERE t.time_key = ps.purchase_date AND
  4 ps.product_id = p.product_id
  5 GROUP BY t.month, t.year, p.product_id;
```

MONTH	YEAR	PRODUCT_ ID	SUM_OF_SALES	TOTAL_SALES
1	1999	SP1000	6185.16	92
1	1999	SP1001	3445.2	96
1	1999	SP1010	4405.88	92
1	1999	SP1011	4405.88	92
1	1999	SP1012	4405.88	92
	:			

```
162 rows selected.


Execution Plan
```

```
  0 SELECT STATEMENT Optimizer=CHOOSE
            (Cost=1 Card=162 Bytes=4050)
  1 0 TABLE ACCESS (FULL) OF 'PRODUCT_SALES_BY_MONTH'
        (Cost=1 Card=162 Bytes=4050)
```

In addition, query rewrite depends on the integrity of your dimension and constraint definitions. Does each product in the product table roll up to one and only one category, as specified in your dimension definition? Does each product in the purchases table have a corresponding product_id in the products table, as specified by your references constraints?

Use QUERY_REWRITE_INTEGRITY is ENFORCED when your application absolutely requires that the same result be obtained from using the summary as from querying the detail tables. You must also enforce all referential integrity constraints, using the ENABLE VALIDATE clause.

Use QUERY_REWRITE_INTEGRITY is TRUSTED if you have summaries based on prebuilt tables. You are responsible for ensuring that the summary data represents all the data in the underlying detail tables. You are saying, "Trust me. This summary can be used for rewrite purposes."

Use QUERY_REWRITE_INTEGRITY is TRUSTED if you have declared referential integrity constraint definitions but not enforced them, using the ENABLE NOVALIDATE RELY clause. You are saying, "Trust me. I've already verified the integrity myself. I know there is a primary key in the dimension table for each foreign key in the fact table, and all foreign keys are non-null."

Use QUERY_REWRITE is STALE_TOLERATED when the approximate result obtained from the materialized view is good enough for your application. New data may have been added, or the constraint and dimension relationships may not be accurate, but the result obtained from using the materialized view is "close enough."

3.5   ORACLE SUPPLIED FUNCTIONS

Another facility that the database designer may like to take advantage of is using an Oracle-supplied function in a query. Oracle 8*i* has many functions, and two that are of specific interest to the data warehouse user are:

- CUBE
- ROLLUP

The Cube and Rollup functions simply extend what is possible with the standard GROUP BY clause.

Multidimensional queries often involve aggregating data and comparing aggregations across several dimensions. To facilitate these types of operations, the CUBE and ROLLUP operators have been added to SQL in Oracle 8*i*. The ROLLUP operator is used to compute subtotals, and the CUBE operator is used to compute cross-tabulations. In the past these types of operations have been done using report-writing tools. By executing them within the server, they can be executed in parallel, and optimizations can be applied to improve performance. ROLLUP and CUBE are extensions to the GROUP BY clause of the SQL SELECT statement.

All of these functions, and the other ones supplied, may be used either in a SQL query or in a materialized view definition, which is how they are illustrated here.

3.5.1   Cube

The CUBE function groups all of the selected rows by all of the possible combinations. Referring to our example where we are creating a materialized view that records the total sales of a product for a product by date category.

Below you can see the sample materialized view and the results of the query. As you can see, when the query results are displayed, the query returns one row for every possible combination of date and product category.

```
CREATE MATERIALIZED VIEW product_cube_sum
 PCTFREE 0 TABLESPACE summ
 STORAGE (initial 2k next 2k pctincrease 0)
 BUILD IMMEDIATE
 REFRESH COMPLETE
 ENABLE QUERY REWRITE
AS
SELECT p.category, t.time_key, SUM(purchase_price)
 FROM product p, purchases f, time t
 WHERE p.product_id = f.product_id AND
  t.time_key = f.time_key
  GROUP BY CUBE (p.category, t.time_key);

SVRMGR> select * from product_cube_sum;
CATE TIME_KEY SUM(PURCHASE_PRICE)
---- --------- ----------
ELEC 01-JAN-99 1766098.6
ELEC 02-JAN-99 1766098.6
ELEC 01-FEB-99 1766098.6
ELEC 02-FEB-99 1766098.6
ELEC 01-MAR-99 3532085.16
ELEC 02-MAR-99 1766042.58
ELEC 12362522.1

HDRW 01-JAN-99 18741.32
HDRW 02-JAN-99 18741.32
HDRW 01-FEB-99 18741.32
HDRW 02-FEB-99 18741.32
HDRW 01-MAR-99 37482.64
HDRW 02-MAR-99 18741.32
HDRW 131189.24

MUSC 01-JAN-99 20182.96
MUSC 02-JAN-99 20182.96
MUSC 01-FEB-99 20182.96
MUSC 02-FEB-99 20182.96
```

```
MUSC 01-MAR-99 40365.92
MUSC 02-MAR-99 20182.96
MUSC 141280.72

 01-JAN-99 1805022.88
 02-JAN-99 1805022.88
 01-FEB-99 1805022.88
 02-FEB-99 1805022.88
 01-MAR-99 3609933.72
 02-MAR-99 1804966.86
 12634992.1
28 rows selected.
```

3.5.2   Rollup

The ROLLUP function is very similar to the CUBE function except that it groups the selected rows and returns a single result. ROLLUP creates subtotals, rolling data up from a lower level to a higher level. It also produces a grand, or final, total. The ROLLUP operator is useful for totaling data across a hierarchical dimension such as time.

Referring to our example again, this time it still returns one row for each date and product category, but now the entries that do not have a category are rolled up into one line, thus resulting in only 22 rows being displayed.

```
CREATE MATERIALIZED VIEW product_rollup_sum
 PCTFREE 0 TABLESPACE summ
 STORAGE (initial 2k next 2k pctincrease 0)
 BUILD IMMEDIATE REFRESH COMPLETE
 ENABLE QUERY REWRITE
AS
SELECT p.category, t.time_key,
 SUM(purchase_price)
 FROM product p, purchases f, time t
 WHERE p.product_id = f.product_id AND
  t.time_key = f.time_key
  GROUP BY ROLLUP (p.category, t.time_key);

SVRMGR> select * from product_rollup_sum;

CATE TIME_KEY SUM(PURCHASE_PRICE)
---- --------- ----------
ELEC 01-JAN-99 1766098.6
ELEC 02-JAN-99 1766098.6
ELEC 01-FEB-99 1766098.6
ELEC 02-FEB-99 1766098.6
ELEC 01-MAR-99 3532085.16
```

```
ELEC  02-MAR-99  1766042.58
ELEC  12362522.1

HDRW  01-JAN-99  18741.32
HDRW  02-JAN-99  18741.32
HDRW  01-FEB-99  18741.32
HDRW  02-FEB-99  18741.32
HDRW  01-MAR-99  37482.64
HDRW  02-MAR-99  18741.32
HDRW  131189.24

MUSC  01-JAN-99  20182.96
MUSC  02-JAN-99  20182.96
MUSC  01-FEB-99  20182.96
MUSC  02-FEB-99  20182.96
MUSC  01-MAR-99  40365.92
MUSC  02-MAR-99  20182.96
MUSC  141280.72

   12634992.1
22 rows selected.
```

3.6　QUERY OPTIMIZATION TECHNIQUES

There are several different ways to retrieve any given row in the database. An index could be used to locate the row, or, if the table is small, it might be faster to perform a full table scan, reading each row sequentially. If there are multiple indexes, the optimizer chooses the best one to use. If there is a materialized view, the query may be rewritten to use it. The job of the optimizer is to choose a strategy to execute the query in the fastest possible time. Oracle uses two approaches to optimization:

- Rule-based optimization
- Cost-based optimization

The *rule-based optimizer* uses a set of rules to rank each of the possible different access paths available according to the speed of execution of each path. It chooses the access path with the best rank. The rule-based optimizer does not take into account the size of the table or the data distribution. Thus, it will always choose to use an index on a small table even though a full table scan may be more efficient.

The rule-based optimizer is no longer being enhanced by Oracle. New features such as partitioning, star query optimization, and query rewrite are only available using the cost-based optimizer. You should plan to use the cost based optimizer for your data warehouse.

The *cost-based optimizer* considers the available access paths and statistics in the data dictionary such as the number of rows or table cardinality to determine which access path costs the least.

To use the cost-based optimizer statistics, describing the cardinality and data distribution must be collected for each table and index using the using the DBMS_STATS package or the ANALYZE command. Statistics may either be gathered by reading all rows or estimated reading only a sample of rows. When a table is analyzed, statistics can also be gathered for each index on the table.

The cost-based optimizer uses these statistics to determine how much I/O, CPU time, and memory are required to execute a statement for a particular access path, and assigns a cost to each possible plan. You can also use hints in your SQL statement to influence the optimizer's choice of strategy. This is useful in cases where you may have a better understanding of the data than the optimizer has and are able to choose a more efficient execution plan than the optimizer.

The following statements analyze the tables and indexes in the "easydw" database.

```
ANALYZE TABLE customer COMPUTE STATISTICS;
ANALYZE TABLE todays_special_offers COMPUTE STATISTICS;
ANALYZE TABLE product COMPUTE STATISTICS;
ANALYZE TABLE time COMPUTE STATISTICS;
ANALYZE TABLE purchases COMPUTE STATISTICS;
```

You also need to analyze the materialized views to gather statistics.

```
ANALYZE TABLE total_products_by_month COMPUTE STATISTICS;
```

When using the summary advisor, gather statistics for each LEVEL column in your dimensions, each JOIN KEY column, and key columns in the fact table. An example of the analyze command to gather statistics for the columns in the product table is listed below.

```
ANALYZE TABLE products COMPUTE STATISTICS FOR COLUMNS
product.product_id, product.product_category
```

Statistics should be gathered after data is loaded and again whenever changes made to the data are likely to have altered the distribution, to ensure the cost-based optimizer has up-to-date data to base its decision upon. When partitioned tables are used, only the newest partition or subpartition where rows have been added need to be analyzed.

In Oracle 8*i* you can automatically gather statistics for a table by enabling monitoring of Data Manipulation Language activity for that table using the

ALTER TABLE command. You can then use the GATHER STALE option in the GATHER_DATABASE_STATS package to gather statistics for just those tables whose statistics need to be updated.

Hint: Run analyze to gather optimizer statistics after each data load, prior to creating the summaries. Run analyze again after creating the materialized views and again after refreshing them with large amounts of data

---

Set the "init.ora" parameter OPTIMIZER_MODE to CHOOSE, which causes the optimizer to choose between the rule-based optimizer and the cost based optimizer, depending on whether statistics are available.

3.6.1   Join Optimization

A join operation combines data from two or more tables, based on a common column, called the "join condition." The query optimizer chooses the *join method* from one of the following:

Sort-Merge Join

The data from each table is sorted by the values of the columns in the join condition. The sorted tables are then merged, so that each pair of rows with matching columns are combined. The SORT_AREA_SIZE initialization parameter specifies the amount of memory available for sorting. Once this is exceeded, intermediate data is written to temporary segments in the TEMPORARY TABLESPACE on disk.

Nested Loop Join

One table is chosen as the outer table the other, as the inner table. For each row in the outer table, all matching rows that satisfy the join condition in the inner table are found.

Hash Join

Hash join processing can dramatically improve performance of equijoins for complex queries involving large amounts of data. This is especially useful *when there are no indexes on the columns being joined.* Given the ad hoc nature of decision support queries, it is not always possible for the DBA to index all the columns the users may use to join tables together. When using

Oracle as the staging area for data transformations, data may be moved from one temporary table into another. It may be more efficient to use a hash join than to take the time to build indexes on.

Hint: Hash join optimization will improve performance for some of your queries, so be sure to enable it by using the initialization parameter HASH_JOIN_ENABLED. Alternatively, if you know you want it to be used for a particular query, you can use the USE_HASH hint on that query.

The hash join is performed by loading the smaller table into memory, and applying a hashing function to the join key to build a hash table. The second table is then scanned, its keys are hashed, and compared to the hash table in memory to look for matching rows. If there is not sufficient memory to hold the smaller table, the tables will be broken into smaller partitions.

Partition Wise Join

When the tables being joined are partitioned, the optimizer may choose to perform a *partition-wise join*. Rather than performing a large join between the tables, the join operation is broken up into a series of smaller joins between the partitions or subpartitions.

A full partition-wise join can be done when the tables being joined are equipartitioned by the join key in the query. When executing the query in parallel, each join can be executed on a separate processor.

If only one of the tables is partitioned by the join key, a partial partition-wise join can be done when executing the query in parallel. The table that is not partitioned by the join key is dynamically repartitioned, and each query server joins a pair of partitions from the two tables. When possible, the optimizer combines partition pruning and partition-wise join.

The decision to use partition-wise join or any of its variants is taken by the optimizer based on cost. To display the execution plan chosen by the optimizer, use the EXPLAIN PLAN statement.

3.6.2   Star Queries

A star query is a typical query executed on a star schema. Each of the dimension tables is joined to the fact table using the primary key/foreign key relationship. Oracle 8*i* optimizes the performance of star queries using the star transformation algorithm and bitmap indexes. First, bitmap indexes are used to retrieve the necessary rows from the fact table. The result is then joined to the dimension tables.

Rather than computing a Cartesian product of the dimension tables, the star transformation is based on combining bitmap indexes on the fact table columns that correspond to the constrained dimensions. The star transformation works by generating new subqueries that can be used to drive a bitmap index access path for the fact table.

If your data warehouse has a star schema, you should enable star transformation. This is done by setting the STAR_TRANSFORMATION_ENABLED initialization parameter to TRUE. Alternatively, you can use the STAR_TRANSFORMATION hint on queries that join the fact and dimension tables.

Hint: Be sure to create a bitmap index for each key column in the fact table.

3.7　PARALLELISM

Many operations in a data warehouse involve processing large amounts of data. Bulk loading, creating indexes, creating summaries, fetching rows, sorting, and joining data from multiple tables can all take a considerable amount of time.

When running Oracle 8*i* on machines with multiple processors, parallelism can be used to reduce the time it takes to execute a task. Parallelism allows certain SQL statements to be divided transparently into several concurrently executing operations. By dividing the work among several processes on different processors, the statement can be completed faster than with only a single process.

Because of the data throughput requirements of a warehouse, parallel execution is critical; thus it is important that the hardware selected for the data warehouse or data mart be a mutliprocessor machine, either a Symetlnc Multi-Processor (SMP), cluster, or Masswely Parallel Processor (MPP) system. Uniprocessors have only a single CPU and are, therefore, appropriate only for small data marts.

SMPs have multiple CPUs that share memory and disks via a common bus. There is only one version of the operating system running, which schedules tasks to execute on each CPU in a symmetric fashion.

Clusters combine multiple nodes of a uniprocessor, or SMP system, together. Any node in the cluster may access any disk in this "shared disk" architecture. The nodes are connected by a system interconnect used to support the distributed lock manager.

MPPs have many separate nodes connected together by a high-speed interconnect. In this "shared nothing" architecture, each node has its own local memory and local disks and runs its own version of the operating system.

Parallelism improves performance only if you have the necessary hardware resources available. If your system is already heavily loaded, upgrade your hardware configuration before enabling parallelism. Since additional work needs to be done to set up and control parallel execution, it will only increase the system load.

In order to execute a statement in parallel, the parallel execution coordinator partitions the work to be done among a pool of parallel execution servers. It ensures that the load is balanced among the processes and redistributes work to any process that may have finished before the others. The coordinator receives the results from the parallel execution servers and assembles them into the final result.

The type of query whose performance improves the most by executing it in parallel is one that processes large amounts of data and returns a small result, such as an aggregation. For example, obtaining the total sales for the first four months of the year is shown in Figure 3.16.

Figure 3.16 Parallel Query

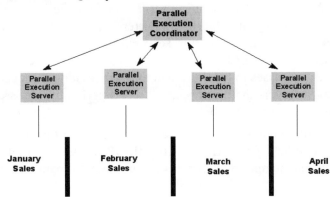

The work to be executed in parallel can be broken up in various ways. If a table or index is partitioned, as in the previous example, the coordinator may assign each parallel execution server to work on one or more partitions. Alternatively, a table or index may be divided up into blocks of rowid ranges. Each parallel execution server works in parallel on different ranges. If a table is not partitioned, new rows can be inserted in parallel by dividing the work among the parallel execution servers, where they are inserted into free space.

Parallel execution server should not be confused with Oracle Parallel Server. In an Oracle Parallel Server, the parallel execution servers may be spread across multiple instances. When using Oracle Parallel Server, the number of database *instances* that can be used to execute the query may be specified.

The query optimizer decides whether to execute the operations in parallel and determines the degree of parallelism. This determines the number of parallel execution servers allocated to do the work. The degree of parallelism is determined by default based on the number of CPUs. Alternatively, you can set the degree of parallelism for a table or an index using the PARALLEL clause on CREATE or ALTER TABLE or on an SQL statement using optimizer hints or the PARALLEL clause. This statement sets the degree of parallelism to four for the purchases table.

```
ALTER TABLE purchases PARALLEL 4;
```

A pool of parallel execution servers are created when the database instance is started up. These are available for use by any parallel operation. The query coordinator obtains the required number of parallel execution servers from the pool when needed to execute a parallel operation. When processing is complete, the coordinator returns the parallel execution servers to the server pool.

Use the PARALLEL_MIN_SERVERS initialization command to specify the number of parallel execution servers that should be created on startup. If there are a large number of concurrent users executing parallel statements, additional parallel execution servers can be created. The initialization parameter, PARALLEL_MAX_SERVERS, specifies the maximum number of server processes to create. When they are no longer needed, the parallel execution servers that have been idle for a period of time are terminated. The pool is never reduced below the PARALLEL_MIN_SERVERS parameter.

A parallel operation can be executed with fewer than the requested number of processes. The PARALLEL_MIN_PERCENT initialization parameter specifies the minimum percentage of requested parallel execution servers.

4   Loading Data into the Warehouse

4.1   THE ETT PROCESS

Populating a data warehouse involves all of the tasks related to getting the data from the source operational systems, cleansing and transforming it to the right format and level of detail, loading it into the target data warehouse, and preparing it for analysis purposes.

Figure 4.1 The ETT Process

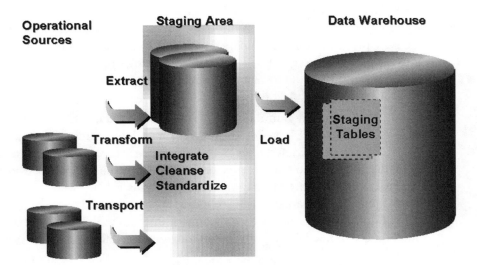

Figure 4.1 shows the steps making up the Extraction, Transformation, and Transportation (ETT) process. Data is extracted from the source operational systems and transported to the staging area. The staging area is a temporary holding place used to prepare the data. The staging area may be a set of *flat files*, or staging may be done in temporary staging tables in the *Oracle warehouse*. The data is integrated with other data, cleansed, and transformed into a common representation. They are then loaded into the target data warehouse tables. Sometimes this process is referred to as *ETL*, extraction, transformation and load. Sometimes this process is referred to as ETL, extraction, transformation, and load.

During the initial population of the data warehouse, historical data is loaded. The data in the warehouse may often be in multiple formats. If, for instance, the point-of-sales operational system was replaced two years ago, the current two years of history will be in one format, while data older than two years will be in another format.

After the initial historical load, new transaction and event data needs to be loaded on a periodic basis. This is typically done on a regular time schedule, such as at the end of the day, week, or month. During the load and while the indexes and summaries are being refreshed, the data is unavailable to warehouse users for querying. The period of time allowed for inserting the new data is called the "batch window." The batch window is a continuously shrinking amount of time, as more businesses are on-line for longer periods of time. Higher availability can be achieved by partitioning your fact table. While data is loaded into a new partition, the rest of the partitions are still available for use.

A large portion of the work in building a data warehouse will be devoted to the ETT process. Finding the data from the operational systems, creating extraction processes to get it out, filtering, cleansing, transforming, integrating data from multiple sources, and loading them into the warehouse all can take a considerable amount of time.

If you are not already familiar with the company's data, part of the difficulty of developing the ETT process is gaining an understanding of the data. One object can have different names in different systems. Even worse, two different things could have the same name. It can be a challenge to discover all of this, particularly in a company where the systems are not well-documented. Each column in the target data warehouse must be mapped to the corresponding column in the source systems. Some of the data will be mapped directly; other data will need to be derived and transformed into a different format.

Once the data is loaded into the warehouse, further processing to integrate it with existing data, updating indexes, gathering statistics, and refreshing summaries need to take place prior to it being "published" as ready for users to access. Once the data is published, it should not be updated again until the next batch window, to ensure users do not receive different answers to the same query asked at a different time.

4.1.1   **Extracting Data From the Operational Systems**

Once you have identified the data you need in the warehouse for analysis purposes, you need to locate the operational systems within the company that contain that data. The data needed for the warehouse is extracted from the source operational systems and written to the staging area, where it will later be transformed. To minimize the performance impact on the production database, data is generally downloaded without applying any transformations to it.

Often the owners of the operational systems will not allow the warehouse developers direct access to those systems but will provide periodic extracts. These extracts are generally in the form of flat, sequential operating system files, which will make up the "staging area."

Application programs need to be developed, to select the fields and records needed for the warehouse. If the data is stored in a legacy system, these may be written in COBOL and require special logic to handle things such as repeating fields in the "COBOL occurs clause." The data warehouse designers need to work closely with the application developers for the OLTP systems that are building the extract scripts to provide the necessary columns and formats of the data.

As part of designing the ETT process, you need to determine how frequently data should be extracted from the operational systems. It may be at the end of some time period or business event, such as at the end of the day or week or upon closing of the fiscal quarter. It should be clearly defined what is meant by the "end of the day" or the "last day of the week." The extraction may be done at different times for different systems and staged to be loaded into the warehouse during an upcoming batch window.

Some operational systems may be in relational databases such as Oracle8, Oracle Rdb, DB2/MVS, SQL/Server, Sybase, or Informix. Others may be in a legacy database format such as IMS or Oracle DBMS. Others may be in VSAM, RMS indexed files, or some other structured file system.

If you are able to access the source systems directly, you can get the data out by a variety of techniques depending on the type of system it is. For small amounts of data, you can use a gateway or ODBC. For larger amounts of data, a custom program directly connecting to the source database in the database's native Application Programming Interface (API) can be written.

Many ETT tools simplify the extraction process by providing connectivity to the source. In Chapter 5, we'll see an example of extraction using the Oracle Data Mart Builder component of the Data Mart Suite.

Capturing Changed Data

After the initial load of the warehouse, as the source data changes, the data in the warehouse must be updated or refreshed to reflect those changes on a regular basis. A mechanism needs to be put into place to monitor and capture changes of interest from the operational systems. Rather than rebuilding the entire warehouse periodically, only the changes need to be applied. By isolating changes as part of the extraction process, less data needs to be moved across the network and loaded into the data warehouse.

Changed data includes both new data that has been added as well as updates and deletes to existing data. For example, in the EASYDW warehouse, we are interested in all new orders as well as updates to existing product information and customers. If we are no longer selling a product, the product is deleted from the order-entry system. We may still want to retain the history in the warehouse.

In the data warehouse, it is not uncommon to change the dimension tables because, say, a product description may change. However, you should try to avoid updates to the fact table because problems may arise if this data changes.

There are various ways to identify this new data. One technique to determine the changes is to include a time stamp to record when each row in the operational system was changed. The data extraction program then selects the source data based on the time stamp of the transaction and extracts all rows that have been updated since the time of the last extraction. When moving data from the order processing system into the EASYDW warehouse, this technique can be used by selecting rows based on the order_date.

If the source is a relational database, triggers can be used to identify the changed rows. Triggers are stored procedures that can be invoked before or after an event, such as when an insert, update, or delete occurs. The trigger can be used to save the changed records in a table from where the extract process can later retrieve the changed rows. Be very careful of triggers in high volume applications, as they can add significant overhead to the operational system.

Sometimes you may not be able to change the schema to add a timestamp or trigger. Your system may already be heavily loaded, and you do not want to degrade the performance in any way. Or the source may be a legacy system, which does not have triggers. Therefore, you may need to use a file comparison to identify changes. This involves keeping before and after images of the extract files to find the changes. For example, you may need to compare the recent extract with the current product or customer list to identify the changes.

Changes to the metadata or data definitions must also be identified. Changes to the structure of the operational system, such as adding or dropping a column, impact the extraction and load programs, which may need to be modified to account for the change.

4.1.2   Transforming the Data into a Common Representation

Once the data has been extracted from the operational systems it is ready to be cleansed and transformed into a common representation. Differences between naming conventions, storage formats, data types, and encoding schemes must all be resolved. Duplicates are removed, relationships are validated, and unique key identifiers are added. In this section, various types of transformations will be introduced. In Chapter 5, some of these transformations will be demonstrated using Oracle Data Mart Builder.

Integrating Data from Multiple Sources

Often the information needed to create a table in the warehouse comes from multiple source systems. If there is a field in common between the systems, the data can be joined via that column.

Integrating data from multiple sources can be very challenging. The operational systems may have been designed by different people, at different times, using different technology, e.g. hardware platforms, database management systems, and operating system software. If data is coming from an IBM mainframe, the data may need to be converted from EBCDIC to ASCII.

To compound the problem, there may not be a common identifier in the source systems. For example, when creating the customer dimension, there may not be a customer_id in each system. You may have to look at customer names and addresses to determine that it is the same customer. These may have different spacing, case, and punctuation. There is no SQL join operator that allows fuzzy matching, this type of transformation must be done another way. Special tools can be purchased for name and address validation and correction.

Cleansing Data

The majority of operational systems contain dirty data, which means that there may be:

- Duplicate records

- Data missing
- Data contains invalid values

Sometimes business rules have been enforced by the applications; other times, by integrity constraints within the database; and sometimes there may be no enforcement at all.

Data must be standardized. For example, any given street address, such as 1741 Coleman Ave., can be represented in many ways. The word "Avenue" may be stored as "Ave," "Ave.," "Avenue," or "AVE." *Search & Replace transforms* allow you to search for any of these values and replace them with the standard value you've chosen for your warehouse.

You may want to check the validity of certain types of data. If a product is sold only in three colors, you can validate that the data conform to a list of values, such as red, yellow, and green. You may want to validate data against a larger list of values stored in a table, such as the states within the United States. *Table lookup transforms* retrieve the value of a column by looking it up in a dimension table in the database.

Some types of cleansing involve combining and separating character data. You may need to *concatenate* two string columns. For example, combining last name, comma, and first name into the customer_name column. Or you may need to use a *substring* operation to divide a string into separate parts, such as separating the area code from a phone number.

An important data integrity step involves enforcement of one-to-one and one-to-many relationships. Often these are checked as part of the transformation process rather than by using referential integrity constraints in the warehouse.

Deriving New Data

While loading the data, you may want to perform *calculations* or derive new data from the existing data. For example, you may want to keep a running total or count of records as they are moved from the source to the target database.

During the design process, the appropriate level of granularity for the warehouse is determined. It is often best to store data at various levels of granularity with different retention and archive periods. The most fine-grained transaction data will usually be retained for a much shorter period of time than data aggregated at a higher level. Transaction granular sales data is necessary to analyze which products are purchased together. Daily sales of a product by store is used to analyze regional trends and product performance.

Data may be aggregated as part of the transformation process. If you did not want to store the detailed transactions in your data warehouse, the data can be *aggregated* prior to moving it to the data warehouse.

Generating Warehouse Keys

Instead of using the keys that were used in the operational system, a common design technique is to make up a new key, called the *synthetic key*, to use in the warehouse. The synthetic key is usually a generated sequence of integers.

Synthetic keys are used for a variety of reasons. The keys used in the operational system may be long character strings, with meaning embedded into the components of the key. Because synthetic keys are integers, the fact tables and B*tree indexes are smaller, with fewer levels, and take less space, improving query response time. Synthetic keys provide a degree of isolation from changes in the operational system.

If the operational system changes the product-code naming conventions, or format, all data in the warehouse does not have to be changed. In these days of company acquisitions, if you need to load products from a newly acquired company into your warehouse, it is highly unlikely that both companies used the same product encoding schemes. The use of synthetic keys can greatly help integrate the data.

Both the synthetic keys and operational system keys are stored in the dimension table, as shown in Figure 4.2. The synthetic key is used in the fact table as the column that joins the fact table to the dimension table. In this example, there are two different formats for product codes. Some are numeric, separated by a dash "123-118." Others are a mix of alphanumeric and numeric characters "SR125." As part of the ETT process, as each fact record is loaded, the synthetic key is looked up from the dimension tables and stored in the fact table.

Choosing the Optimal Place to Perform the Transformations

Transformations of the data may be done at any step in the ETT process. You need to decide the most efficient place to do each transformation—at the source, in the staging area, during the load operation, or in temporary tables once the data is loaded into the warehouse.

- **Transformations can be done as part of the extraction process.** In general, it is best to do *filtering* types of transformations whenever possible at the source. This allows you to select only the records of interest for loading into the warehouse. Ideally, you want to extract only the data that has been changed since your last extraction. While other transformations could be done at the source operational system, an important consideration is to minimize the additional load the extraction process puts on the operational system.

Figure 4.2 The Use of Synthetic Keys in the Warehouse

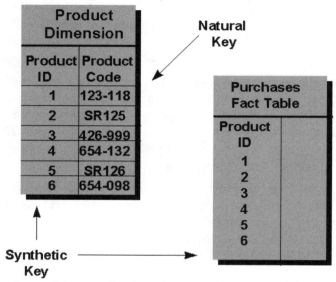

- **Transformations can be done in a staging area prior to loading the data into the data warehouse.** When data needs to be integrated from multiple systems, it cannot be done as part of the extraction process. You can use flat files as your staging area, your Oracle database as your staging area, or a combination of both. If your incoming data is in a flat file, it is probably more efficient to finish your staging processes prior to loading the data into the Oracle warehouse. If your data is already in Oracle, it may be more efficient to perform your transformations in temporary tables within the database. Transformations that require sorting, sequential processing, and row-at-a-time operations can be done efficiently in the flat file staging area.

When the data can be processed in bulk using SQL set operations, which can be done in parallel, the transformations can be efficiently done in staging tables in the Oracle server. If some of the data needed for the transformation purposes is already in the warehouse, it may be more efficient to do the transformation in the warehouse. For example, key lookups to obtain the synthetic key from the dimension table can be efficiently performed in staging tables in the database. If your source is an Oracle 8*i* database, transportable tablespaces make it easy to move data into the warehouse without first extracting the data into an external table. In this case, it makes sense to do the transformations in temporary staging tables once the data is in the warehouse.

- **Transformations may be done during the load process.** Some simple types of transformations can be done as the data is being loaded. For example, SQL*Loader conventional path mode can be used to change the case of a character column to uppercase. This is best done when a small number of rows need to be added; for example, when initially loading a dimension table.

4.1.3   Loading the Warehouse

When loading the warehouse, load the dimension tables first. The dimension tables contain the synthetic keys or other descriptive information needed by the fact tables. When loading the fact tables, information is looked up from the dimension tables and added to the columns in the fact table.

When loading the dimension table, you need to both *add new rows* and *make changes to existing rows.* For example, a customer dimension may contain tens of thousands of customers. Usually, only ten percent or less of the customer information changes. You will be adding new customers and sometimes modifying the information about existing customers.

When adding new data to the dimension table, you need to determine if the record already exists. If it does not, you can add it to the table. If it does exist, there are various ways to handle the changes based on whether you need to keep the old information in the warehouse for analysis purposes.

If a customer's address changes, there is no need to retain the old address, so the record can simply be updated. In a rapidly growing company the sales regions will change often. For example, "Canada" rolled up into the "rest of the world" until 1990, then rolled up into the "Americas," after a reorganization. If you needed to understand both the old geographic hierarchy as well as the new one, you can create a new dimension record containing all the old data plus the new hierarchy, giving the record a new synthetic key. Alternatively, you could create columns in the original record to hold both the previous and current values. In either case, loading the dimension table requires the use of special programming logic.

The *time dimension* contains one row for each unit of time that is of interest in the warehouse. In the EASYDW shopping example, purchases can be made on-line 365 days a year, so every day is of interest to us. For each given date, information about the day is stored, including the day of the week, the week number, the month, the quarter, the year, and if it is a holiday. The time dimension may be loaded on a yearly basis. New data for each day of the year can be added.

When loading the fact table, you typically append new information to the end of the existing fact table. You do not want to alter the existing rows, because you want to preserve that data. For example, the PURCHASES fact table contains three months of data. New data from the source order entry system is appended to the purchases fact table monthly. Partitioning the data by month facilitates this type of operation.

4.2   LOAD TECHNIQUES

In this section we will take a look at two common techniques to load data. If your data is in an a flat file, external to the database, you can use SQL*Loader to move the data into the tables in your warehouse. Data can be inserted into a new table, or new rows can be appended to an existing table. If your operational data is in an Oracle 8*i* database, transportable tablespaces can be used to move the data from between the operational system and the warehouse.

One of the most popular tools for loading data is SQL*Loader, because it has been designed to load records as fast as possible. It can be used either from the operating system command line or via its wizard in Oracle Enterprise Manager (OEM), which we will first see how to use.

4.2.1   Using the SQL*Loader Wizard

Figure 4.3 shows the Oracle Enterprise Manager Data Management Pack Load wizard, which can be used to help automate the scheduling of your SQL*Loader jobs. The wizard guides you through the process of loading data from an external file into the database according to a set of instructions in a control file.

You can launch the data management tools through the Oracle Enterprise Management console, or from either Schema Manager or Storage Manager if they are connected to the Oracle Management Server. From the Schema Manager, choose the *Tools* menu, then the *Data Management* menu, and then click on *Load option*.

The Control File

The *control file* is a text file that describes the load operation. The role of the control file, which is illustrated in Figure 4.4, is to tell SQL*Loader which data file to load, how to interpret the records and columns, and what tables the data should be inserted into.

Figure 4.3 Schema Manager Load Wizard

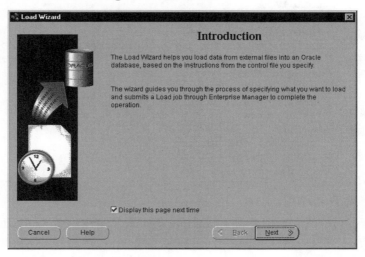

Figure 4.4 The Control File

The control file is written in SQL*Loader's data definition language. Figure 4.5 shows the control file that would be used to add new product data into the product table in the EASYDW warehouse. The data is stored in the file product.dat. New rows will be appended to the existing table.

Figure 4.5 Control File to Load Product Dimension Table

```
— Load product dimension
LOAD DATA
INFILE 'product.dat' append
INTO TABLE product
FIELDS TERMINATED BY ',' OPTIONALLY ENCLOSED BY "'"
(product_id,
 product_name,
 category,
 cost_price,
 sell_price,
 weight,
 shipping_charge,
 manufacturer,
 supplier)
```

The Data File

Figure 4.6 shows a small sample of the data file product.dat. Each field is separated by a comma and optionally enclosed in a single quote. Each field in the input file is mapped to the corresponding columns in the table. As the data is read, it is converted from the data type in the input file to the data type of the column in the database.

Figure 4.6 Sample Data File

```
'SP1242', 'CD LX1','MUSC', 8.90, 15.67, 2.5, 2.95, 'RTG', 'CD Inc'
'SP1243', 'CD LX2','MUSC', 8.90, 15.67, 2.5, 2.95, 'RTG', 'CD Inc'
'SP1244', 'CD LX3','MUSC', 8.90, 15.67, 2.5, 2.95, 'RTG', 'CD Inc'
'SP1245', 'CD LX4','MUSC', 8.90, 15.67, 2.5, 2.95, 'RTG', 'CD Inc'
```

The data file in Figure 4.6 is an example of data stored in stream format. Each record is terminated by a record separator, often a line feed or carriage return/ line feed. Each field is separated by a delimiter character, often a comma. The fields may also be enclosed in single or double quotes.

In addition to the stream format, SQL*Loader supports fixed-length and variable-length format files. In a fixed-length file, each record is the same length. Normally each field in the record is also the same length. In the control file, the input record is described by specifying the starting position, length, and data type. In a variable-length file, each record may be a different length. The first field in each record is used to specify the length of that record.

SQL*Loader Modes of Operation

Figure 4.7 shows SQL*Loader's two modes of operation: *conventional* and *direct path.*

Conventional path load should only be used to load small amounts of data, such as initially loading a small dimension table. The *conventional path load* issues SQL INSERT statements. As each row is inserted, the indexes are updated, triggers are fired, and constraints are evaluated.

When loading large amounts of data in a small batch window, *direct path load* can be used to optimize performance. *Direct path load* bypasses the SQL layer. It formats the data blocks directly and writes them to the database files. When running on a system with multiple processors, the load can be executed in parallel.

Hint: Use direct path mode if you plan to use FAST refresh to refresh your summaries.

Figure 4.7 SQL*Loader Modes of Operation

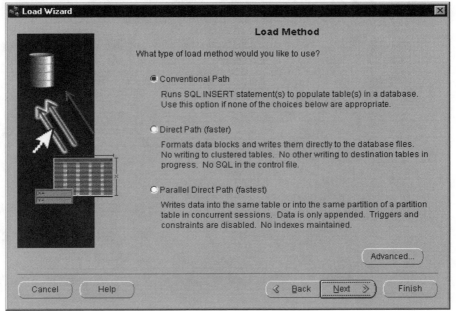

Handling SQL*Loader Errors

You can create additional files during the load operation to aid in the diagnosis and correction of any errors that may occur during the load. A log file is created to record the status of the load operation. This should always be reviewed to ensure the load was successful.

Copies of the records that could not be loaded into the database because of data integrity violations can be saved in a *bad file*. This file can later be re-entered once the data integrity problems have been corrected.

If you receive an extract file with more records than you are interested in, you can load a subset of records from the file. The WHERE clause in the control file is used to select the records to load. Any records that are skipped are written to a *discard file*.

Select which optional files you would like created using the *Advanced* option, as shown in Figure 4.8. In this example, we've selected a bad file, a discard file, and a log file.

Figure 4.8 SQL*Loader Advanced Options

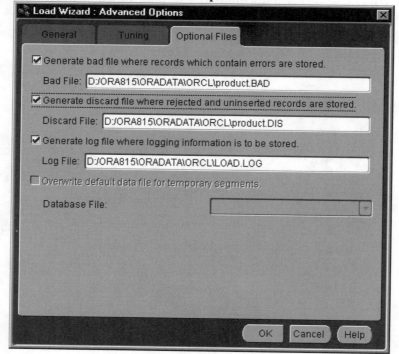

Scheduling the Load Operation

Enterprise Manager's job scheduling system allows you to create and manage jobs, schedule the jobs to run, and monitor progress. You can run a job once or choose how frequently you would like the job to run. If you will run the job multiple times, you can save the job in Enterprise Manager's jobs library so that it can be rerun in the future. In Figure 4.9, the job will be scheduled to run at the end of every month.

Figure 4.9 Scheduling the Load

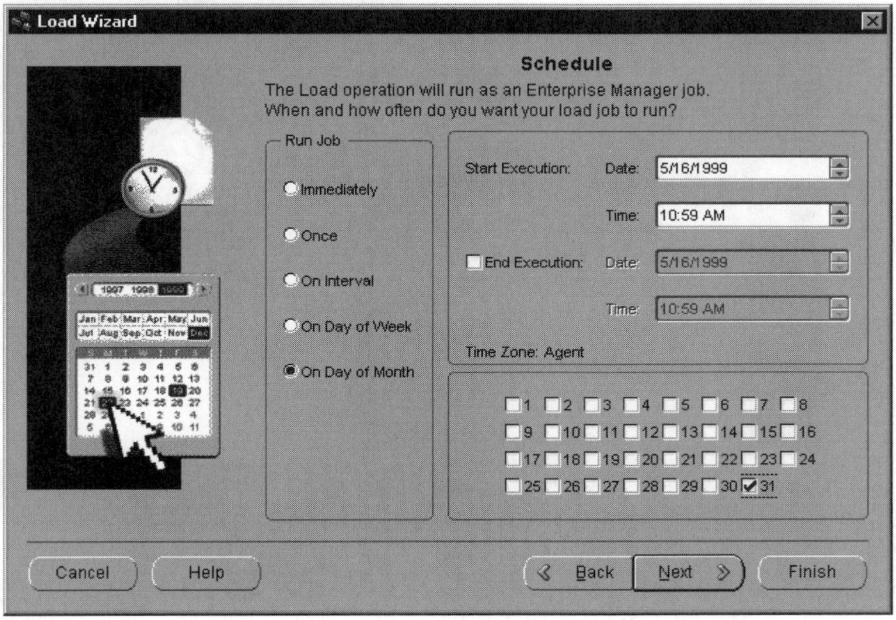

Monitoring Progress of the Load Operation

You can monitor the progress of a job while it is running from the jobs pane on the Enterprise Manager Console, shown in Figure 4.10. The Active page lists all jobs that are either running or are scheduled to run. By clicking on the job in the active jobs page, information about the job's state and progress can be displayed. Load 0012 is running. The History Page contains a list of jobs that have been run previously. You can check to see if the job has run successfully after it has completed.

Figure 4.10 Monitoring Jobs from the OEM Console

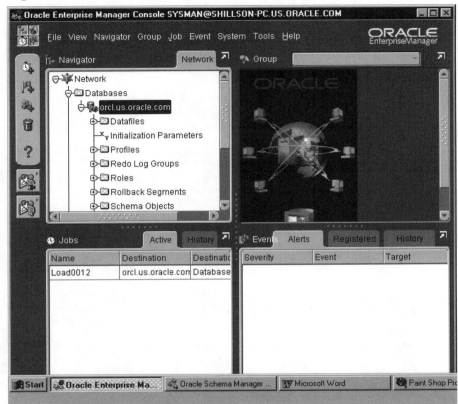

Analyzing the SQL*Loader Log

Figure 4.11 shows a portion of the log file from a sample load session. Twenty-seven rows were appended to the product table. One record was rejected due to invalid data. A copy of that record can be found in the file, bad.dat.

Figure 4.11 SQL*Loader Log File

```
SQL*Loader:Release 8.1.5.0.0 -Production on Tue May 4 20:10:23 1999

(c) Copyright 1998 Oracle Corporation. All rights reserved.

Control File: f:/book/product.ctl
Data File: f:\book\product.dat
```

```
Bad File: f:/book/product.bad
Discard File: none specified

(Allow all discards)

Number to load: ALL
Number to skip: 0
Errors allowed: 50
Bind array: 64 rows, maximum of 65536 bytes
Continuation: none specified
Path used: Conventional

Table PRODUCT, loaded from every logical record.
Insert option in effect for this table: APPEND
```

Column Name	Position	Len	Term	Encl	Datatype
PRODUCT_ID	FIRST	*	,	O(')	CHARACTER
PRODUCT_NAME	NEXT	*	,	O(')	CHARACTER
CATEGORY	NEXT	*	,	O(')	CHARACTER
COST_PRICE	NEXT	*	,	O(')	CHARACTER
SELL_PRICE	NEXT	*	,	O(')	CHARACTER
WEIGHT	NEXT	*	,	O(')	CHARACTER
SHIPPING_CHARGE	NEXT	*	,	O(')	CHARACTER
MANUFACTURER	NEXT	*	,	O(')	CHARACTER
SUPPLIER	NEXT	*	,	O(')	CHARACTER

```
Record 28: Rejected - Error on table PRODUCT, column PRODUCT_ID.
Column not found before end of logical record
  (use TRAILING NULLCOLS)
```

```
Table PRODUCT:
 27 Rows successfully loaded.
 1  Row not loaded due to data errors.
 0  Rows not loaded because all WHEN clauses were failed.
 0  Rows not loaded because all fields were null.
```

4.2.2   Optimizing SQL*Loader Performance

When loading large amounts of data in a small batch window, a variety of techniques can be used to optimize performance:

- **Using direct path load**. By formatting the data blocks directly and writing them to the database files, much of the work needed to execute a SQL insert statement is eliminated. Direct path load requires *exclusive access to the table or partition being loaded.* In addition, *triggers* *are automatically disabled,* and *constraint evaluation is deferred* until the load completes.

- **Disabling integrity constraint evaluation prior to loading the data.** When loading data with direct path, SQL*Loader automatically disables all CHECK and REFERENCES integrity constraints. When using parallel direct path load or loading into a single partition, other types of constraints must be disabled. You can manually disable evaluation of not null, unique, and primary key constraints during the load process, as well. When the load completes, you can have SQL*Loader reenable the constraints, or do it yourself manually.

- **Loading the data in sorted order.** Presorting data minimizes the amount of temporary storage needed during the load, enabling optimizations to minimize the processing during the merge phase to be applied. To tell SQL*Loader what indexes the data is sorted on, use the SORTED INDEXES statement in the control file.

- **Deferring index maintenance.** Indexes are maintained automatically whenever data is inserted or deleted, or the key column updated. When loading large amounts of data with direct path load, it may be faster to *defer index maintenance* until after the data is loaded. You can either drop the indexes prior to the beginning of the load or skip index maintenance by setting SKIP_INDEX_MAINTENANCE=TRUE on the SQL*Loader command line. Index partitions that would have been updated are marked "index unusable," because the index segment is inconsistent with respect to the data it indexes. After the data is loaded the indexes must be rebuilt.

- **Disabling redo logging.** All changes made to the database are also written to the redo log so they can be used to recover the database after failures. *Media recovery* is the process of recovering after the loss of a database file—often due to a hardware failure such as a disk head crash. *Crash recovery* is used to recover from a system failure in which data in memory was modified but not yet written to the database files on disk.

  Since you already have a copy of the data being loaded into the warehouse, you have an alternative to using the redo log to recover. If the system fails in the middle of loading the data, you could restart the load rather than using the redo log for recovery.

  To disable logging of redo during the SQL*Loader session, use the UNRECOVERABLE option in the control file.

- **Loading the data into a single partition.** While you are loading a partition of a partitioned or subpartitioned table, other users can continue to access the other partitions in the table. Loading the April transactions will not prevent users from querying the existing data for January through March. Thus, overall availability of the warehouse is increased.

- **Loading the data in parallel.** When a table is partitioned, the direct path loader can be used to load multiple partitions in parallel. You can also set up multiple, concurrent sessions to perform a direct path load into the same table or into the same partition of a partitioned table.

4.2.3   SQL*Loader Direct Path Load of a Single Partition

We will look at an example of loading data into a single partition. In the EASYDW warehouse, the fact table is partitioned by date. At the end of April 1999, the April sales transactions are loaded into the EASYDW warehouse.

In the example below, we create a tablespace, add a partition to the purchases table, and then use SQL*Loader direct path load to insert the data into the April 1999 partition.

(1)   Create a Tablespace

```
CREATE TABLESPACE purchases_apr99
datafile 'd:\ora815\oradata\orcl\PURCHASESAPR99.f' size 5m
reuse autoextend on
default storage
(initial 64k next 64k pctincrease 0 maxextents unlimited);
```

(2)   Add a Partition

```
ALTER TABLE easydw.purchases
ADD PARTITION purchases_apr99
values less than (TO_DATE('30-04-1999', 'DD-MM-YYYY'))
pctfree 0 pctused 99
storage (initial 64k next 64k pctincrease 0)
tablespace purchases_apr99;
```

(3)   Disable all Referential Integrity Constraints and Triggers

When using direct path load of a single partition, referential and check constraints on the table partition must be disabled along with any triggers .

```
ALTER TABLE purchases disable constraint fk_time;
ALTER TABLE purchases disable constraint fk_product_id;
ALTER TABLE purchases disable constraint fk_customer_id;
```

(4)   Load the Data

Figure 4.12 shows the SQL*Loader control file to load new data into a single partition. Media recovery is possible to get the data file back, however the table is not recoverable and will have to be reloaded. Any data that cannot be loaded will be written to the file "purchases.bad." Data will be loaded into the "purchases_apr99" partition. The file, purchases.dat, is a fixed-length file. Each field in the input record is described by specifying the starting position, its ending position, and its data type. Note, these are SQL*Loader data types, not the data types in an Oracle table. When the data is loaded into the tables, each field is converted to the data type of the column if necessary.

Figure 4.12 SQL*Loader Control File to Load into a Single Partition

```
UNRECOVERABLE LOAD DATA
INFILE 'purchases.dat' BADFILE 'purchases.bad'
APPEND
 INTO TABLE purchases
 PARTITION (purchases_apr99)
 (product_id         position (1-6) char,
 time_key           position (7-17)
 date "DD-MON-YYYY",
 customer_id        position (18-25)      char,
 purchase_date position (26-36)       date "DD-MON-YYYY",
 purchase_time position (37-40)       integer external,
 purchase_price position (41-45)       decimal external,
 shipping_charge position (46-49) integer external,
 today_special_offer    position (50) char)
```

Figure 4.13 shows a sample of the purchases data file. The product_id starts in column 1 and is six bytes long. "Time_key" starts in column 7 and is 17 bytes long. The data mask "DD-MON-YYYY" is used to describe the input format of the date fields.

Figure 4.13 Sample Purchases Data File

```
 1 2  3  4  5
1234567890123456789012345678901234567890123456789012345678901
     |          |          |          |    |    |    |
SP100101-APR-1999AB12345601-APR-1999002428.014.50Y
SP100101-APR-1999AB12345701-APR-1999102428.014.50Y

Sqlldr userid=easydw/easydw control=purchases.ctl
  log=purchases.log direct=true skip_index_maintenance = true
```

To invoke SQL*Loader direct path mode from the command line, set direct=true. In this example, skip_index_maintenance is set to true, so the indexes will need to be rebuilt after the load.

(5) Analyze the Log

Figure 4.14 shows a portion of the SQL*Loader log file from the load operation. Rather than generating redo to allow recovery, invalidation redo was generated to let Oracle know this table cannot be recovered. The indexes were made unusable. The column starting position and length are described.

(6) Reenable all Constraints

When loading into a single partition, all references to constraints and triggers must be reenabled after the load. If you have already ensured data integrity, and do not want to incur the overhead of revalidating the data, use the ENABLE NOVALIDATE clause.

```
ALTER TABLE purchases enable constraint fk_time;
ALTER TABLE purchases enable constraint fk_product_id;
ALTER TABLE purchases
      enable novalidate constraint fk_customer_id;
```

(7) Rebuild Indexes

All local indexes for the partition can be maintained by SQL*Loader. Global indexes are not maintained on single partition or subpartition direct path loads and must be rebuilt. In the example above, the indexes must be rebuilt since index maintenance was skipped.

```
ALTER INDEX product_pk_index REBUILD ;
ALTER INDEX purchase_customer_index
      REBUILD PARTITION purchases_apr99;
ALTER INDEX purchase_product_index
REBUILD PARTITION purchases_apr99;
ALTER INDEX purchase_time_index
      REBUILD PARTITION purchases_apr99;
ALTER INDEX purchase_SPECIAL_index
      REBUILD PARTITION purchases_apr99;
```

Figure 4.14 SQL*Loader Log File

```
SQL*Loader: Release 8.1.5.0.0-Production on Mon May 17 18:33:18 1999

(c) Copyright 1998 Oracle Corporation. All rights reserved.

Control File: f:\book\purchases.ctl
Data File: f:\book\purchases.dat
Bad File: f:\book\purchases.bad
Discard File: none specified
 (Allow all discards)

Number to load: ALL
Number to skip: 0
Errors allowed: 50
Continuation: none specified
Path used: Direct
Load is UNRECOVERABLE; invalidation redo is produced.
Table PURCHASES, partition PURCHASES_APR99, loaded from every
  logical record.
Insert option in effect for this partition: APPEND

Column Name          Position  Len   Term  Encl    Datatype

PRODUCT_ID             1:6      6                   CHARACTER
TIME_KEY               7:17     11                  DATE DD-Mon-YYYY
CUSTOMER_ID            18:25    8                   CHARACTER
PURCHASE_DATE          26:36    11                  DATE DD-Mon-YYYY
PURCHASE_TIME          37:40    4                   CHARACTER
PURCHASE_PRICE         41:45    5                   CHARACTER
SHIPPING_CHARGE        46:49    4                   CHARACTER
TODAY_SPECIAL_OFFER    50       1                   CHARACTER

The following index(es) on table PURCHASES were processed:
index EASYDW.PURCHASE_PRODUCT_INDEX partition PURCHASES_APR99 was
 made unusable due to: ORA-26025: SKIP_INDEX_MAINTENANCE option
    requested
index EASYDW.PURCHASE_CUSTOMER_INDEX partition PURCHASES_APR99 was
    made unusable due to:ORA-26025: SKIP_INDEX_MAINTENANCE option
    requested
index EASYDW.PURCHASE_SPECIAL_INDEX partition PURCHASES_APR99 was
 made unusable due to:ORA-26025: SKIP_INDEX_MAINTENANCE option
    requested
index EASYDW.PURCHASE_TIME_INDEX partition PURCHASES_APR99 was
made unusable due to: ORA-26025: SKIP_INDEX_MAINTENANCE option
requested
```

4.2.4   SQL*Loader Parallel Direct Path Load

When a table is partitioned, the direct path loader can be used to load multiple partitions in parallel. Each parallel direct path load process should be loaded into a partition of a table stored on a separate disk, to minimize I/O contention.

Since data is extracted from multiple operational systems, you will often have several input files that need to be loaded into the warehouse. These files can be loaded in parallel, and the workload distributed among several concurrent SQL*Loader sessions.

Figure 4.15 SQL*Loader Parallel Direct Path Load

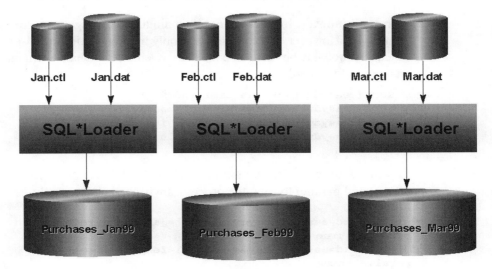

Figure 4.15 shows an example of how parallel direct path load can be used to initially load the historical transactions into the purchases table. You need to invoke multiple SQL*Loader sessions. Each SQL*Loader session takes a different data file as input. In this example, there are three data files, each containing the purchases for one month: January, February, and March. These will be loaded into the purchases table, which is also partitioned by month. Each data file is loaded in parallel into its own partition.

It is suggested that the following steps are followed to load data in parallel using SQL*Loader:

(1) **Disable all constraints and triggers.** Constraints cannot be evaluated, and triggers can not be fired during a parallel direct path load. If you forget, SQL*Loader will issue an error.

```
ALTER TABLE purchases disable constraint not_null_time;
ALTER TABLE purchases disable constraint fk_time;
ALTER TABLE purchases disable constraint not_null_product_id;
ALTER TABLE purchases disable constraint fk_product_id;
ALTER TABLE purchases disable constraint not_null_customer_id;
ALTER TABLE purchases disable constraint fk_customer_id;
ALTER TABLE purchases disable constraint special_offer;
```

(2) **Drop all indexes.** Indexes cannot be maintained during a parallel direct path load. However, if we are loading only a few partitions out of many, then it is probably better to skip index maintenance and have them marked as unusable instead.

```
DROP INDEX easydw.purchase_time_index;
DROP INDEX easydw.purchase_product_index;
DROP INDEX easydw.purchase_customer_index;
DROP INDEX easydw.purchase_special_index;
```

(3) **Load the data.** By invoking multiple SQL*Loader sessions and setting direct and parallel to true, the processes will load concurrently.

```
Sqlldr userid=easydw/easydw control=jan.ctl direct=true
    parallel=true
Sqlldr userid=easydw/easydw control=feb.ctl direct=true
    parallel=true
Sqlldr userid=easydw/easydw control=mar.ctl direct=true
    parallel=true
```

(4) **Anaylze the log.** A portion of one of the log files is listed below. Note, the mode is direct with the parallel option.

```
SQL*Loader:Release 8.1.5.0.0-Production on Sun May 23 12:13:48 1999
(c) Copyright 1999 Oracle Corporation. All rights reserved.

Control File: f:\book\feb.ctl
Data File: f:\book\FEB.dat
 Bad File: f:\book\FEB.bad
 Discard File: none specified
 (Allow all discards)
```

```
Number to load: ALL
Number to skip: 0
Errors allowed: 50
Continuation: none specified
Path used: Direct - with parallel option.
```

(5) Reenable all constraints. After using parallel direct path load, constraints must be reenabled.

```
ALTER TABLE purchases enable constraint not_null_time;
ALTER TABLE purchases enable constraint fk_time;
ALTER TABLE purchases enable constraint not_null_product_id;
ALTER TABLE purchases enable constraint fk_product_id;
ALTER TABLE purchases enable constraint not_null_customer_id;
ALTER TABLE purchases enable constraint fk_customer_id;
ALTER TABLE purchases enable constraint special_offer;
```

(6) Recreate all indexes.

```
CREATE BITMAP INDEX easydw.purchase_time_index ON purchases
 (time_key )
local
 (partition indexJan99 tablespace purchases_jan99_idx,
 partition indexFeb99 tablespace purchases_feb99_idx,
 partition indexMar99 tablespace purchases_mar99 );

CREATE INDEX easydw.purchase_product_index ON purchases
 (product_id )
 local
 pctfree 5 tablespace indx
 storage (initial 64k next 64k pctincrease 0) ;
```

4.2.5   Transformations Using SQL*Loader

If you receive extract files that have data in them that you do not want to load into the warehouse, you can use SQL*Loader to filter the rows of interest. You select the records that meet the load criteria, specifying a WHEN clause to test an equality or inequality condition in the record. If a record does not satisfy the WHEN condition, it is written to the discard file. The discard file contains records that were filtered out of the load because they did not match any record-selection criteria specified in the control file. Note, these records differ from rejected records written to the BAD file. Discarded records do not necessarily have any bad data. The WHEN clause can be used with either conventional or direct path load.

When using conventional path load, you can use SQL*Loader to perform simple types of transformations on character data. For example, portions of a string can be inserted using the substring function; two fields can be concatenated together using the CONCAT operator. You can trim leading or trailing characters from a string using the trim operator. The control file in Figure 4.16 shows an example, changing the format of the product_id column to uppercase and discarding any rows with a blank product_id.

Figure 4.16 Using SQL*Loader to Uppercase Column Values

```
LOAD DATA
INFILE 'product.dat' append
INTO TABLE product WHEN product_id != BLANKS
FIELDS TERMINATED BY ',' OPTIONALLY ENCLOSED BY "'"
(product_id "upper(:product_id)",
 product_name,
 category,
 cost_price,
 sell_price,
 weight,
 shipping_charge,
 manufacturer,
 supplier)
```

The *discard* file is specified when invoking SQL*Loader from the command line as shown below.

```
sqlldr userid=easydw/easydw control=product.ctl
log=product.log bad=product.bad discard=product.dis
```

4.2.6   Loading the Warehouse Using Transportable Tablespaces

If both your operational system and data warehouse are running Oracle 8*i* a tablespace can be moved from one database to another. *Transportable Tablespaces*, a new feature in Oracle 8*i*, provide a mechanism to move one or more tablespaces from one Oracle database into another.

Transportable tablespaces can be used to move data from the operational database to the staging area if you are using an Oracle database to do your staging. After the data is transformed in the staging area, transportable tablespaces can be used again to move data from the staging area into the data warehouse. Transportable tablespaces are also useful to move data from the data warehouse to a dependent data mart.

To transport a tablespace, use the export utility to unload the metadata describing the objects in the tablespace, *copy* the data files and export dump file containing the metadata to the target system, and then use the *import* utility to load the metadata descriptions into the target database.

Figure 4.17 Transportable Tablespaces

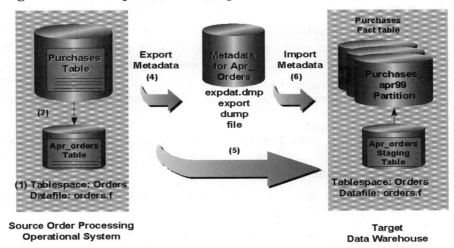

Moving data using transportable tablespaces is much faster than using either export/import or unload/load of the same data. Rather than processing the data a row at a time when transporting a tablespace, the entire file or set of files are physically copied and then integrated into the database by importing the metadata describing the files. In addition, index data can also be moved, eliminating the need to rebuild indexes after importing data.

In Oracle 8*i*, you can transport tablespaces only between Oracle databases that use the same data block size and character set and that run on compatible platforms from the same hardware vendor. Figure 4.17 illustrates using transportable tablespaces to move data.

One of the sources for data in the EASYDW Warehouse is an Oracle 8*i* order-processing system. In this example, the order-entry system has a record for every order stored in the purchases table. At the end of April, all the orders for April 1999 will be copied into a new table called apr_orders in the orders tablespace stored in the datafile "orders.d."

The metadata describing the orders tablespace is exported and stored in the export dump file "expdat.dmp." The datafile, "orders.f" and the export dump file, "expdat.dmp," are copied to the target data warehouse system. The metadata describing the orders tablespace is imported using the import utility. The apr_orders table can be used as a staging table. Once the data has been transformed and cleansed, a new partition is created in the purchases fact table, and the apr_orders are moved into the new partition.

Here are the steps that are required to transport a tablespace from one database to another.

(1) Create a tablespace in the OLTP system. Choose a name that is unique on both the source and target system. In this example, the tablespace orders is created, and its corresponding data file is "orders.f."

```
CREATE TABLESPACE orders
DATAFILE 'd:\ora815\oradata\orcl\orders.f' SIZE 5M REUSE
AUTOEXTEND ON
DEFAULT STORAGE
(INITIAL 64K NEXT 64K PCTINCREASE 0 MAXEXTENTS  UNLIMITED);
```

(2) Move the data for April 1999

In this example, a table is created and populated using the CREATE TABLE AS SELECT statement.

```
CREATE TABLE apr_orders AS SELECT * FROM .purchases
WHERE purchase_date BETWEEN '01-APR-1999' AND '30-APR-1999';
```

Each tablespace must be self-contained and cannot reference anything outside the tablespace. If there were a global index on the April orders table, it would not be self-contained, and the index would have to be dropped before the tablespace could be moved.

(3) Alter the tablespace so that it is read-only.

```
ALTER TABLESPACE orders READ ONLY;
```

(4) Unload the dictionary definitions.

Using the EXPORT command, we extract the metadata definitions for our tablespace orders.

```
EXP 'system/manager as sysdba' TRANSPORT_TABLESPACE=y
  TABLESPACES=orders TRIGGERS=n CONSTRAINTS=n GRANTS=n
  FILE=expdat.dmp LOG=export.log
```

When transporting a set of tablespaces, you can choose to include referential integrity constraints. However, if you do include these, you must move the tables with both the primary and foreign keys.

Hint: When exporting and importing tablespaces, be sure to connect 'as sysdba.'

The following is a copy of the log file, export.log, generated from the export. Only the tablespace metadata is exported, not the data.

```
Connected to: Oracle 8i Enterprise Edition Release 8.1.5.0.0
With the Partitioning option
PL/SQL Release 8.1.5.0.0 - Production
Export done in WE8ISO8859P1 character set and WE8ISO8859P1 NCHAR
 character set
Note: table data (rows) will not be exported
Note: grants on tables/views/sequences/roles will not be exported
Note: constraints on tables will not be exported
About to export transportable tablespace metadata...
For tablespace ORDERS ...
. exporting cluster definitions
. exporting table definitions
. . exporting table  APR_ORDERS
. end transportable tablespace metadata export
Export terminated successfully without warnings.
```

(5) Transport the Tablespace.

Now copy the files

- datafile, orders.f
- export dump file, expdata.dmp

to the physical location on the system containing the staging database. You can use any facility for copying flat files, such as an operating system copy utility or FTP. In our example, orders.f was copied to d:\ora815\oradata\orcl\orders.f.

(6) Import the Metadata.

By importing the metadata, you are plugging the tablespace into the target database.

```
IMP 'system/manager as sysdba' transport_tablespace=y
datafiles='d:\ora815\oradata\orcl\orders.f'
```

Check the import logs to ensure no errors have occurred. Note, the transportable tablespace metadata was imported.

```
Connected to: Oracle8i Enterprise Edition Release 8.1.5.0.0
With the Partitioning option
PL/SQL Release 8.1.5.0.0 - Production
Export file created by EXPORT:V08.01.05 via conventional path
```

```
About to import transportable tablespace(s) metadata...
import done in WE8ISO8859P1 character set and WE8ISO8859P1
  NCHAR character set
. importing SYS's objects into SYS
. importing OLTP's objects into OLTP
. . importing table  "APR_ORDERS"
Import terminated successfully without warnings.
```

(7) **Alter the orders tablespace so that it is in read-write mode.** You are ready to perform your transformations!

SQL> ALTER TABLESPACE orders READ WRITE;

Exchanging a partition

Another technique to bear in mind is the use of the EXCHANGE PARTITION clause, which changes the data and index. You would use this to *convert:*

- a partition or subpartition into a nonpartitioned table
- a nonpartitioned table into a partitioned or subpartitioned table

This technique could be considered as a means of getting data into the warehouse quickly when using the transportable tablespace facility.

4.2.7   Moving Data From a Staging Table into the Fact Table

If you are doing transformations in the Oracle data warehouse, you typically load data into temporary staging tables, transform the data, then move it to the warehouse detail fact tables. In Figure 4.18, the April purchases have been moved into temporary staging tables in the warehouse using transportable tablespaces.

Figure 4.18 Moving Data from a Staging Table into the Fact Table

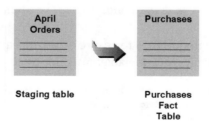

After transforming the data using SQL or PL/SQL, we are ready to move the data into our purchases fact table.

(1) Create a new tablespace for the April purchases. Since the purchases table is partitioned by month, a new tablespace will be created to store the April purchases. This can be achieved using either SQL as shown below or via Storage Manager, as illustrated in Figure 4.19.

```
SQL> CREATE TABLESPACE purchases_apr99
   DATAFILE 'd:\ora815\oradata\orcl\purchasesapr99.f' SIZE 5M
REUSE AUTOEXTEND ON
   DEFAULT STORAGE
   (INITIAL 64K NEXT 64K PCTINCREASE 0 MAXEXTENTS UNLIMITED);
```

Figure 4.19 Using Storage Manager to Create a Tablespace

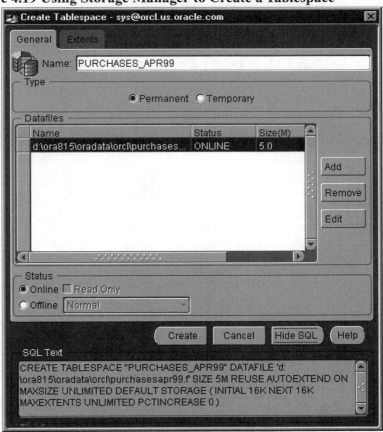

(2) Add a partition to the purchases table.

Since the PURCHASES table in our EASYDW data warehouse is partitioned, we must now add a partition for this new data.

```
SQL>ALTER TABLE easydw.purchases
ADD PARTITION purchases_apr99
values less than (TO_DATE('30-04-1999', 'DD-MM-YYYY'))
pctfree 0 pctused 99
storage (initial 64k next 164 pctincrease 0)
tablespace purchases_apr99;
```

Using Schema Manager, we can see the new partition we have just added, in Figure 4.20

(3) Move the table into the new partition using direct path insert.

When the fact table already exists you can add more data to it by using the *Direct path* INSERT statement. A direct load enhances performance during insert operations by formatting and writing data directly into the data files without using the buffer cache. This functionality is similar to SQL*Loader direct path mode.

Figure 4.20 Using Schema Manager to View a Table's Partitions

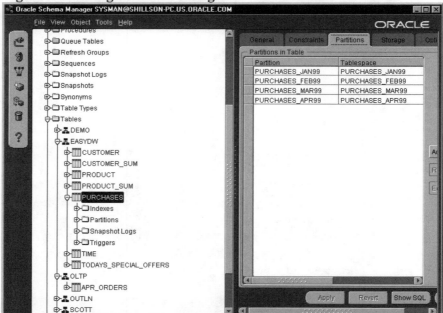

Hint: Be sure you have disabled all *references* constraints before executing the direct load insert. If you do not, the *append hint* will be ignored, no warnings will be issued, and a conventional insert will be used. The insert will take a long time, and you will have to completely refresh your materialized views.

Direct path INSERT appends the inserted data after existing data in a table; free space within the existing data is not reused. Data can be inserted into partitioned or nonpartitioned tables, either in parallel or serially. Direct path INSERT updates the indexes of the table.

In the EASYDW database, since the purchases table already exists and is partitioned by month, we'll use the direct path insert to move the data into the table. Direct path INSERT is executed when you include the APPEND hint and are using the SELECT syntax of the INSERT statement. Beware, conventional path is used when using the INSERT...with the VALUES clause.

```
SQL>INSERT /*+ APPEND */ INTO easydw.purchases
   SELECT * FROM oltp.apr_orders
```

In our example, the purchases fact table already existed, and new data was added into a separate partition. If the detail fact table does not yet exist, you can create a new table selecting a subset of one or more tables using the CREATE TABLE AS SELECT statement. The table creation can be done in parallel. You can also disable logging of redo. In the example below, temp_products is the name of the *staging* table. After performing the transformations and data cleansing, the products table is created by copying the data from temp_products table.

```
SQL> CREATE TABLE products PARALLEL NOLOGGING AS
        SELECT * FROM temp_products;
```

Hint: When moving data between tables in a database, always use either the direct load insert or the CREATE TABLE AS SELECT, if you are using summary management. These techniques or SQL*Loader direct path mode are required in order to do a FAST REFRESH of your summaries.

4.3   POSTLOAD OPERATIONS

After the data is loaded, you need to validate its quality, rebuild indexes, update the cost based optimizer statistics, and refresh the summaries prior to making the data available to the warehouse users.

(1) Analyze the logs to ensure the data was loaded successfully. Validate that the correct number of rows have been added.

(2) Process the load exceptions. If using SQL*Loader, look in the .bad file and the exceptions table to find out which rows were not loaded. Records that fail NOT NULL constraints are rejected and written to the SQL*Loader bad file.

(3) Reenable data integrity constraints. Ensure referential integrity if you have not already done so. Make sure that each foreign key in the fact table has a corresponding primary key in each dimension table. For the EASYDW warehouse, for each row in the purchases table, we need to ensure that each customer has a valid customer_id and that each product has a valid product_id.

When using direct path load, CHECK and REFERENCES integrity constraints were disabled. When using parallel direct path load, all constraints were disabled. An easy way to determine which constraints are disabled is to look in the table user_constraints and check for any disabled constraints, as illustrated below:

```
SQL> SELECT constraint_name, status from user_constraints;

CONSTRAINT_NAME                             STATUS
------------------------                    --------

PK_CUSTOMER                                 ENABLED
COST_PRICE_NOT_NULL                         ENABLED
SELL_PRICE_NOT_NULL                         ENABLED
SHIPPING_CHARGE_NOT_NULL                    ENABLED
PK_PRODUCT                                  ENABLED
NOT_NULL_PRODUCT_ID                         DISABLED
NOT_NULL_TIME                               DISABLED
NOT_NULL_CUSTOMER_ID                        DISABLED
SPECIAL_OFFER                               DISABLED
FK_PRODUCT_ID                               DISABLED
FK_TIME                                     DISABLED
FK_CUSTOMER_ID                              DISABLED
PUBLIC_HOLIDAY                              ENABLED
PK_TIME                                     ENABLED
PK_SPECIALS                                 ENABLED

15 rows selected.
```

In this example, we can see that several of our constraints have been disabled.

When constraints are reenabled, all rows in the entire table are evaluated, and any rows that violate integrity are reported as errors.

```
SQL>ALTER TABLE purchases enable constraint not_null_time;
SQL>ALTER TABLE purchases enable constraint
        not_null_product_id;
SQL>ALTER TABLE purchases enable constraint fk_product_id;
SQL>ALTER TABLE purchases    enable constraint fk_customer_id;
```

(4) Handle constraint violations.

To find the rows with bad data, you can create an exceptions table. Create the table named "exceptions" by running the script UTLEXCPT1.SQL. When enabling the constraint, list the table name the exceptions should be written to.

```
SQL> ALTER TABLE purchases ENABLE CONSTRAINT fk_product_id
        EXCEPTIONS INTO exceptions;
```

In our example, two rows had bad product_id's. A sale was made for a product that does not exist in the product dimension.

```
SQL> SELECT * FROM EXCEPTIONS;
```

ROW_ID	OWNER	TABLE_NAME	CONSTRAINT
AAAC/ZAAMAAAAADAAF	EASYDW	PURCHASES	FK_PRODUCT_ID
AAAC/ZAAMAAAAADAAI	EASYDW	PURCHASES	FK_PRODUCT_ID

To find out which rows have violated referential integrity, select the rows from the purchases table where the rowid is in the exception table. In this example, there are two rows where there is no matching product in the products dimension.

```
SQL> SELECT * from purchases WHERE
 rowid in (select row_id from exceptions);
```

PRODUCT_	TIME_KEY	CUSTOMER_I	PURCHASE_	PURCHASE_TIM	PURCHASE_PRICE
XY1001	01-MAR-99	AB123457	01-MAR-99	1024	28.01 4.5 Y
AB1234	01-MAR-99	AB123456	01-MAR-99	24	28.01 4.5 Y

Hint: It is important to fix any referential integrity constraint problems, particularly if you are using summary management, which relies on the correctness of these relationships to perform query rewrite.

---

(5) Ensure data integrity without validating constraints.

If integrity checking is maintained in an application or the data has already been cleansed, and you know it will not violate any integrity constraints, enable the constraints with the NOVALIDATE clause. Include the rely clause for query rewrite. Since summary management and other tools depend on the relationships defined by references constraints, you should always define the constraints, even if they are not validated.

```
ALTER TABLE purchases ENABLE NOVALIDATE CONSTRAINT
  fk_product_id;
ALTER TABLE purchases MODIFY CONSTRAINT fk_product_id RELY;
```

(6) Rebuild any unusable indexes. An index becomes unusable when it no longer contains index entries to all the data. Some of the reasons an index may be unusable are:

- You requested that index maintenance be deferred, using the skip_index_maintenance parameter when invoking SQL*Loader.
- UNIQUE constraints were not disabled when using SQL*Loader direct path. At the end of the load, the constraints are verified when the indexes are rebuilt. If any duplicates are found, the index is not correct and will be left in an "Index Unusable" state.

The index must be dropped and re-created or rebuilt to make it usable again. If one partition is marked UNUSABLE, the other partitions of the index are still valid.

(7) Check for any unusable indexes.

Prior to publishing data in the warehouse, you should check to determine if any indexes are in an unusable state by querying the table USER_INDEXES as illustrated below. Here we can see that the PRODUCT_PK_INDEX is unusable. If an index is partitioned, its status is "N/A."

```
SQL> SELECT INDEX_NAME, STATUS FROM USER_INDEXES;

INDEX_NAME                     STATUS

CUSTOMER_PK_INDEX              VALID
I_SNAP$_CUSTOMER_SUM          VALID
PRODUCT_PK_INDEX              UNUSABLE
PURCHASE_CUSTOMER_INDEX       N/A
PURCHASE_PRODUCT_INDEX        N/A
PURCHASE_SPECIAL_INDEX        N/A
PURCHASE_TIME_INDEX          N/A
TIME_PK_INDEX                VALID
TSO_PK_INDEX                 VALID

9 rows selected.
```

Next check to see if any index partitions are in an unusable state by checking the table USER_IND_PARTITIONS. In the example below all indexes for the "purchases_apr99" partition are unusable since index maintenance was skipped during the load.

```
SELECT INDEX_NAME, PARTITION_NAME, STATUS FROM
   USER_IND_PARTITIONS WHERE STATUS != 'VALID';
```

INDEX_NAME	PARTITION_NAME	STATUS
PURCHASE_TIME_INDEX	INDEXFEB99	USABLE
PURCHASE_TIME_INDEX	INDEXMAR99	USABLE
PURCHASE_PRODUCT_INDEX	PURCHASES_FEB99	USABLE
PURCHASE_PRODUCT_INDEX	PURCHASES_MAR99	USABLE
PURCHASE_CUSTOMER_INDEX	PURCHASES_JAN99	USABLE
PURCHASE_CUSTOMER_INDEX	PURCHASES_FEB99	USABLE
PURCHASE_CUSTOMER_INDEX	PURCHASES_MAR99	USABLE
PURCHASE_SPECIAL_INDEX	PURCHASES_JAN99	USABLE
PURCHASE_SPECIAL_INDEX	PURCHASES_FEB99	USABLE
PURCHASE_SPECIAL_INDEX	PURCHASES_MAR99	USABLE
PURCHASE_SPECIAL_INDEX	PURCHASES_APR99	UNUSABLE
PURCHASE_TIME_INDEX	INDEXJAN99	USABLE
PURCHASE_PRODUCT_INDEX	PURCHASES_JAN99	USABLE
PURCHASE_CUSTOMER_INDEX	PURCHASES_APR99	UNUSABLE
PURCHASE_PRODUCT_INDEX	PURCHASES_APR99	UNUSABLE
PURCHASE_TIME_INDEX	PURCHASES_APR99	UNUSABLE

```
16 rows selected.
```

You can also use Schema Manager to determine if any indexes are unusable, as shown in Figure 4.2.1. There it advises us that the "purchases_apr99" partition of the purchase_time_index is unusable.

(8) Rebuilding unusable indexes.

If you have any indexes that are unusable, you must rebuild them prior to accessing the table or partition. In the example below, the product_pk_index is rebuilt, and each partitioned index of the newly added "purchases_apr99" partition is rebuilt.

```
SQL> ALTER INDEX product_pk_index rebuild;
SQL> ALTER INDEX purchase_customer_index
        REBUILD PARTITION purchases_apr99;
SQL> ALTER INDEX purchase_product_index
        REBUILD PARTITION purchases_apr99;
SQL> ALTER INDEX purchase_time_index
        REBUILD PARTITION purchases_apr99;
SQL>ALTER INDEX purchase_SPECIAL_index
        REBUILD PARTITION purchases_apr99;
```

Figure 4.21 Using Schema Manager to Look for Unusable Indexes

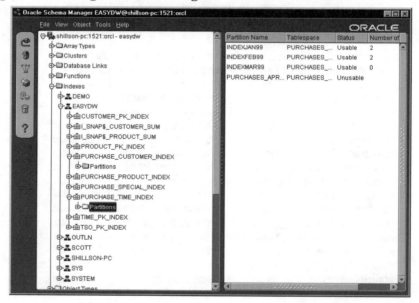

(9) Gather optimizer statistics for the tables.

Run the ANALYZE utility to update the optimizer statistics on any tables where you have added a significant amount of data. Statistics can be gathered for an index, index partition, table, partition or subpartition, and a materialized view.

Since we added an entire partition to the purchases fact table, the example below will gather statistics for the purchases_apr99 partition.

```
ANALYZE TABLE purchases
 PARTITION( purchases_apr99) COMPUTE STATISTICS;
```

(10) Verify the dimensions. If using summary management, run the DBMS_OLAP.VALIDATE_DIMENSION procedure for each dimension to verify that the hierarchical, attribute, and join relationships are correct. It can also be used to determine if any level columns in a dimension are NULL. You can either verify the newly added rows or all the rows. Any exceptions are logged in the table MVIEW$_EXCEPTIONS, which is created in the user's schema.

In the following example, the product_dim dimension (parameter 1) in the EASYDW schema (parameter 2) is verified for correctness. All rows will be validated (parameter 3 is set to *false*), and we'll check for *nulls* (parameter 4 is set to *true*).

```
SQL> EXECUTE DBMS_OLAP.VALIDATE_DIMENSION
         ('product_dim','easydw', FALSE ,TRUE);

PL/SQL procedure successfully completed.

SQL> select * from mview$_exceptions;
no rows selected
```

(11) Refresh the summaries. If using Summary Management, refresh the materialized views using the DBMS_MVIEW.REFRESH PL/SQL package.

After loading the April data into the purchases table, in the examples earlier in the chapter, the "product_sales_by_month" summary becomes stale. It only contains information on the sales for January through March and must be refreshed to add April's data.

In order to use refresh, make sure you have started job queues. These can be started by setting the number of job_queue_processes in your init.ora parameter file or via altering a system parameter. In addition, you can also set the job_queue_interval to determine how frequently the job queue scheduler checks to see if there is a new job to execute. When using *Fast Refresh,* set the job_queue_processes equal to the number of processors you can devote to the refresh process.

```
SQL> ALTER SYSTEM set job_queue_processes =2;
```

It is also helpful to create a refresh log file to verify the results of the refresh. In order to have a log created for you, you must set the init.ora parameter UTL_FILE_DIR to the where the log should be written.

To refresh the materialized views, execute the DBMS_MVIEW.REFRESH procedure. Since the same procedure is used to refresh both materialized views that are summaries and materialized views used for replication, some of the parameters are not meaningful in a warehouse environment.

In the following example, product_sales_by_month (parameter 1) will be refreshed using a *Fast refresh*, "F" (parameter 2). In order to be able to execute a fast refresh of a materialized view that contains joins and aggregates, such as the product_sales_by_month summary, the new data in the purchases fact table must have been inserted in bulk using a direct path operation such as SQL*Loader direct path mode, *Direct Load Insert,* or *Create Table* as Select.

Use "A" to always completely rebuild the materialized view and "F" to perform a fast refresh. Use "?" to use the default refresh method specified when the materialized view was created. When the default refresh method is FORCE, the materialized views will be refreshed in the optimal way. A fast refresh will be used if possible, otherwise a complete refresh will be done.

You can also specify a specific rollback segment to use (parameter 3) and whether to continue after errors when refreshing multiple materialized views (parameter 4) are specified next. It is important to set atomic refresh (parameter 5) to FALSE for the refresh methods optimized for the data warehouse environment to be used.

```
SQL> EXECUTE
        dbms_mview.refresh('easydw.product_sales_by_month',
        'F',null,true,false,atomic_refresh=>false);
```

(12) Gather optimizer statistics for the materialized views. Run *analyze* to update optimizer statistics on any materialized views that may have significantly changed in size.

```
SQL>ANALYZE TABLE product_sales_by_month COMPUTE STATISTICS;
```

(13) Backup the database, table or partition after the load is complete if you used the UNRECOVERABLE option. Since media recovery is disabled for the table being loaded, you will not be able to recover in the event of media failure. Refer to Chapter 7 for a discussion on backup techniques.

(14) Publish the data. Send E-mail to notify the users of what data has been loaded the previous day and is ready for their use.

4.4   USING TOOLS FOR THE ETT PROCESS

In addition to the Oracle tools mentioned in this chapter, several tools are available on the marketplace to help automate parts of the ETT process. These tools provide the mechanisms to connect to the heterogeneous data sources, generally to either relational databases or flat files, and perform the data extraction functions. They control the transfer of data across a network, provide data transformation services, data cleansing capabilities, and load the data into your data warehouse.

Some tools generate COBOL, C, or C++ code to extract data from the operational systems. This code then needs to be compiled and linked, requiring many steps for the management of multiple intermediate files. These types of tools can often access data in legacy systems.

Other tools provide an integrated development and management environment but may not be able to move large amounts of data through the network. Some tools aid in the management of the data extraction, filtering, and transport. Others help with the analysis process prior to the extract phase, processing metadata to abstract and documenting the business rules. Still others specialize in data quality and cleansing.

In the next chapter, we'll look at the Oracle Data Mart Suite, which provides many of the functions discussed in this chapter to help you create and manage your data marts.

5 Oracle Data Mart Suite

5.1 COMPONENTS OF THE DATA MART SUITE

Data warehouses provide detailed data for an entire enterprise. Building an enterprise-wide data warehouse is complex and can take anywhere from 18 months to three years to deploy. Data marts arose from the realization that many of the benefits of a warehouse could be realized on a smaller scale.

Data marts are subject-specific and contain information about one particular subject or application within the enterprise. A data mart may contain data for only one department, a geographic area, or a line of business such as sales, marketing, or finance. The major difference between *data warehouses* and *data marts* is the scope of the information contained. The source of the data for a data mart may be the enterprise data warehouse, or the operational systems.

Because data marts are more bounded, they are faster and easier to build—sometimes being built as quickly as three months. The Data Mart Suite makes the process of building data marts much easier. The suite contains a set of components that can be used to design, build, manage, and access a data mart.

The Data Mart Suite consists of:

- *Oracle Data Mart Designer*, a database design tool to design data marts
- *Oracle Data Mart Builder*, a tool to build the data extraction, transformation, transport, and load processes
- *Oracle8 Enterprise Edition*, which is used as a repository for both the data and the metadata
- *Oracle Enterprise Manager*, which administers and manages the data mart
- *Oracle Discoverer*, which analyzes and queries the data
- *Oracle Reports*, which generates reports
- *Oracle Web Application Server,* which enables Internet access

All components are integrated into a single installation procedure, and the metadata is shared between components. The tools all have graphical user interfaces, making it possible to build a data mart in a short amount of time without writing any application code. The suite includes a *cookbook*, which helps new users learn the basic functionality of each component quickly.

At the time of writing, the Data Mart Suite is Version 2.5.1, which is available on Windows NT and Sun Solaris and supports Oracle8. There is also a Sales and Marketing Suite, which is a prepackaged solution for building data marts for sales and marketing applications. It includes all the components above, plus Oracle Sales Analyzer and the Rolap Option.

Oracle Sales Analyzer is a business-intelligence application used to analyze sales and marketing data. It can be used to evaluate trends and marketing campaigns, profitability product life cycles, and promotional effectiveness.

The Rolap option includes the Express multidimensional server, the relational access manager, to access the data in Oracle 8, the Web agent, and a Microsoft Excel add-on, which provides a spreadsheet interface.

Oracle has announced its intention to replace some components in the suite with Oracle Warehouse Builder in the future.

This chapter will provide a brief overview of Oracle Data Mart Designer, Oracle Data Mart Builder, and Oracle Reports. Oracle Discoverer will be discussed in Chapter 6, and Web access will be presented in Chapter 8. Oracle Enterprise Manager has been discussed throughout the book and, therefore, will not be described here.

5.2   DATA MART DESIGNER

Oracle Data Mart Designer is a visual toolset for modeling, designing, and generating databases. It is a subset of Oracle Designer.

It can be used to model the design for your data mart and generate the SQL needed to create it. Oracle Designer can also be used to capture the design of an existing system. This is useful for "reverse engineering" the source systems. If you do not have the schema designs for some of the legacy systems that are sources for your data mart, obtaining a visual representation can help in determining the table and column names.

All data from Data Mart Designer is stored in a central *repository*, where it is shared with other tools in the Data Mart Suite. Figure 5.1 shows the Oracle Designer Front Panel, from where each of the tools is launched.

Oracle Data Mart Designer is composed of the following tools:

- The *Entity Relationship Diagrammer* is used to model the system requirements.

- The *Database Design Transformer* is used to generate a preliminary database design based on the entity relationship diagram.

Figure 5.1 The Oracle Designer Front Panel

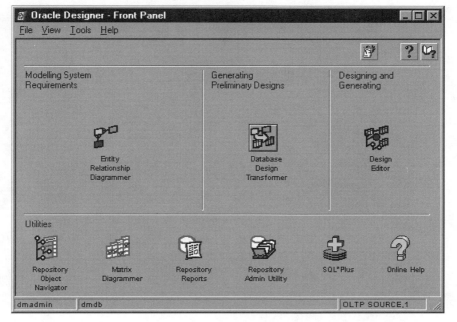

- The *Design Editor* is used to edit the design and generate the database.
- The *Utilities* are used to manage the repository.

Before you begin to use Designer, you must have a user account and password. New users are created using the Repository Admin Utility.

5.2.1   Creating a Designer Application

The information in the Designer repository is organized into *applications*. An application is a grouping of logically related information. In the examples in this chapter, one application will be created to store the design of the EASYDW data mart. A separate application will be created to store the design of the ORDER ENTRY system, which is the source for the EASYDW database. New applications can be created by users who are of type MANAGER.

To create an application, choose *File* menu then *Change Application System* from the Designer front panel. The application system dialog box, shown in Figure 5.2, is displayed.

Figure 5.2 Creating a Designer Application

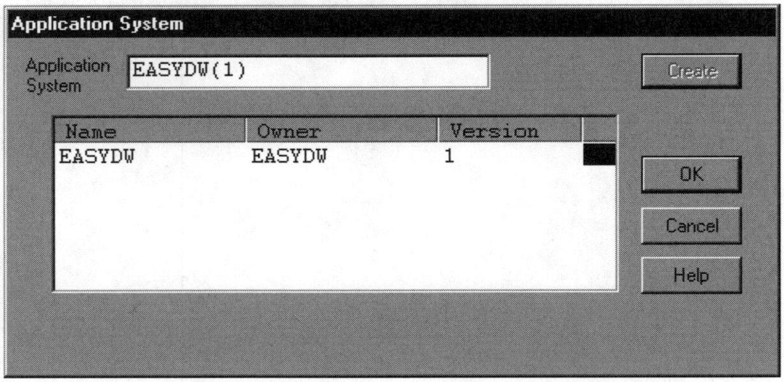

In this example, the application system, EASYDW, is being created to store the design of the data mart. This is the first version of the design. If major changes are being made to a design, the original application can be frozen and a new version created.

5.2.2   Designing a Data Mart

Designing a data mart using Data Mart Designer involves the following steps:

(1) Creating the data model using the *Entity Relationship Diagrammer*.

(2) Translating the data model into the database design using the *Database Design Transformer*.

(3) Generating the SQL to create database objects using the *Design Editor*.

Creating the Data Model

The Entity Relationship Diagrammer is used to create the data model. Entity Relationship (E-R) modeling involves identifying the entities, attributes, and relationships. Entities are things that are important to the business, such as products, customers, and purchases. Attributes are the properties of those things, such as product name, selling price, and cost. Relationships describe how things are related to each other. For example, a customer purchases products.

In a relational database, entities correspond to tables, attributes correspond to columns, and relationships are represented by referential integrity constraints.

Creating the Entities

The Entity Relationship Diagrammer is started by clicking the button in the Oracle Designer front panel shown in Figure 5.1. Figure 5.3 shows the process of creating the data model for the EASYDW star schema. The customer entity has been created, and we are in the process of creating the product entity.

Entities are created using the *Entity* button, currently highlighted on the toolbar.

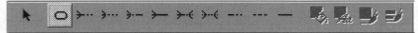

After positioning the box where you want it on the screen, the *Create Entity* dialog box appears. The name of the entity, an abbreviation or short name, and the plural of the entity name are entered.

Figure 5.3 Entity Relationship Diagrammer—Creating the Entities

Creating the Attributes

After creating the entities, the attributes are created. Attributes correspond to columns in the tables. By double-clicking on the entity in the Entity Customer, Relationship Diagrammer, the Edit Entity dialog box is displayed, as shown in Figure 5.4. The type of entity, such as fact or dimension table or volume of data and growth rate expected, are entered.

Figure 5.4 The Edit Entity Dialog Box

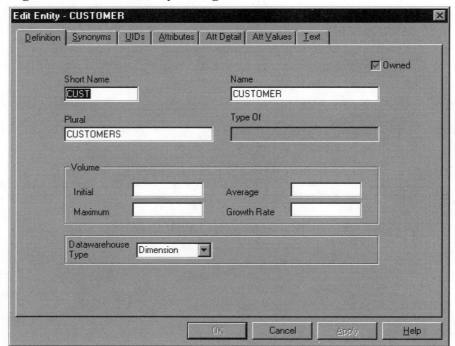

The *Attributes* tab is used to define attributes as shown in Figure 5.5. The attribute's name, its sequence in the record, whether it's mandatory or optional, whether it uniquely identifies the record are entered, and the data type and length.

In this example, the CUSTOMER_ID column is required. The rest of the columns are optional. The columns that uniquely identify the row, or the UID, are indicated by checking the primary box. The UIDs tab is used to change the composition of the UID or to create alternate UIDs.

Figure 5.5 Entity Relationship Diagrammer—Create Attributes

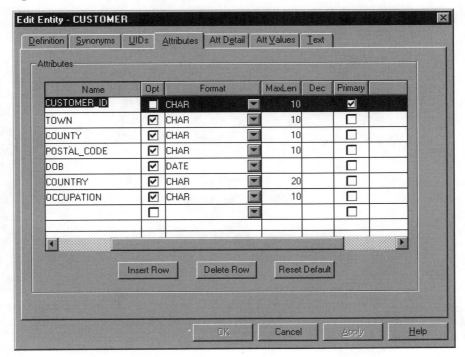

Creating the Relationships

Relationships are associations between two entities. In Figure 5.6, a relationship is created between the purchases fact table and the customer dimension table. The type of relationship (One-to-One, Many-to-One, or Many-to-Many) and whether the relationship is mandatory or optional is determined by the button chosen on the toolbar.

Since one customer can make many purchases, the relationship between customers and purchases is a one-to-many relationship. Since a customer may not make any purchases, the customer side of the relationship is optional. One could argue that a person isn't a customer if he doesn't make any purchases, but that discussion will be left to the database designers.

The *Many-to-One* (Mandatory to Optional) relationship toolbar button is clicked. The relationship is created by clicking on the entity that is on the many side of the relationship (product) and dragging the pointer to the entity on the one side of the relationship (customer). A line with crow's feet appears between the two entities, and the Create Relationship dialog box is opened.

Each side of the relationship is named. The names of the two ends of the relationship appear on the entity relationship diagram. In this example, "One customer makes *many* purchases."

Figure 5.6 Creating the Relationships

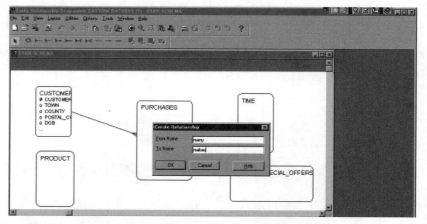

After you have added all attributes and defined all relationships, the entity relationship model is stored in the repository. Figure 5.7 shows the diagram created for the EASYDW star schema.

Figure 5.7 E-R Diagram of the EASYDW Star Schema

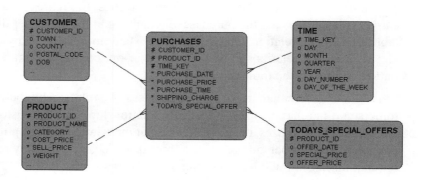

5.2.3   Translating the Data Model into the Database Design

After the E-R diagram is created, it is transformed into a database design, called a server model, using the Database Design Transformer, which is launched from the Designer Front Panel. Table definitions are created from the entities, and column definitions are created from the attributes. FOR-EIGN key constraints are defined to implement the relationships between entities. PRIMARY key constraints are created for the UNIQUE identifiers. Not NULL constraints are generated for all columns that were not optional.

The name chosen for the table is the plural version of the entity name, with spaces converted to underscores. The names of the column definitions are the attribute names preceded by the table name and an underscore. These and other settings can be customized.

Figure 5.8 shows the database design transformer window, which is launched from the Designer Front Panel. Press the *Run* button to transform the E-R diagram to the server model which represents the database design. The server model is stored in the repository.

Figure 5.8 Database Design Transformer Window

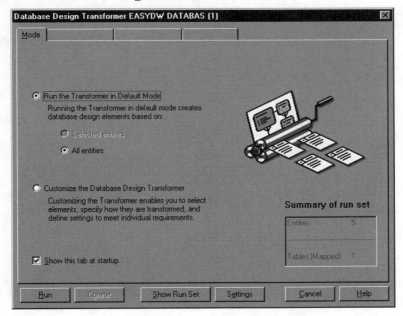

5.2.4 Generating the SQL to Create the Database Objects

After the server model has been created using the Database Design Transformer, Data Mart Designer can create the tables, indexes, and constraints in your target database. Alternatively, it can create SQL scripts containing the DDL to create the objects in your database, saving you the task of typing the

SQL. Usually you will want to generate SQL scripts, make any desired changes, and use them to create the objects in the database. By generating scripts, you also have a record of the SQL used to generate the objects.

Launch the Design Editor from the Oracle Designer Front Panel shown in Figure 5.1. From the *Generate* menu in the Design Editor, select *Generate,* then *Generate Database from Server Model*. This opens the Generate Database from Server Model dialog box, shown in Figure 5.9. In this example, the DDL to create an Oracle 8*i* database will be created in files with the name of EASYDW.

Figure 5.9 Generating the Database Design

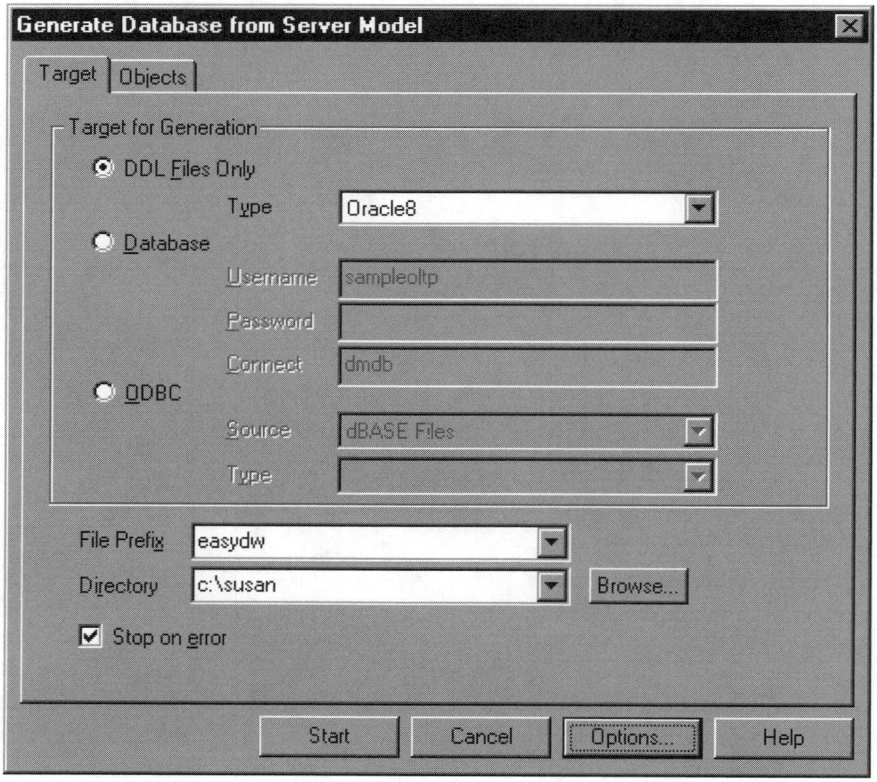

To select which objects the DDL will be generated for, choose the objects tab. Objects are moved from the *Don't Generate* list to the *Generate* list by selecting the item and clicking the double right-arrow button. In the example in Figure 5.10, DDL will be generated for all the relational tables.

Figure 5.10 Selecting Objects for the Design

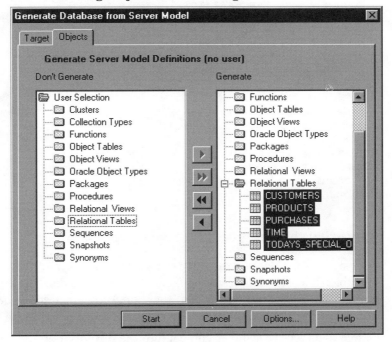

By pressing the *Start* button, the following files were created:

(1) easydw.tab—contains the DDL to create the tables

(2) easydw.ind—contains the DDL to create the indexes

(3) easydw.con—contains the DDL to create the constraints

(4) easydw.sql—a script executee using SQL*Plus that invokes the other three files.

Inspect the files generated, and make any changes required to implement the physical design. For example, you may want to change the index types to bitmaps and partition the fact table. You may not like some of the names generated, so these can be changed, as well.

A portion of the files are displayed below.

```
— c:\susan\easydw.tab
—
— Generated for Oracle 8 on Fri Jun 11 19:58:07 1999 by
  Server Generator 2.1.24.3.0

PROMPT Creating Table 'CUSTOMERS'
CREATE TABLE    CUSTOMERS
  (CUSTOMER_ID  VARCHAR2(10) NOT NULL
```

```
  ,TOWN           VARCHAR2(10)
  ,COUNTY         VARCHAR2(10)
  ,POSTAL_CODE    VARCHAR2(10)
  ,DOB            DATE
  ,COUNTRY        VARCHAR2(20)
  ,OCCUPATION     VARCHAR2(10) )
/
        :

— Generated for Oracle 8 on Fri Jun 11 19:58:07 1999 by
  Server Generator 2.1.24.3.0

PROMPT Creating Primary Key on 'PRODUCTS'
ALTER TABLE   PRODUCTS
ADD CONSTRAINT PROD_PK PRIMARY KEY
  (PRODUCT_ID)
/
```

5.2.5   Capturing the Design of an Existing Database

In designing the data extraction processes needed to build your data mart, the tables and columns from the source systems are determined. If you are not familiar with the systems or if there is insufficient documentation, this can be a difficult task.

Oracle Data Mart Designer can capture the design of an existing database and create a server model of the design in its repository. You can then view the design with the navigator or visually, as a server model diagram, to determine the tables, columns, data types, indexes, primary keys, and constraints.

By generating a server model for each of your source systems, the process of identifying the data needed for the data mart is much easier. Oracle Data Mart Builder can use the server model designs to obtain the metadata for the source systems for the ETT process.

Designs can be captured for Oracle databases, from Oracle or ANSI SQL DDL scripts, or for relational databases from other vendors. When capturing designs for non-Oracle databases, connectivity is via ODBC.

From the Designer Front Panel, shown in Figure 5.1, click on the *Design Editor*, and when asked where you would like to start, choose the *server model*. Run the *Design Capture*, as shown in Figure 5.11.

The connection information for the source database is entered in the source tab. The schema objects to capture are selected in the objects tab. In the example in Figure 5.12, data for all relational tables in the OLTP schema will be captured. In the examples in this chapter, the source of data is the OLTP order entry system.

Figure 5.11 The Server Model Guide

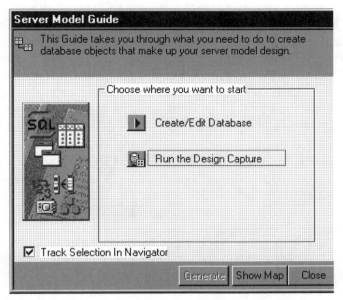

Figure 5.12 Capturing a Server Model from the Database

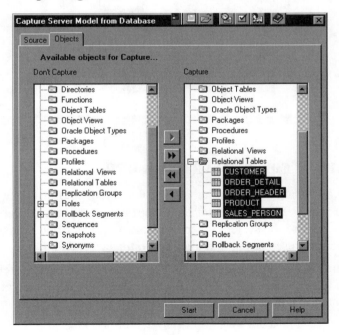

Figure 5.13 shows the server model diagram for objects captured from the order-entry system. For each table, the columns and data types are displayed. Characters are represented by the letter *A* preceding the column name, numbers are represented by *789*, and dates with a calendar page. Columns with NOT NULL constraints are preceded by a "*," and primary key columns are preceded by the "#" sign. Relationships between tables have been determined from references constraints and are represented in the diagram by arrows with the crow's foot. The symbols at the top of each table, for example, the sunglasses, allow you to choose what will be displayed on the diagram.

Figure 5.13 Server Model Diagram of Order-Entry Source System

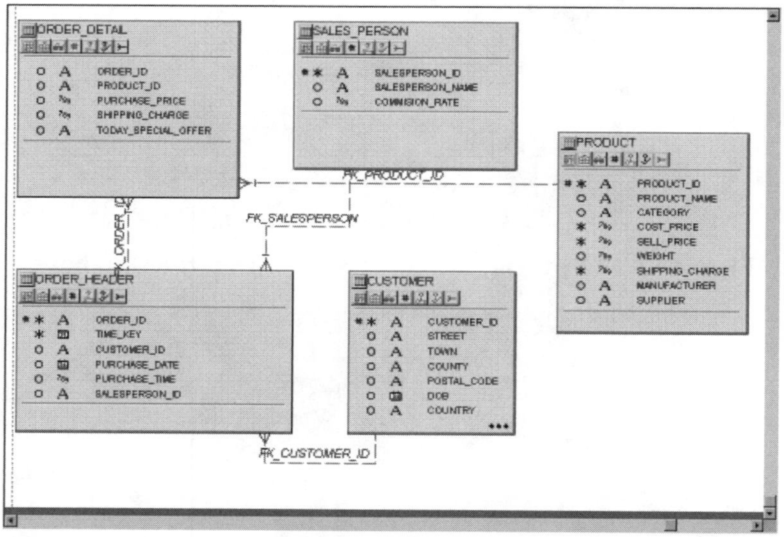

5.3   ORACLE DATA MART BUILDER

Oracle Data Mart Builder is a graphical tool set for managing the ETT process. It is used to extract data from a source system, transport it across a network to the system where the data mart is located, transform it to a common representation, and load it into the target data mart.

The ETT process is described in a "plan," which visually represents the flow of information. Data flows from one or more data sources to a target. The sources of data may either be relational database systems or flat files.

Depending on the architecture chosen for your warehouse, the sources may be the operational systems, a staging area where data has previously been moved to, or the data warehouse, if you are building a dependent data mart. The target is usually the data mart, but Oracle Data Mart Builder could also be used to create a flat file for intermediate processing prior to loading the data mart.

Native connectivity is available to access Oracle, Sybase, Microsoft SQL Server, and Informix databases. Support through ODBC is used to access data in IBM DB2 and other relational databases. The flat files may either be stored in character-delimited or fixed-length formats.

Plans contain a sequence of steps, called *transforms*. Transforms are used to manipulate the data, manage the data flow, and populate the data mart. Predefined transforms are supplied to provide data cleansing, integration, aggregation, and key generation. Custom transforms can also be developed using VBScript or C++.

Data Mart Builder consists of three components:

(1) A client front-end, which includes the Data Mart Builder user interface used to build plans, the Data Mart Builder Admin interface used to manage the repository, and the data collector agent.

(2) The back-end repository, where the metadata, ETT plans, and administrative statistics are stored. The repository can be stored in the same database as the data mart.

(3) The Data Collection (DC) Agent, which executes the plans. The DC Agent can run on an NT or Solaris server and is usually located on the same server as the target data mart.

The basic capabilities of Data Mart Builder will be illustrated with plans that perform the following tasks:

(1) Populate the product dimension from a flat file

(2) Populate the time dimension

(3) Populate the purchases fact table from the order-entry system

Before using Data Mart Builder, you must have a user name and password to log in. Accounts are created using the Oracle Data Mart Builder Admin tool.

Figure 5.14 shows the Oracle Data Mart Builder graphical user interface. The workspace is divided into three areas:

(1) Data Flow Editor, which is displayed on the top right of the screen

(2) Grid, displayed on the bottom right

(3) Bins, displayed on the left

Some of the terminology used in Data Mart Builder comes from a traditional warehouse in a business. For example, tools and parts are stored in bins.

Figure 5.14 The Data Mart Builder User Interface

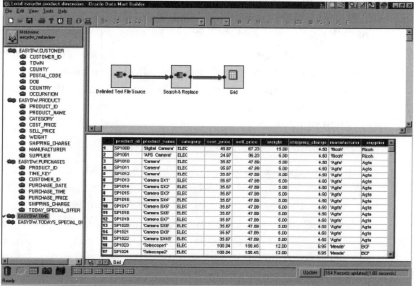

When you log into Data Mart Builder, you will see a screen similar to the one in Figure 5.14, which shows a plan under development that will load the product dimension from a flat file. The *plan* has three transforms: a *Delimited Text File Source*, a *Search & Replace* transform, and a *Grid*.

Transforms can be classified as:

- source transforms
- sink transforms
- data manipulation transforms

All plans start with a *source* transform, which describes the source of the data to be loaded. Plans end with a *sink* transform, which determines where the data will be loaded. The transforms between the sources and the sink change the data in some way or control the flow of the plan. In this example, the source of the plan is a delimited text file, and the sink is a grid. The data will be modified using the search & replace transform.

The *grid* is used to display the results of a plan while the plan is being developed. Prior to loading the products into the database, the results can be displayed on the grid for debugging purposes.

Plans are created using tools stored in *bins*. Bins are opened by clicking the buttons in the gallery at the bottom left of the screen.

Items contained in the bins are included in a plan by dragging them into the *workspace*. Looking at the bins from left to right:

- The *recycle bin* is represented by the garbage can icon. It contains objects that have been deleted.

- The *parts bin* is grayed out because it is currently in use. The tables and columns are stored in the parts bin. Each table is referred to as a part, and each column as a category.

- The *plan bin* contains plans that have been saved so they can be scheduled to run at a later time.

- The *snap bin,* depicted by the camera, is where the results of a plan execution can be saved.

- The *tools bin* contains the built-in and custom transforms.

A plan is executed by pressing the *Update* button at the bottom of the screen.

5.3.1   Creating the BaseViews and MetaViews

In order to access a database, you must specify what type of database it is, where it's located, and be able to log in as a user with sufficient privileges to read the metadata. This is done by creating a *BaseView* for each relational database you will be accessing. This includes all relational database sources as well as the target data mart.

A *BaseView* is a metadata layer that Oracle Data Mart Builder uses to reference database schema objects. Multiple BaseViews can be created for the same database. One may be for the DBA so he can see all tables, while another BaseView may be set up for a user who may have access only to the tables in his schema.

A *MetaView* is a logical layer built on top of one or more BaseViews. You can have more than one MetaView for any BaseView.

When combining data from multiple heterogeneous sources, a MetaView is created that contains the tables and columns from each of the BaseViews. Figure 5.15 shows a diagram of the metadata layers. A BaseView is created for each database, and a MetaView is created to describe the objects of interest in each database. In this case, a third MetaView is created that describes columns and tables from the two databases.

Figure 5.15 Data Mart Builder BaseViews and MetaViews

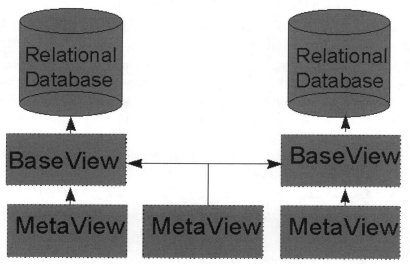

A new BaseView is created using the *BaseView Editor*. The BaseView Editor is invoked by selecting *Tools* then *BaseView Editor*. In the BaseView Editor toolbar, shown in Figure 5.16, click the New BaseView button on the far left

Figure 5.16 BaseView Dialog Box

The *Define BaseView* dialog box is shown in Figure 5.17. An arrow next to a field indicates that the field is required or that an invalid value has been entered. The following information is entered:

- *BaseView Name*—Each BaseView is given a unique name.

- *Database Type*—Choose from Oracle, SQL/Server, Sybase, Redbrick, Informix, or an ODBC source. In this example, the BaseView for the EASYDW target data mart will be created, which is an Oracle database.

- *Data Dictionary Type*—Used to specify where to obtain the metadata from the database or the Oracle Data Mart Designer Repository. In this example, the metadata will come from the database.

- *Service Name*—This field is used to specify the physical location of the database. Since this is an Oracle database, you are prompted for the *service name*. If this was a BaseView for a database from another vendor, you would be prompted for the *server* name. If the source was accessed via ODBC, you would be prompted for the *Data Source*. In this example, we used the starter database that comes with the Data Mart Suite, whose service name is "dmdb."

- *Database*—The name of the database from which to create the BaseView. It is used for access to non-Oracle databases and is left blank for Oracle BaseViews since the database name is determined by the service name.

- *User Name* and *Password*—Used to gain access to the database. The value entered for User Name is automatically entered for the *Database User*. In this case, we will log into the database as user EASYDW.

The tables that make up the BaseView are selected by clicking on the *tables* button at the bottom of Figure 5.17. All tables in the EASYDW schema have been selected from the list of available tables.

A MetaView is created using the MetaView Editor. You can either start with all of the items in the BaseView, or you can start with an empty MetaView and populate it with the tables and columns you are interested in.

If you want to include all of the objects in the BaseView, a MetaView can be created automatically when the BaseView is created. In the example in Figure 5.17, the MetaView named "easydw_MetaView" is *autocreated*.

MetaViews can be modified using the MetaView Editor. Columns can be added, deleted, or renamed. New columns can be calculated from the existing columns by applying mathematical functions.

After creating the BaseView, a visual representation of the schema, such as the one shown in Figure 5.18, is displayed. On the right are the tables shown in graphical form, and on the left are the same tables in a hierarchy.

The tables can be moved around to create a visually pleasing display of the schema. Referential integrity constraints are represented as joins between the tables and are shown with arrows. These are used by Data Mart Builder to generate the SQL needed to join the tables together.

In this diagram, there is no arrow between the EASYDW.TODAYS_SPECIAL_OFFERS and the EASYDW.PURCHASES table because no referential integrity constraint has been defined.

Figure 5.17 Defining a BaseView

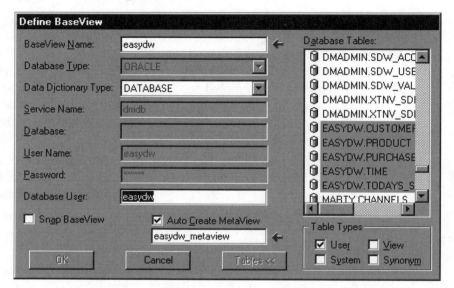

A join can be added in the BaseView, which would provide Data Mart Builder the columns needed to join the two tables together. Adding a join in a BaseView does not modify the underlying database.

Figure 5.18 Creating the Tables in the EASYDW BaseView

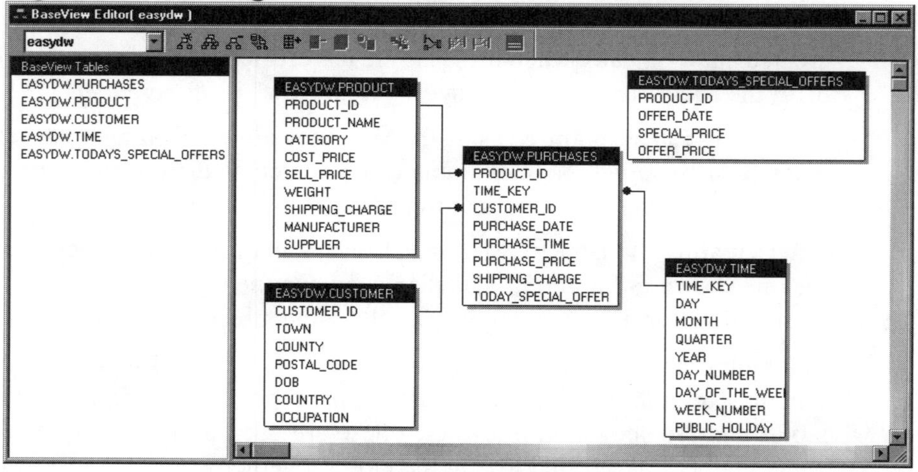

5.3.2   Loading Data from a Flat File

Figure 5.19 shows the final plan to load the product dimension. To create a plan, the tools bin is opened, and the transforms are dragged into the workspace. The names of the transforms that can be used in a plan are listed in the bin.

Data will be loaded from the file named, "products.csv." Prior to running the plan, the file must be copied to the server that the DC Agent is running on. A portion of the data file is shown in Figure 5.20. The data in the first column, the "product_id," has been entered in several different ways: ("SP-1000," "SP 1010", and "SP1012.") Some product-id's have a hyphen between the characters and the numbers, some have a space, and some have neither. Prior to loading the data, the hyphen and spaces will be removed using the search and replace transform.

By double-clicking on the delimited text file source transform, its dialog box is opened, as shown in Figure 5.21. The file attributes including the *File Name*, *Character Set*, *Separator, Quote,* and *Comma* characters are entered. In this example, the data is stored in the ASCII character set, and each field is separated by a comma and may be enclosed in a single quote.

Figure 5.19 Data Mart Builder Plan to Load the Product Dimension

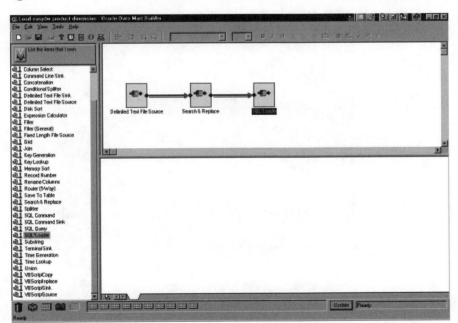

Figure 5.20 Sample Comma Separated Data File

```
'SP-1000', 'Digital Camera','ELEC', 45.67, 67.23, 15.00 4.50,
  'Ricoh','Ricoh'
'SP-1001', 'APS Camera','ELEC', 24.67, 36.23, 5.00, 4.50,
  'Ricoh','Ricoh'
'SP 1010', 'Camera','ELEC', 35.67, 47.89, 5.00, 4.50,
  'Agfa','Agfa'
'SP 1011', 'Camera','ELEC', 35.67, 47.89, 5.00, 4.50,
  'Agfa','Agfa'
'SP1012', 'Camera','ELEC', 35.67, 47.89, 5.00, 4.50,
  'Agfa','Agfa'
```

BaseViews and MetaViews are not created for flat files. Instead, the record layout is described in the Field List shown in Figure 5.21. The *Column Name, Output Type*, *Length*, and *Scale* are entered for each column. Product_id is a string eight characters in length. Data Mart Builder uses the column names to map the fields in the input file to the columns in the table. If the file contains extra fields that don't need to be loaded, name those fields "filler" or any name that has not been used as a column name in the table. To see how each field is interpreted prior to loading the data, supply a sample data file. Data Mart Builder can also sample a portion of the actual data file. In this example, the data file "C:\susan\product2.csv" is sampled.

Figure 5.21 Delimited Text "txt" Source

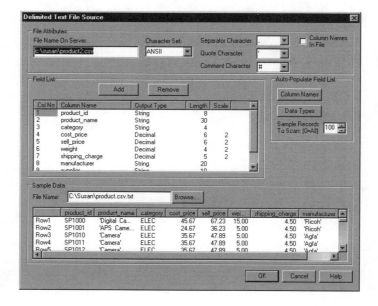

If the column names are stored in the first row of the file, check the *Column Names In File* box, and use the sample file to *autopopulate* the *field list* column names and data types. The *search & replace transform* will be used to remove the hyphen and spaces from the product_id field. The transform is dragged from the tools bin into the workspace. The dialog box shown in Figure 5.22 is displayed by double-clicking on the search & replace transform.

Figure 5.22 Search & Replace Transform

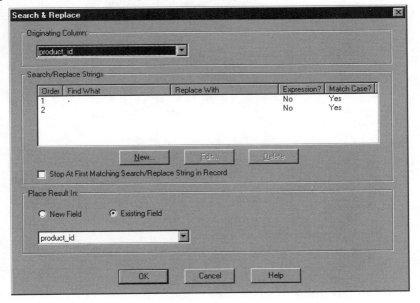

The *search and replace strings* are now entered. In this example, the hyphen, '-', in product_id is replaced with null, ' '. The space, ' ', is replaced with null ' '. The result will be placed back into the same field, product_id. If you want to keep both the old and new values, a new field could have been created.

After debugging the plan, the grid is replaced with one of the load transforms to populate the data mart. These include:

- Batch loader transform, to insert rows using the SQL INSERT statement
- Batch update transform, to update existing rows
- SQL*Loader transform, to load data using the SQL*Loader utility

Figure 5.23 shows the SQL*Loader dialog box, which is displayed by double-clicking on the SQL*Loader transform. The *Destination table* name and how the table will be updated are specified. In this example, data will be loaded into the EASYDW.PRODUCT table in the EASYDW BaseView. The data will be inserted into an empty table that has already been created.

Figure 5.23 SQL*Loader Transform

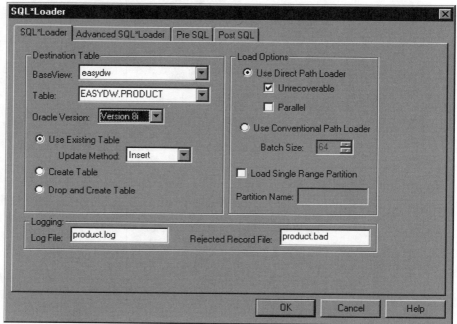

Data Mart Builder can use either *Conventional* or *Direct Path* load.

Conventional path load issues SQL INSERT statements. As each row is inserted, indexes are updated, triggers are fired, and constraints are evaluated.

Direct path load optimizes performance by bypassing the SQL layer and formatting the data blocks directly and writing them to disk. Therefore, it is much faster than a conventional load, especially when large volumes of records are being added to the data mart.

To disable logging, check the *Unrecoverable* option box. The new rows being inserted will not be written to the redo log used for recovery. Therefore, be sure to back up the database, partition, or subpartition after the load is complete when using the unrecoverable option.

A load may be executed in *Parallel,* or data can be loaded into a single partition. A *Log File* and a *Rejected Record File* can be created. The log file contains a record of the status of the load operation. It should always be created and reviewed to ensure the load was successful. Copies of records that could not be loaded because of data integrity errors can be saved in the rejected record file. Refer to Chapter 4 for more details on SQL*Loader.

Oracle Data Mart Builder automatically generates the SQL*Loader control file. While debugging the plan it is sometimes helpful to see the control file that has been generated. *The Advanced SQL*Loader* tab gives you the ability to save the SQL*Loader Control File or edit it manually to add capabilities not included by default.

5.3.3 Populating the Time Dimension

The time dimension contains one row for each unit of time that is of interest in the data mart. In the EASYDW shopping example, the unit of time is a day, since people shop on-line every day of the year. *The Time Generation Transform,* shown in Figure 5.24, makes it easy to populate the time dimension. The data is actually generated and not read from any source.

Figure 5.24 Data Mart Builder Plan to Load the Time Dimension

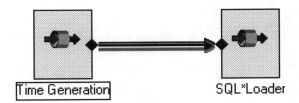

Time Generation   SQL*Loader

Click on the time generation transform to open the dialog box shown in Figure 5.25. One record is created for each day starting at the *Start Date* for the length of time specified in the *Duration.*

The primary key for the time dimension is generated by checking the *Date* box. In this example, it will be stored in the "time_key" column. Any of the other columns in the table can also be generated for any given date. The types of data that are of interest are checked, and the output column name is listed. Figure 5.26 shows a sample of the data generated for the EASYDW time dimension. All columns except for "public_holiday" are automatically generated. The time dimension is listed again for reference purposes to help match the column names with the names used by Data Mart Builder.

Figure 5.25 Time Generation Dialog Box

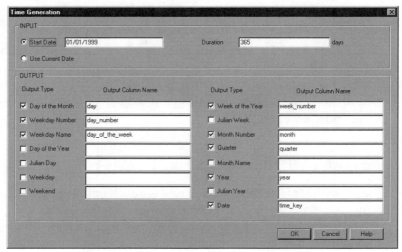

Julian dates can be generated by checking the *Julian Day, Julian Week,* and *Julian Year* boxes. Julian dates are the number of days, weeks, or years since January 1, 4713 B.C.

```
CREATE TABLE easydw.time
(time_key        DATE,
 day                    NUMBER (2,0),
 month                  NUMBER (2,0),
 quarter                NUMBER (2,0),
 year                   NUMBER (4,0),
 day_number             NUMBER (3,0),
 day_of_the_week        VARCHAR2(9),
 week_number            NUMBER (2,0),
 public_holiday         VARCHAR2(1)
  CONSTRAINT public_holiday
   CHECK (public_holiday IN ('Y','N')) )
PCTFREE 0 PCTUSED 99
TABLESPACE dimensions
STORAGE (INITIAL 16K NEXT 16K PCTINCREASE 0) ;
```

In Figure 5.26, the output of the time generation transform is displayed on the grid. The grid can be used to ensure the correct data is being generated for each column, since the names of all the date-related columns can be somewhat confusing.

Figure 5.26 Time Generation Grid

	time_key	day	month	quarter	year	day_number	day_of_the_week	week_number
1	01/01/1999 12:00:00 AM	1	1	1	1999	5	Friday	0
2	01/02/1999 12:00:00 AM	2	1	1	1999	6	Saturday	0
3	01/03/1999 12:00:00 AM	3	1	1	1999	7	Sunday	0
4	01/04/1999 12:00:00 AM	4	1	1	1999	1	Monday	0
5	01/05/1999 12:00:00 AM	5	1	1	1999	2	Tuesday	0
6	01/06/1999 12:00:00 AM	6	1	1	1999	3	Wednesday	0
7	01/07/1999 12:00:00 AM	7	1	1	1999	4	Thursday	0
8	01/08/1999 12:00:00 AM	8	1	1	1999	5	Friday	1
9	01/09/1999 12:00:00 AM	9	1	1	1999	6	Saturday	1
10	01/10/1999 12:00:00 AM	10	1	1	1999	7	Sunday	1
11	01/11/1999 12:00:00 AM	11	1	1	1999	1	Monday	1
12	01/12/1999 12:00:00 AM	12	1	1	1999	2	Tuesday	1
13	01/13/1999 12:00:00 AM	13	1	1	1999	3	Wednesday	1
14	01/14/1999 12:00:00 AM	14	1	1	1999	4	Thursday	1
15	01/15/1999 12:00:00 AM	15	1	1	1999	5	Friday	2
16	01/16/1999 12:00:00 AM	16	1	1	1999	6	Saturday	2
17	01/17/1999 12:00:00 AM	17	1	1	1999	7	Sunday	2

5.3.4   Loading Data from a Relational Source

After loading the dimension tables, the fact table can be loaded. Prior to creating the plan, a BaseView and MetaView must be created describing the order- entry schema. In this example, the metadata for the source system will come from the Designer Repository. The Data Dictionary Type is Oracle Data Mart Designer, as shown in Figure 5.27.

Figure 5.27 Creating a BaseView Using Metadata from Repository

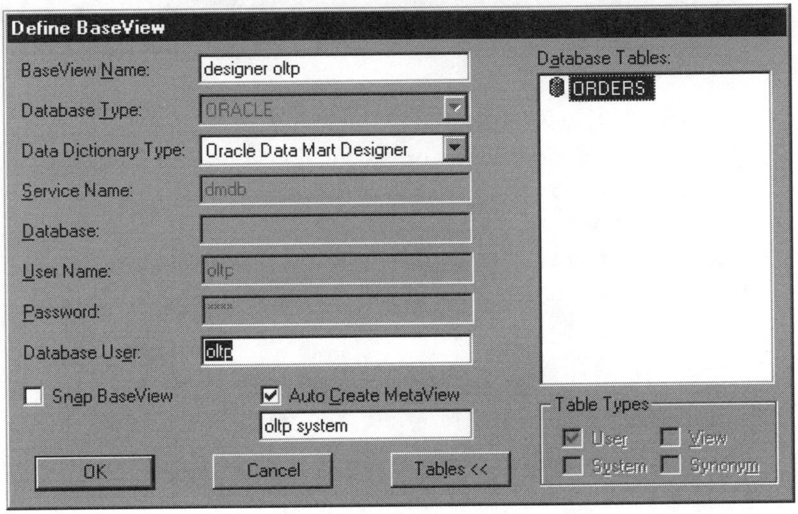

When the source of data is the Designer Repository, the Oracle Data Mart Designer dialog box appears, as shown in Figure 5.28. The designer user, password, application name, and version are all entered. The database user name must also entered.

Figure 5.28 Specifying the Designer Application for a BaseView

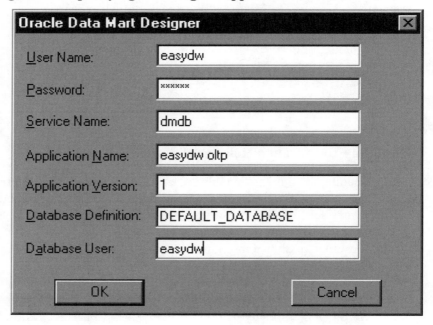

Figure 5.29 shows a plan that extracts the orders for the month of May 1999 from the orders table in the operational system and loads them into the purchases fact table in the EASYDW database.

Figure 5.29 Data Mart Builder Plan to Load Purchases Fact Table

The plan is composed of a SQL query transform, which extracts the data from the source order-entry database and a SQL*Loader transform to load the data into the purchases table in the EASYDW data mart.

A new plan is created by selecting New Plan from the File menu. The tables and columns in the OLTP schema are displayed by clicking on the parts bin and selecting the MetaView just created. The tables or columns that contain the data to be loaded into the data mart are dragged into the workspace.

When you drag parts (tables and columns) into the workspace, the SQL Query transform is automatically added to the plan. A SQL statement is generated to select the columns from the tables in the source database. The SQL query can be edited by double-clicking on the SQL Query transformation icon.

Figure 5.30 Applying Filters With the Query Editor

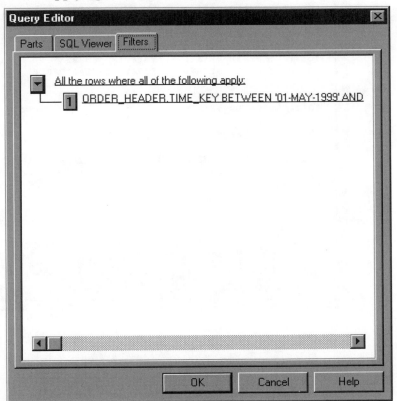

In Figure 5.30, a filter has been added to the query to select only the rows for the month of May 1999.

For debugging purposes, the SQL that was generated for the query can be checked by selecting the SQL Viewer tab shown in Figure 5.31. The order_header and order_detail tables have been joined by order_id. This was entered automatically based on the referential integrity constraint definitions. Only the rows between "01-May-1999" and "31-May-1999" will be retrieved.

Figure 5.31 Viewing the SQL Generated to Extract Data

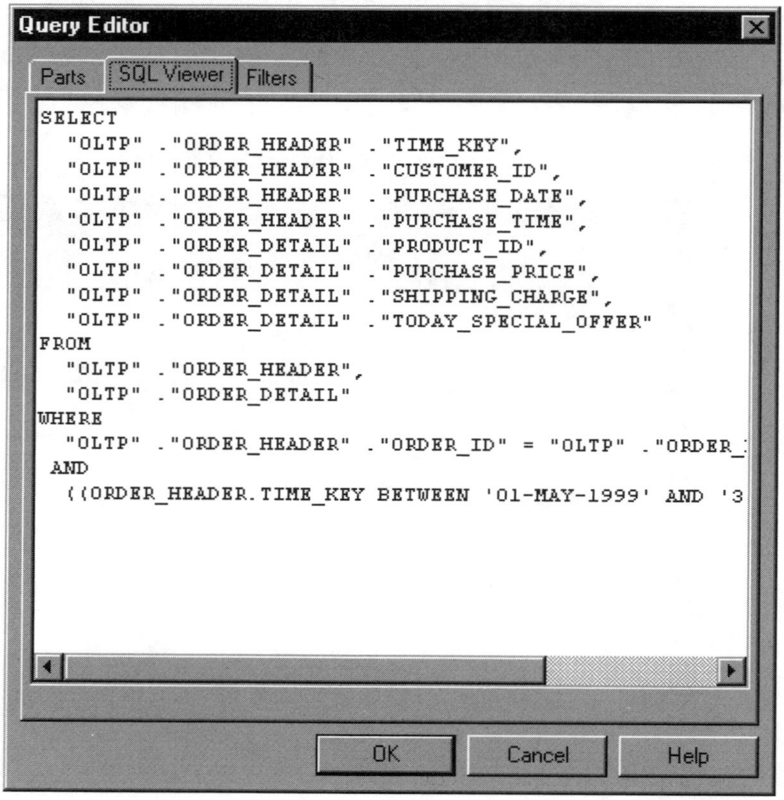

```
Query Editor                                              [X]

 Parts | SQL Viewer | Filters

 SELECT
   "OLTP" ."ORDER_HEADER" ."TIME_KEY",
   "OLTP" ."ORDER_HEADER" ."CUSTOMER_ID",
   "OLTP" ."ORDER_HEADER" ."PURCHASE_DATE",
   "OLTP" ."ORDER_HEADER" ."PURCHASE_TIME",
   "OLTP" ."ORDER_DETAIL" ."PRODUCT_ID",
   "OLTP" ."ORDER_DETAIL" ."PURCHASE_PRICE",
   "OLTP" ."ORDER_DETAIL" ."SHIPPING_CHARGE",
   "OLTP" ."ORDER_DETAIL" ."TODAY_SPECIAL_OFFER"
 FROM
   "OLTP" ."ORDER_HEADER",
   "OLTP" ."ORDER_DETAIL"
 WHERE
   "OLTP" ."ORDER_HEADER" ."ORDER_ID" = "OLTP" ."ORDER_
 AND
   ((ORDER_HEADER.TIME_KEY BETWEEN '01-MAY-1999' AND '3



        [    OK    ]    [  Cancel  ]    [   Help   ]
```

5.3.5   Scheduling Plans

Once a plan has been developed, it can be run immediately, or it can be scheduled to run at a later time. A plan is scheduled by clicking the clock icon. The scheduler window shown in Figure 5.32 is displayed.

Figure 5.32 Scheduling a Plan

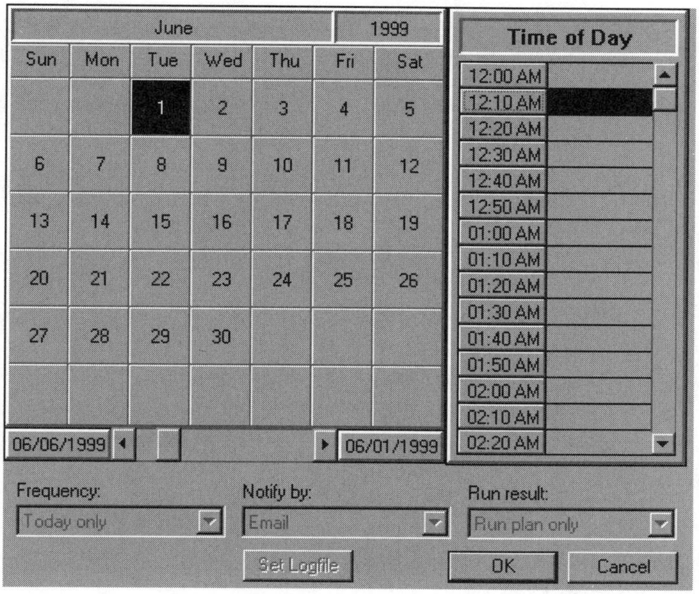

The date and time the plan will be run are entered. In order to schedule the run, click on the desired date and time, and drag the plan to it. Plans can be run just once or on a daily, weekly, or monthly basis. Upon completion of the plan, a log can be created, and a user can be notified via E-mail. In this example, the plan will be run on June 1, and E-mail will be sent when it has completed.

Plan scheduling relies on the Windows NT Scheduling Service, which must be started for plans to run.

5.4   ORACLE REPORTS

Oracle Reports is used to create, publish, and distribute reports from information stored in your Data Mart. Reports can be formatted in a variety of styles and can be enhanced by adding graphs such as pie charts or bar charts. Reports can be based on predefined templates, or the Template Editor can be used to create new templates.

A report can be distributed in multiple ways. It can be printed on paper, distributed electronically through E-mail, or made available through the Internet (or a company's intranet), where it can be accessed via a Web browser. Oracle Reports is a component of Oracle Developer.

The components of Oracle Reports include:

- *Report Builder:* a wizard-based tool used to create reports
- *Graphics Builder:* a declarative tool for the graphical display of data
- *Reports Runtime* and *Graphics Runtime:* Runtime engines for client/server deployment
- *Reports Server:* A server that enables multitier deployment of reports.

To build a report, the following steps are taken:

(1) Create a report using the *Report Wizard.*

(2) Edit the report using the *Live Previewer.*

(3) Run the report.

5.4.1   Creating a Report Using the Report Wizard

The Report Wizard guides you through the steps of creating a report. To invoke Report Builder, select Report Builder from the Developer R2.1 program group. Figure 5.33 shows the Report Wizard screen where you select how the report is to be built.

Also, if you are new to Oracle Reports then you may want to begin by selecting the Quick Tour and also reviewing the cue cards.

Figure 5.33 The Report Wizard

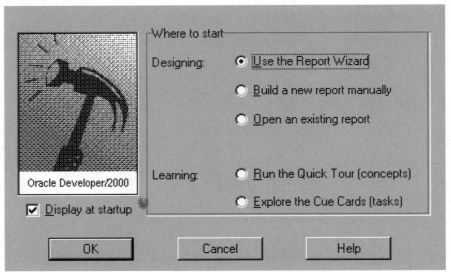

Choosing the Report Style and Title

Figure 5.34 shows the next screen, the styles available for the basic structure of a report. When a style is selected, a thumbnail sketch is displayed on the left side of the screen.

Figure 5.34 Choosing a Report Style

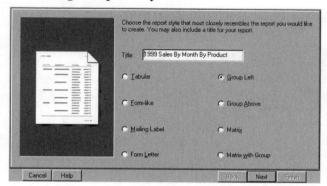

The title of this report will be "1999 Sales by Month by Product." The data will be grouped by month and product, using the Group Left style.

Selecting the Data for the Report

The data to include in the report is specified using an SQL query. The query can be typed directly, can be created using the Query Builder, or the SQL can be imported from a file. In the example in Figure 5.35, the SQL statement was created using SQL*Plus, saved in a file, and then imported into the Report Builder.

For users not familiar with SQL, the Query Builder can simplify the creation of the SQL statement.

Figure 5.35 Specifying the Data for the Report

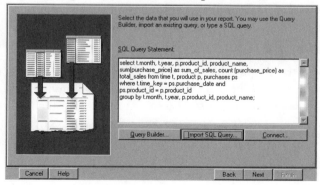

Selecting the Grouping Columns

A report with a group contains one or more levels of subtotals. The fields the data will be grouped by are selected from the list of available fields. In the example in Figure 5.36, subtotals will be generated for each month, so month has been selected as the first level.

Figure 5.36 Choosing the Grouping Columns

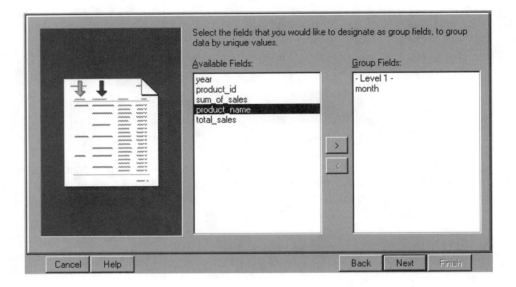

Selecting the Fields in the Report

The columns that will be printed in the report are selected next. All the columns in the query, or a subset of them, may be chosen. In the example in Figure 5.37, the month, product_name, total_sales, and sum_of_sales will be included in the report. Year and product_id will not be displayed.

Creating the Totals

Totals are computations performed on all of the records in a column. The columns chosen in this screen will be the columns that the subtotals at the end of each group and final totals at the end of the report are based on. In Figure 5.38, the sum_of _sales and sum of total_sales will be calculated.

Figure 5.37 Selecting the Fields in a Report

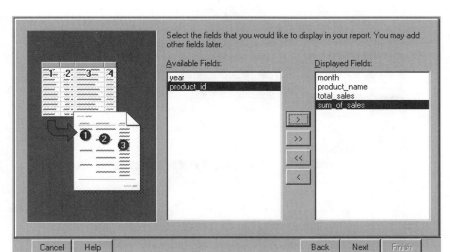

Figure 5.38 Creating Subtotals and Final Totals

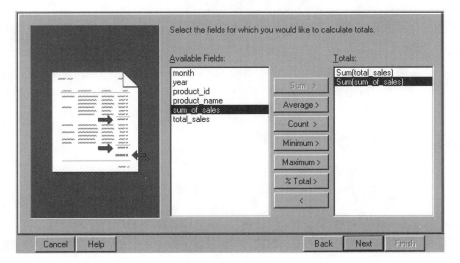

Running the Report

You can choose labels for column headings and from a variety of predefined templates for the output report format. When you're done specifying options for your report, click *Finish*. The report is now run and displayed in the Live Previewer, as shown in Figure 5.39.

The picture at the top of the report is Oracle Headquarters in Redwood Shores, California. You can substitute your company picture or logo.

Figure 5.39 Looking at a Report with the Live Previewer

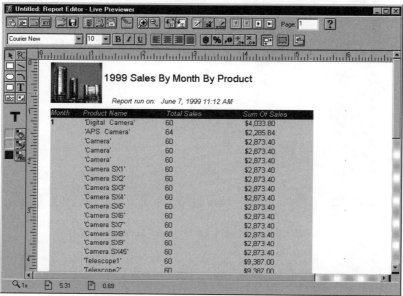

You can step through each page of the report. Figure 5.40 shows the last page of the report with the subtotals for the month of May and grand totals for all sales to date.

Figure 5.40 Report Totals

1999 Sales By Month By Product

Report run on: June 7, 1999 11:12 AM

Month	Product Name	Total Sales	Sum Of Sales
5	Total:	4	$112.04
Total:		4,970	$2,509,608.10

5.4.2　Editing a Report

The Live Previewer is a WYSIWYG (what you see is what you get) editor that lets you look at the report and modify the layout, allowing you to see the effect of the changes immediately. You can add currency symbols, commas, and decimal points. You can change the font, and bold, underline, or italicize text, and you can format numbers to represent dollar figures.

After you create a report with the Report Wizard and enter it from the Live Previewer, the Report Wizard is tabbed. You can go to any page of the Wizard, and make changes to the report. Figure 5.41 shows some of the different templates you can use for the output format of your report. To see how another template would look, select it, and click the *Apply* button.

Reports can also be customized with the *Object Navigator*, a high-level browser for defining, locating, and working with the objects in a report.

Figure 5.41 Editing a Report

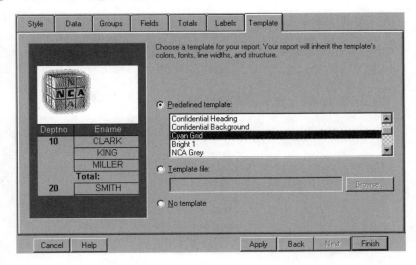

Oracle Reports has a Chart Wizard ,which allows you to display your data pictorially. You can add a bar chart, pie chart, or line graph to your reports. The Chart Wizard is invoked by clicking the *Chart* button on the Live Previewer toolbar.

5.4.3   Report Deployment

Oracle Reports allows you to generate multiple output formats and distribute them to multiple destinations from a single run of the report. Reports can be deployed on the Web, embedded in forms or in Graphics Builder displays, and can be E-mailed via the Microsoft Messaging Application Programming Interface (MAPI).

A report can be output in several formats, including ASCII, Postscript, formatted for HP-PCL printers, hypertext markup language (HTML), HTML Cascading Style Sheets (CSS), and Adobe Portable Document Format (PDF). PDF and HTML formats give you the ability to view the reports using a Web browser. Refer to Chapter 8 for a discussion on creating reports for the Web.

Running Reports

A report can be run using the *Report Builder Live Editor*. It can be printed or E-mailed by pressing the print or E-mail buttons on the toolbar.

To run a report at a later time, you can use the *Reports Runtime* utility. After a report is created, the report definition is saved in a file with the extension ".rdf." Prior to running the report, it must be converted to a report binary run only file (.rep) using the Report Compiler, as shown in Figure 5.42.

Figure 5.42 Compiling a Report

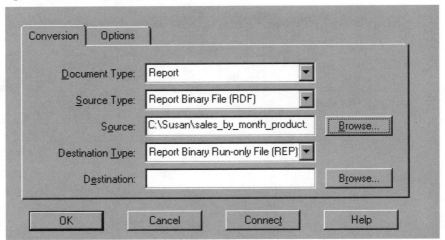

The Report Compiler and Reports Runtime are invoked from the Developer R2.1 program group. The .rep files of the reports that will be run multiple times can be saved so they do not need to be recompiled.

Once the file has been compiled, the report can be run using Reports Runtime. When the report is run, it can be reviewed in the Live Previewer. It can then be printed or E-mailed using the buttons on the toolbar. A file can be generated, as shown in Figure 5.43. Once you know you have the right file, the runtime options allow you to bypass viewing it on the screen first.

Figure 5.43 Reports Runtime

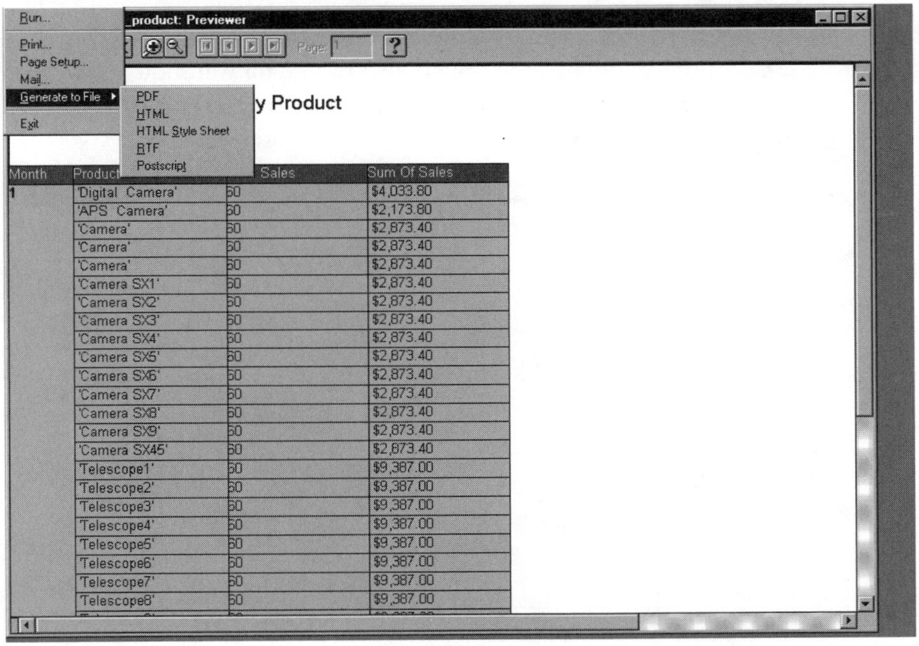

Reports can also be run in a multitier environment using an application server, eliminating the need to install and maintain software on each user's desktop PC. Users launch report requests and receive report output using a Web browser.

The Developer Reports Server allows reports to be run on a remote server. The Reports Server takes execution requests from the clients and schedules and runs the reports. Requests are entered into a job queue and dispatched to run on one of the Reports Server's runtime processes. When the report is complete, the output is returned back to the client. For Web clients, the output is displayed from a Web browser. The Queue Manager can be used to monitor jobs submitted to the Reports Server.

5.5   SUMMARY

The Data Mart Suite provides several components useful in the creation, management, and access of a data mart. Oracle Data Mart Designer provides the ability to model and create the data mart. It also is helpful in reverse-engineering the source schemas. Oracle Data Mart Builder allows you to create and run plans for the ETT process. Oracle Reports provides an easy way to disseminate the information in the data mart.

Some of these tools are obviously useful in data warehouse environments in addition to data marts. In the next chapter, tools used to access the data warehouse, including Oracle Discoverer, will be presented.

6   **Oracle Warehousing Tools**

6.1   WHICH TOOL

It is easy to think that all of your problems are over once you have built the warehouse,but, of course, they are just beginning. Hopefully, you have decided to store inside your data warehouse all of the information that you require and at the appropriate level, so that all you have to do is obtain access to it.

It is at this point that you must decide which tool or tools to use to access your data. The choice is not easy, because there are many to choose from. Since there is a wide choice, this chapter will review three quite different tools from Oracle that provide access to your warehouse data:

- Oracle Discoverer
- Oracle Express
- Oracle Time Series

Where Oracle Discoverer is a typical end user tool for querying your warehouse data directly. Oracle Express is a tool designed for queries involving the dimensions in your warehouse and needs to have its data in its own format database. Oracle Time Series is a set of functions and packages that are used to perform time-based analysis on data in an Oracle 8*i* database.

6.2   ORACLE DISCOVERER

Oracle Discoverer is a very easy to use GUI tool, that has been designed for users who are not computer literate. Therefore in order for them to be able to use the tool easily, some setup is required from the DBA group. Once this has been done, however, your end users should really like using this tool. Oracle Discoverer is available in two editions:

- User
- Administration

The *Administration* edition is the version that is used by the DBA's of the data warehouse to set up the environment for the general Discoverer users.

The *User* edition is the version that the majority of your users will use to query the data in the data warehouse because it is has been designed especially for people who are not familiar with writing computer programs, and also for anyone who is not familiar with SQL and prefers to deal with data using familiar business entities. Also, for those users who may be concerned that they could change the data within the data warehouse, fear not, because when using the user edition of Discoverer, you can only access the warehouse in read-only mode. The use of Oracle Discoverer is not restricted to Oracle databases only, but that is how we will illustrate its use here.

The databases which is has been certified against using the ODBC driver include, DB2 for NT and MVS, Microsoft SQL Server, Sybase, and Terradata.

6.2.1   Setting Up the Environment

Before you can use Discoverer, some setup is required. Although this may seem like a lot of work initially, once completed, your users will really appreciate the work you have done. The environment that you create will determine exactly which data in the warehouse your users can see and how they see it. To begin using Discoverer, first connect to your Oracle 8*i* database.

Hint: You may prefer to create a special user for Discoverer and connect to your database using that user to ensure that the metadata is loaded under that user name.

End-User Layer

The first time the Administration edition is started, you will be asked to create an *end-user layer*(EUL). The end-user layer comprises all the metadata that is needed by Discoverer; therefore, this task will be performed only once. Figure 6.1 shows the screen where you click on the *Create EUL* button. You must then wait for a few moments while the metadata is loaded into the database.

Figure 6.1 Create the End-User Layer

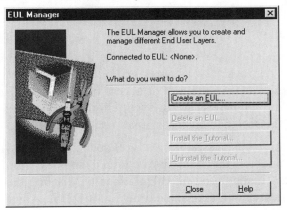

There are many steps involved in setting up the environment for Discoverer. To help you remember them, a window will appear, as shown in Figure 6.2, that lists all of these tasks.

Figure 6.2 Administration Task List

By clicking on any item in this list, you can automatically start that component that provides a very quick start.

Business Area

Once the definition of the end-user layer is complete, a *business area* is named where all of the information needed to query the warehouse must be defined.

The purpose of the business area is to group information into business oriented categories such as *Sales* or *Finance* which are familiar to end users. Business areas are the unit of access control and a user can be assigned to one or more business areas. They will then have access to all of the objects within the assigned business area.

Within this business area, you will specify exactly which data a user may access and how that data may be joined, and describe data aggregations and new data items based on calculations on existing data items. Creating the business area will take some time, but it will reap significant benefits later.

Figure 6.3 Select the Schema

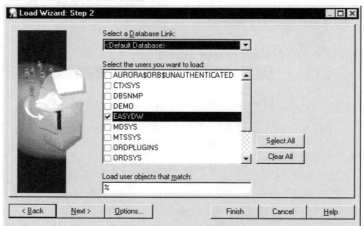

When creating the business area, we must first specify from which schemas the data is to be available to the end user, as illustrated in Figure 6.3. We can select any number of users from the list and also request that it only selects items from the list that match the pattern specified in the box. In our example, we have selected only the user or schema EASYDW.

Once we know from which schema the data will be available, we can then explicitly state from which tables or views we can retrieve data, as shown in Figure 6.4. Using our Easy Shopping example, we have given only the users access to four of the five tables in this data warehouse.

Figure 6.4 Select the Tables and Views

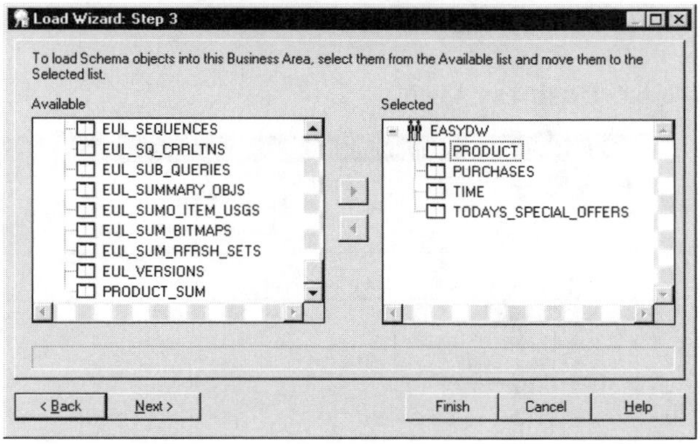

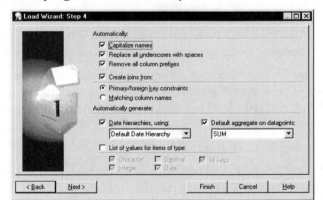

Also at this time, the wizard will ask us if it can make some changes to the data so that it is easier for our end users to handle. In Figure 6.5, we can see some of the ways our data can be modified, such as removing underscores from data names and replacing them with spaces.

The wizard will also automatically create joins based on primary and foreign keys and create hierarchies from the data. By allowing the wizard to perform these tasks, there will be less setup work for you to do.

The first stage in creating our business area is now complete, and Figure 6.6 will now appear. This is where the real work begins. We can now set up the rest of the business area using our task list, shown in Figure 6.2, as a reminder of the steps to complete.

Figure 6.5 Modifying the End-User Layer Data

Although we have shown only the creation of one business area, you could create any number of business areas in your environment, each with their own unique set of data requirements.

Figure 6.6 Business Area

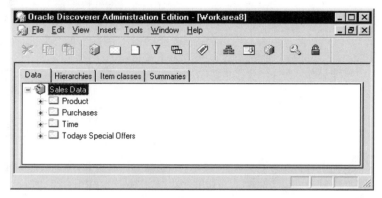

In Figure 6.6, we can see all the tables from the database that we have access to. By default, the end user will have access to every column in those tables. If you click on the table name to expand it, all the columns in that table will appear. To remove any of those columns, simply click on the item using the right mouse button, and a drop-down list will appear. One of the items in that list is *delete item*. Simply select that option, and the item will be removed from the business area, but not from the database.

Before moving on, there is some important terminology that you must familiarize yourself with. In Discoverer, a table or view is known as a *folder* and a column from the table is called an *item*.

A *folder* can be one of two types:

- simple, where it is based on a single database table or view
- complex contain items form other folders and can be nested

An *item* corresponds to a column in a relational database. A simple item is based on a single column in the database, but an item can also be calculated or derived based on a formula using other items, functions, or operators.

Changing Item Details

The attributes of any of the items that you have selected may be modified by selecting the item, clicking on the right mouse button, and then selecting *Properties*. The window illustrated in Figure 6.7 will then appear, and you can then modify whichever properties you like. In this example, we have changed the item's name from Supplier to Main Supplier.

Figure 6.7 Change the Item Details

Specifying Joins

When the business area is first created, Discoverer will automatically create joins between those constraints if the database has primary and foreign keys defined. However, you can specify your own joins by selecting *Insert* from the strip menu and then *Joins*. The window illustrated in Figure 6.8 will appear.

Figure 6.8 Define a Join

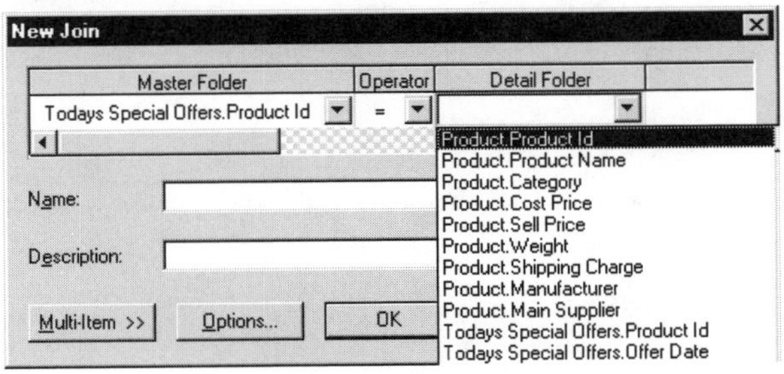

The join is defined by selecting from the drop-down list, which item from the folder is to be joined and the type of join. In our example in Figure 6.8, we have specified a join between the Todays Special Offers table and the Product table using the column Product_id.

Create New Items

Another feature that many DBA's may require is the ability to create new columns or items in the database by calculating their results from other columns.

A *calculation* creates a new item in the End User Layer. It will not add underlying columns to database tables. An item calculation is used to create a new item where there is no underlying database column that contains the data required. Calculations can be simple, such as weight *4.54 or they can be complex mathematical or statistical expressions.

For example, in Figure 6.9, a new column called Total Cost is created in the Purchases table by adding together the columns purchase price and shipping charges. You can create as many of these types of calculations as you require, and they will appear as an item for that folder.

Figure 6.9 Creating a Calculated Item

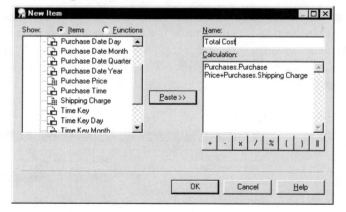

Hierarchies

We have already seen that hierarchies play an important role in our data warehouse. Although in Oracle 8*i* we can create dimensions, at the time of writing, these cannot be used by Discoverer, and we must create our own dimensions, which are known in Discoverer as *hierarchies*.

Hierarchies are very important in Discoverer because if an item is in a hierarchy, then users can:

- Drill Up, changes the query to show a higher level of details
- Drill Down, to show more detail

A hierarchy is created by clicking on *Insert* in the strip menu and then selecting *Hierarchy*. First you will be asked as to the type of hierarchy you want to create, an item or a date. When the business area is first created, it is quite likely that Discoverer will automatically create a time-based hierarchy. Therefore you will probably only have to create non-time-based hierarchies.

Figure 6.10 shows how simple it is to create the hierarchy by selecting the items and then defining the hierarchy relationship. In Figure 6.10, we have created a very simple hierarchy between PRODUCT_ID and CATEGORY.

Figure 6.10 Defining a Hierarchy

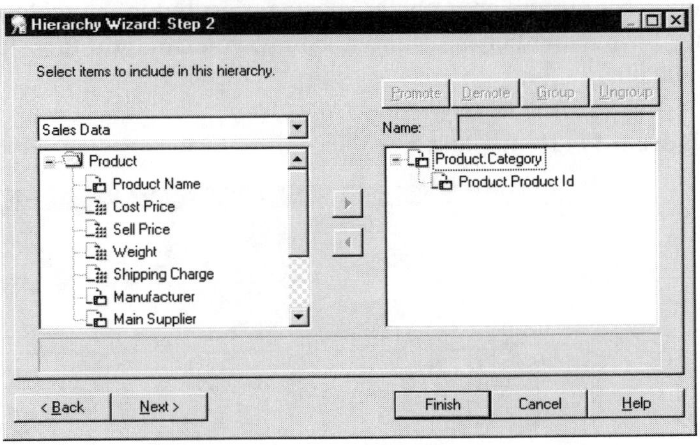

Item Classes—List of Values

When the end users are actually querying the data, there are times when it may be helpful to them if they can see a possible list of values. For example, suppose they want to pick out all of the electrical items if they know which category they are represented in, then this will facilitate rapid query generation.

This is one of the properties of an *item class* which can describe the hierarchical relationship between items, a list of values, alternative sort keys for items, and the display methods. Therefore an item class defines all of the attributes for an item. Once an item class has been defined it can then be assigned to other items which share similar properties.

An item class is created by selecting *Insert* from the strip menu and then *Insert Class* from the list or by clicking on the text in the administration task list shown in Figure 6.2. Several different types of classes of items may be created, but if you select *List of Values,* then all you have to select is the column containing the values and which tables will use it.

When it is complete, click on the tab *Item Classes,* and the window illustrated in Figure 6.11 will appear. In this example a list of values called *Categories* has been created. If we expand the entry categories, the data warehouse can be queried, and all the different values will be displayed. In Figure 6.11, there are only three categories, but in the real world, where you may have a number of different values, you can omit this step of displaying the results.

Figure 6.11 Item Class

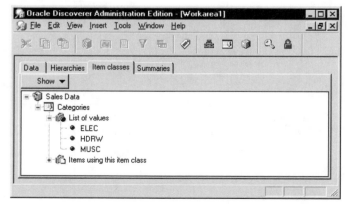

Summaries

We have already seen the importance of creating and using summary tables in our data warehouse. Discoverer allows you to create your own summaries, either by:

- Collecting usage statistics from previous Discoverer sessions
- Manually creating the summary
- Registering a previously built summary

To manually create your summary, click on *Insert* in the strip menu, and then select *Summary*. The first window that appears will ask you the type of summary that you wish to create. If you select *From Items in the End-User Layer* then you can create your own summary.

Then the window illustrated in Figure 6.12 appears. There you select the folders and items from within those tables that are to appear in the summary. In our example, we have selected only the Purchases table, but you could select multiple tables. Then we chose four of the data items in that table. For the item purchase price, we have asked that this value be aggregated.

You will see that Discoverer will automatically supply a range of functions for you to select when a function may be applied to an item. In Figure 6.12, for the item purchase_price, we have asked that the SUM function be applied to this item. Next you are asked to specify which groups of items you require.

Figure 6.12 Creating a Summary

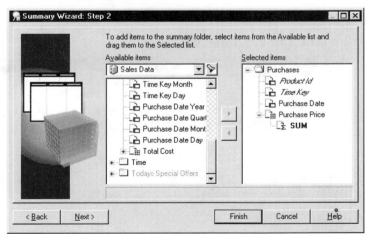

Finally, you will be asked how often this summary is to be refreshed. Remember that, as new data is added to the warehouse, the summaries must be maintained to reflect the latest data. In Figure 6.13, we can see that we have stated that this summary be created now and never refreshed after this time.

Figure 6.13 Refreshing the Summary

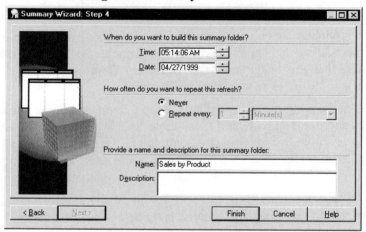

At any time, we can see the summaries that we have created by clicking on the *Summaries* tab, as illustrated by Figure 6.14. Here we can see that we have two summaries defined, one called Sales by product and another Sales by date.

Figure 6.14 List of Summaries

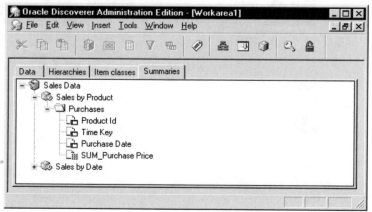

At the time of writing, the summaries created here are specific to Discoverer, and they are not the same as the materialized views that were described in Chapter 3. Hopefully, by the time you read this, a more recent version of Discoverer will be available, one that creates the materialized views described in Chapter 3 and takes advantage of features such as query rewrite.

Security Issues

The final setup task is defining who may access the business area that you have just created. You can start this component by double-clicking on *Grant Business Area Access,* shown in Figure 6.2.

A window will appear that will allow you to state which users can access a business area or which business areas a user can access. In Figure 6.15, we can see that the only user who we will grant access to our business area is EASYDW.

Don't forget that, although in this example we have enabled access via the user name, you can also grant access to the business area via the roles that may be given to a user. When you are satisfied that all the relevant access rights have been given, click on the *Apply* button to complete the changes.

Figure 6.15 Granting Access to the Business Area

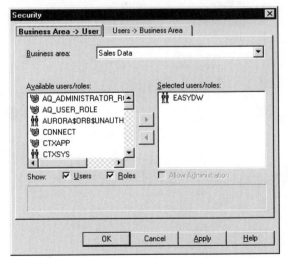

In Figure 6.16, we can now see our complete business area. Expanding just the Purchases table, we can see all the items that are available to our users, the new calculation that we created, called Total Cost, and the functions that we can apply to that column. At the bottom of the window, we can see that joins have been created from the Purchases table to the Product and Time table. Of course, not all the information can be displayed on this one window, so, to see the *Hierarchies* tab you will have to click it. The same is true for item classes and summary information.

We have now completed all of the basic setup tasks for using Discoverer. Don't forget to save all of your work, and please remember that the tool is much more sophisticated that we have shown in these few pages.

6.2.2   Query using the User Edition

Once the environment has been set up for querying via Discoverer, you can now start the *User edition*. Simply connect to the database using your user name and password, and you will be asked whether to create or open an existing workbook, a *workbook* being the place where your queries are stored.

Figure 6.16 Completing the Setup

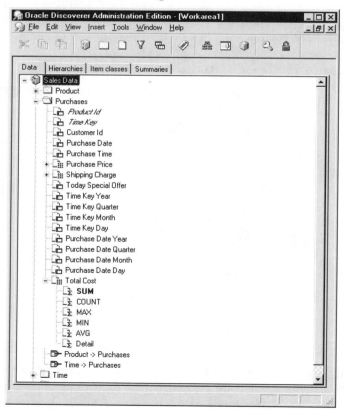

In Figure 6.17, we see the initial window where we specify the workbook and how the results are to be displayed. Discoverer offers a range of display options, such as showing the data in *tabular* or a *crosstab* form. Using the crosstab format is ideal when you have multidimensional data to display.

Now it is time to specify exactly what is to be reported in this query. First you must select the business area that was defined using the Administration edition, to determine the data that you may see. In our example, we have only the Sales Data business area, but there could be several of those to choose from.

Now we have to select the items from those folders. This is a simple process, illustrated in Figure 6.18, involving moving them from the left window (available) to the right window (selected).

Figure 6.17 Using a Workbook

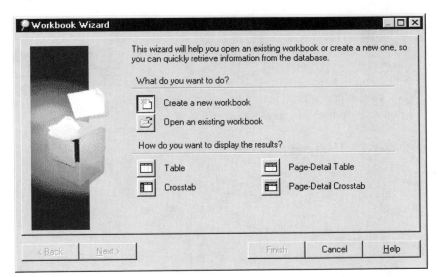

In Figure 6.18, we have selected the item *category* from the product folder and the date from the purchases folder, and then requested that the item purchase price should be aggregated.

Figure 6.18 Selecting Data to Be Displayed

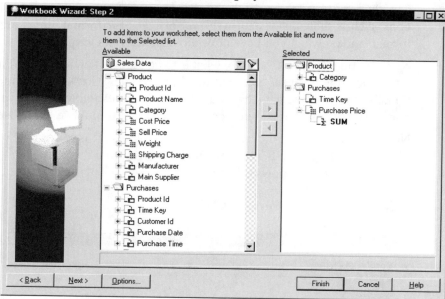

When Discoverer identifies a item upon which functions may be applied, then all possible options are made available to the user.

Figure 6.19 Item Aggregates

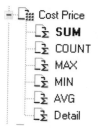

For example, in Figure 6.19, we see that the item cost_price can be summed and counted and Discoverer can calculate the minimum, maximum, or an average. Therefore, to sum purchase price, simply expand the aggregate options for purchase price in the left window, then select the required aggregate, and click the right arrow button to place it on the list of items to display, illustrated in Figure 6.18. This process is repeated for every item required in the report.

Figure 6.20 Laying Out the Report

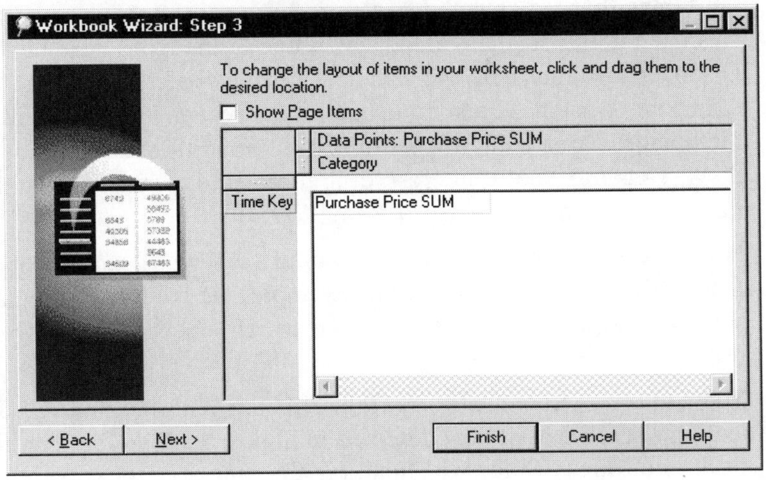

Having chosen our items, we must now drag and drop them onto the worksheet to show how the data is to be reported. Referring to Figure 6.20, we have dragged the item *time key* to the Y axis and placed the *category* on the X axis.

Clicking on the *Finish* button will display the data. Discoverer will now query our data warehouse directly and show us the results, as illustrated in Figure 6.21. There we can see the total sales by category for a given date.

Figure 6.21 Report from Discoverer

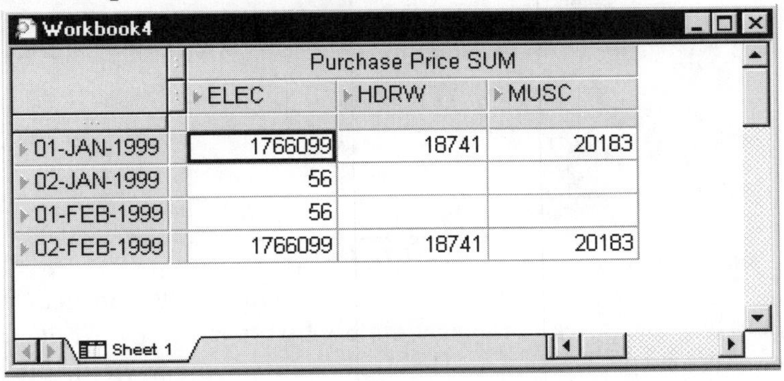

Hint: You may have to format the cells of the report to see the data if the numbers are large, because, by default, it uses small numbers.

Note that in order to report this data, we did not have to specify how to join the tables that we selected because the join information had already been specified in the business area. This is one of the really nice benefits of using Discoverer, because the end user does not have to know about relational joins. All of this work has been done behind the scenes by the person who created the business area using the Administration edition. Now all our user has to do is select the data of interest, drag them onto the repor,t and then click the *Finish* button to request the information.

Now that we have our report, we could very well want to look at the data from a different perspective. For example, we could roll the data up to see sales by month or drill down to see which electrical item generated most revenue.

You can change the report by right clicking with the mouse button and se-lecting *Drill.* The window depicted in Figure 6.22 will appear. Here you can drill up or down. Since we clicked in the time area, Discoverer will use any hierarchies that we described in the business area to help us interrogate the data.

Figure 6.22 Drilling Up/Down the Data

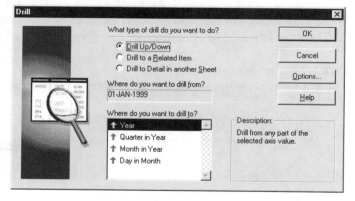

In Figure 6.22, because we have a time hierarchy, we can change our report to sum by year, instead of by day, simply by selecting year from the list and then clicking on the *OK* button. Hopefully now you are beginning to appreciate all of the setup work that we completed using the Administration edition.

In this first example of using Discoverer, we reported all of the data, but you can select a subset, as shown in Figure 6.23.

Figure 6.23 Select Specific Data

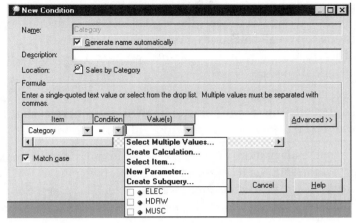

In the window depicted in Figure 6.23, we can give this selection a name. You don't have to know the range of values, because Discoverer will show them in the drop-down list. Therefore, in this example, we could change our report to view only electrical sales from our data warehouse or specify different types of selection criteria.

Earlier we saw how we could create a list of values in the Administration edition. Another nice feature in Discoverer that can help the users query the data faster is that, once created, these values can now appear in the user edition when you are selecting data, as illustrated in Figure 6.24. Here we can see that the category item contains the value "ELEC" for electrical items.

Figure 6.24 Using Lists of Values

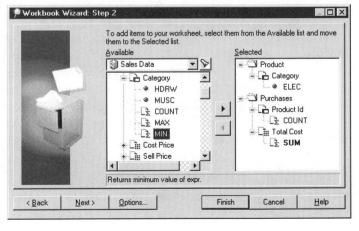

Now we could have just selected the item *category*, but since a list of values has already been defined for this item, by expanding this item, those values are also shown. Consequently, instead of generating a query that returns information on all categories, now we can select which specific categories are of interest. Hence, in this example, we have asked to see only the sales for electrical goods.

Hint: One important point to bear in mind here is that this only works well if the categories are meaningful to the end users.

There are many more facilities available from Discoverer to help you interrogate your data, such as *filters*, which are analogous to WHERE clauses and are used for restricting the rows returned. There is a Schedule Workbook which provides a method of scheduling a workbook for execution later. Discoverer can also take advantage of the Applications security model and there is a Discoverer Viewer which can open existing workbooks.

Hopefully, over these few pages, you now have an appreciation of some of this tool's capabilities and how nice the tool is for end users who may not be very computer literate.

6.3   ORACLE EXPRESS

Another tool available from Oracle for analyzing the data inside your warehouse is called Oracle Express. It is designed for performing multidimensional querying upon your data. Earlier, we defined the terms dimensions in our warehouse, a multidimensional query is one which uses many dimensions. Therefore, in our Easy Shopping Inc. example, a query using dimensions time, product, and customer would be multidimensional.

We have already seen that tools like Discoverer can handle queries involving many dimensions, so why would a tool such as Oracle Express be required. Well, Express uses its own special database, which has been designed specifically for warehouse-style applications because it uses a multidimensional model instead of the traditional entity/relationship model used by relational databases. Therefore, using this special structure enables you to perform complex multidimensional queries very quickly.

Oracle Express can be used on its own or integrated with your Oracle 8i database, which is how we will illustrate its use here. But some setup is required prior to querying the data in your warehouse via Oracle Express.

In order to use Oracle Express against your Oracle 8*i* database, you will first have to use the Relational Access Manager tool to define exactly what information you require from your data warehouse. Then an Oracle Express database is created, and it is linked to the project you created using the Relational Access Manager. Once your relational data have been loaded into the Express database, they can then be queried using Oracle Express Analyzer.

Before attempting to use Oracle Express, you must check that the Express Server is running. On a Windows NT (NT) system, this is achieved by selecting the tool *Express Service Manager.* A window will appear where it asks you which computer you want to attach to. Select your machine, and a list of services will be displayed.

Figure 6.25 Status of Express Service

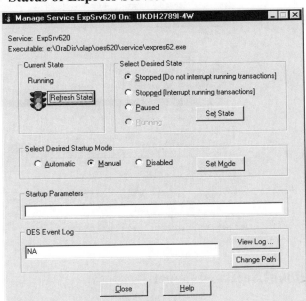

Choose the Express Server from the list, and click on the *OK* button. The window depicted in Figure 6.25 will appear, and you will then see the status of the server. Unfortunately this is a black-and-white book, but trust us when we tell you that the green traffic light is illuminated to show that the Express Server is running.

The Express tool is highly configurable, and, once you are familiar with the tool, you can change numerous options using the Express Configuration

Manager. Once again, you will be asked to select the computer where Express is running. Click the button to *Edit Configuration Settings,* and then press the *Next* button. The window depicted in Figure 6.26 will appear.

As you can see from Figure 6.26 there are numerous parameters that may be changed. In the Oracle Express documentation, there is advice on what these parameters mean and which ones may require adjustment.

Hint: You do not need to have the Express Server running if you are only setting up the environment in Relational Access Manager.

Figure 6.26 Configure Express Service

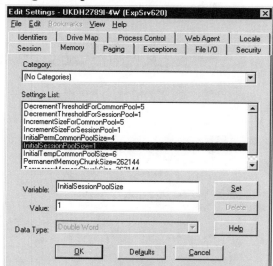

6.3.1   Relational Access Manager

The Relational Access Manager allows you to use Oracle Express against your relational database. Before you can use this tool, there are two scripts files *orathtbl.sql* and *orathidx.sql* that must be run to create the repository tables required by Express. It is probably a good idea to create a new user for the Express repository and then create these tables and indexes under that user. Once this setup phase is complete, you can then define your environment using the Relational Access Administrator.

Relational Access Administrator

When you start the Relational Access Administrator, the first window displayed will ask to which Oracle 8*i* database you want to connect to, using either an ODBC or Net8 connection. Use Net8 whenever possible because it will be more efficient than ODBC; however, in these examples, an ODBC connection has been used. Once connected, the window illustrated in Figure 6.27 will appear which is where you define the Express Data Model, which describes the format of your Express database and how to map your relational data to this structure.

Your *data model* is stored inside a *project*; therefore, if this is the first time you have started Express, don't forget to give your project a name. Otherwise, Express displays a list of known projects, and you can select yours from the list.

Select Tables from the Data Warehouse

The first step is to select the tables from the warehouse that you want to access from Express. Once you have clicked on the table and moved it over to the right window, don't forget to select from the drop-down list whether this is a *lookup* or a *fact* table. Fact tables we have discussed previously, and a lookup table is another name for a dimension.

In Figure 6.27, we have selected six tables from our EASYDW schema, and all of them, apart from the Purchases table, have been identified as lookup tables.

Figure 6.27 Selecting the Tables from the Warehouse

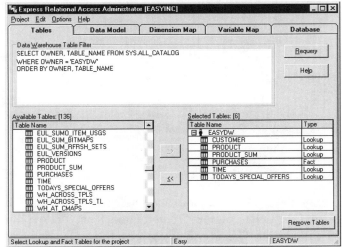

Create the Dimensions

The next step is to click on the *Data Model* tab. This is the section where you have to define the dimensions and variables. Although we have seen in previous chapters that Oracle 8*i* has a dimension object, at the time of writing, Oracle Express is not able to understand that object. Therefore, you will have to define it again. First you describe the dimension, and later you will see how to map the Express dimension object to the tables in your data warehouse.

Although this approach may seem a bit tedious, it will, in fact, not take you very long. If you already have your CREATE DIMENSION statement handy, you can display that window alongside the Express window. Using this approach, all of your dimensions will be defined in a matter of minutes.

In Figure 6.28 we can see all of our dimensions for the Easy Shopping Inc. data warehouse.

Figure 6.28 Defining the Dimensions

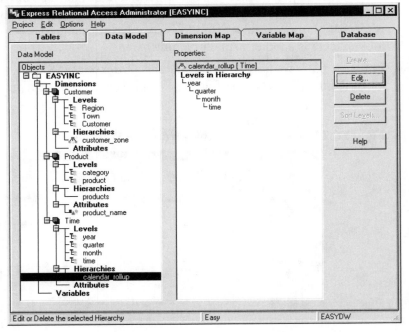

To create the dimension, first click on the word *Dimensions* in the left window, and then click on the *Create* button. The window illustrated in Figure 6.29 will appear. This is where you give the dimension a name.

At this time, you can name each dimension, but you may prefer to close this window and only name one dimension at a time.

Figure 6.29 Naming the Dimension

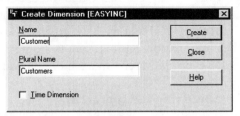

Once the dimension name has been named, all that exists is an empty dimension definition. You must now click on that dimension and specify the levels, attributes, and hierarchy. Levels are created by selecting *level,* as shown in Figure 6.28, and then clicking on the *Create* button. Figure 6.30 appears, where you give each level a name. This is when, if you have your SQL dimension definition handy, you can place the two windows alongside one another and very quickly create the levels.

Figure 6.30 Specifying the Levels in a Dimension

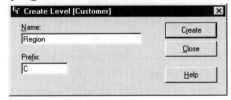

Part of the level definition includes a prefix for each level. Oracle Express expects that all key values within a dimension be unique; however, this is not always possible, and the prefix clause is a mechanism for overcoming this restriction. If all key values are the same, then keep the prefix the same; if they are not, then identify which levels within a prefix are unique.

Hint: If you are unsure whether key values are unique or you get an error message stating that the dimension hierarchy is invalid when you try to save, try using different prefixes .

An example of when multiple prefixes would be required is if we had, say, two hierarchies in the time dimension and the same values could appear in both hierarchies.

Once all the levels are named, they can then be grouped into a hierarchy by selecting *hierarchy* from Figure 6.28 and clicking on the *Create* button. Figure 6.31 will then appear.

Here you give the hierarchy a name and then select the levels from the window on the left in Figure 6.31. Then click on the arrow to move them to the right window. In this example we have created the customer_zone hierarchy that describes the relationship between customer, town, and region. Repeat this process for every hierarchy in each dimension.

Figure 6.31 Specifying the Hierarchy

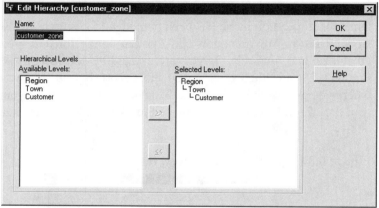

When we saw dimensions being defined in Chapters 2 and 3 you could also define an attribute that has a one-to-one relationship with the level. This can also be described in Express. Figure 6.28 shows that we created an attribute for product_name.

Hint: Create the levels in hierarchy order. Defining the highest level first will facilitate faster hierarchy definition and prevent Express from creating the hierarchy in reverse order.

Mapping the Dimension to the Data Warehouse Dimension Tables

Once the dimensions are created, you can now click on the *Dimension Map* tab to map each level in the dimension to a column in your database. This is achieved using a drag-and-drop technique. Expand the tables in the left window, which contain the columns referenced in your dimension. Referring to Figure 6.32, the product table has been expanded, and the product columns are shown. Then select the column that corresponds to the level in the hierarchy, and drag it over to the appropriate level in the dimension.

The key for the *category* level is the column *category,* and the key for *product* is the column *product_id*. There are some other attributes that must be defined for the level. If the *parent key* is visible, then specify here the column for the next level in the hierarchy. In our example, the parent of product is category; therefore, we specify the category column here by dragging it over from the left window. You must also specify the description for each column. If the item does not have a description, then simply drag over the column name. In our example, category doesn't have a description, so we used category again. It is not necessary to drag the column over three times, because by default, when you select a column and place it in long name, it will automatically be populated into medium and short names.

Figure 6.32 Mapping Dimension to the Database Column

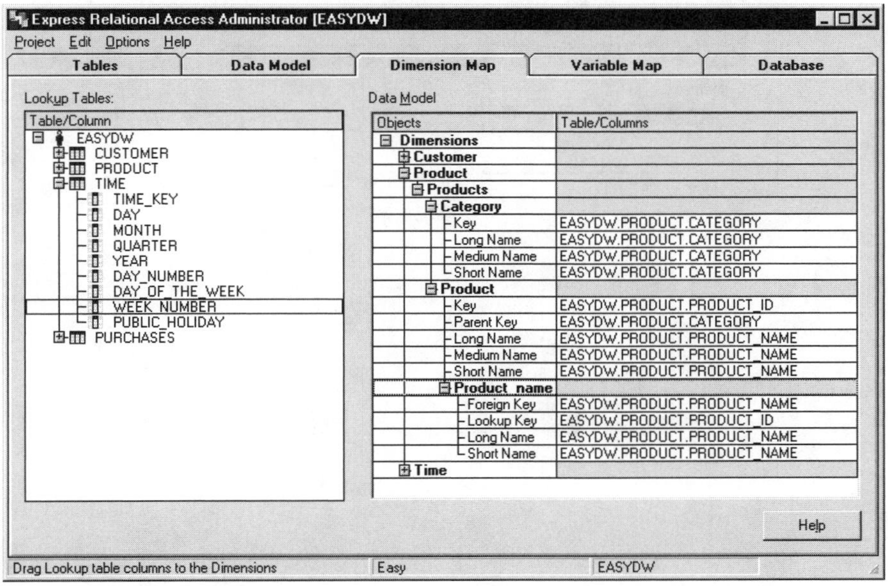

In Figure 6.32, we can also see an example of an attribute definition. Previously, when creating the products dimension we defined an attribute called product_name, which implies that there is a one-to-one relationship between product_id and product_name. Here we can see how we describe that relationship by stating that the column product_name is the foreign key and the column product_id is the look-up key.

Hint: Every item must be mapped to a column in the database; otherwise, an error will be reported by Express that the dimension hierarchy is incorrect.

Don't forget to save your project at this step. Doing so will validate this stage, giving you the chance to correct any problems before proceeding on to the next step in this process.

Creating a Variable

The data model is incomplete until at least one variable has been defined *(variables* identify the data we wish to report upon). They can be any text or numeric data item. A variable is created by clicking on the tab *Data Model,* selecting *Variable* from the hierarchy diagram in the left window, and then clicking on the *Create* button. Figure 6.33 will then appear.

Figure 6.33 Creating a Variable

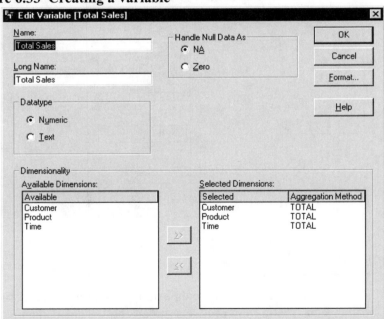

In Figure 6.33, we are creating a variable called Total Sales, which will enable us to report our sales data by customer, product, and time, since these are the chosen dimensions. We have asked for the data to be totaled, but other aggregation methods such as average, first, and large are available.

Mapping a Variable

Once the variables have been defined, you must then map them to the columns in your database. This is achieved by clicking on the Variable Map tab. Figure 6.34 will then appear.

Figure 6.34 Mapping a Variable

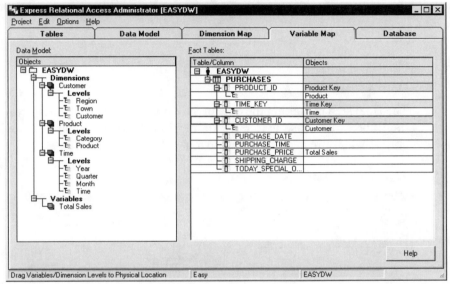

Now you must drag the variables onto the appropriate table in the fact table, which, in our example, is purchase price for the variable total sales. Then you must map the columns in the fact table to the appropriate dimension table. In our example, we have dragged the level customer from the customer dimension and mapped it to the column customer_id in the fact table. This process has been repeated for every dimension defined in this data model.

Hint: If you haven't specified at least one of your tables to be fact table in the Tables section, then no table will appear in the right window.

Once again, the project should be saved, enabling you to check that this stage has been completed correctly. Even though the saving process may report an error with the model, as shown in Figure 6.35, the contents of your project are actually saved. The error message simply advises that you cannot map this model yet into an Express database because there are errors in the design.

Figure 6.35 Error Message for Invalid Project

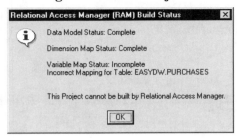

Data Attributes

The final step in making the data in our Oracle 8*i* data warehouse available to the Express database is to click on the *Database* tab. Figure 6.36 will then appear where we specify some attributes for our data.

Figure 6.36 Database Attributes

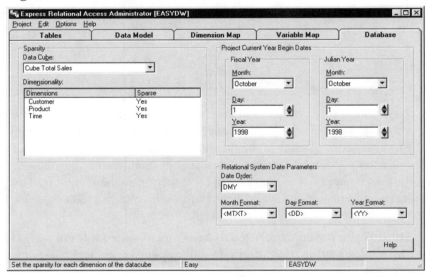

For example, here we can state when our fiscal year begins and the format of our dates. "Sparsity" is a term used by Express to advise that some of the combinations of data do not actually contain data.

Now we should be able to save our project successfully. We are now ready to proceed to the next stage, actually moving the data from our Oracle 8*i* database into the Express database.

6.3.2   **Moving the Data from Oracle 8*i* to the Express Database**

Before you start this step, ensure that your Express server is running, as described in 6.3. Now this is the step that may seem rather strange, because, in order to move your data from Oracle 8*i* to Express, you must select the option *Express Database Maintenance*, which can be found under *Project* on the strip menu in Relational Access Administrator.

Figure 6.37   Defining the Oracle 8*i* Connection

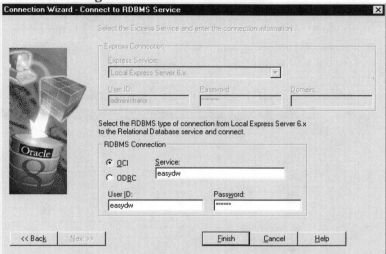

First you will be asked to connect to your Express service. Figure 6.37 will then appear, where you must specify how you will connect to your Oracle 8*i* database. You have the choice of using ODBC or OCI. If you already have defined a service name, then click on OCI, and enter the service name, along with the user name and password required to log in to your Oracle 8*i* database. In our example, we are using the EASYDW service.

Once the connection to the database has been established, you are now given the chance of giving your maintenance procedure a name. Here you have to specify the type of procedure:

- general maintenance
- hybrid maintenance

General maintenance is required when you first create the database or need to update your express database with new dimension data that has been added to the data warehouse.

Hybrid maintenance is also required to obtain the data from the fact tables and load them into your Express database.

Therefore, the first time, you will want to specify both general and hybrid maintenance to ensure that all the data is sent to Express.

Now you may be wondering at what stage the Express database is created. Well the next screen, shown in Figure 6.38, is where you specify the name and location for the Express database. You do not have to worry if it does not already exist because Express will automatically create it for you. If the database already exists but you cannot remember its name, then use the *Browse* button to identify its location and name. The maximum number of characters in an Express database name is six, so you may want to give it some thought as to what you would like it to be called.

Figure 6.38 Specifying the Oracle Express Database

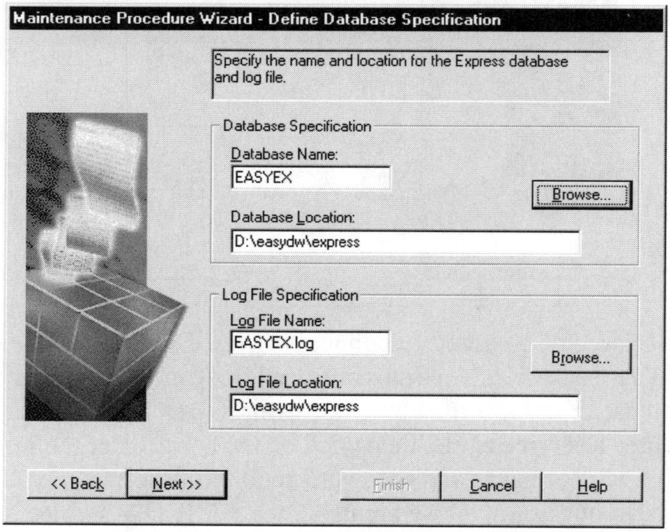

In order to get data into the Express database, you must specify which data is to be loaded, illustrated in Figure 6.39. For example, here we have stated that all data is loaded, but you could selectively choose not to load the product data, for example.

Figure 6.39 Specifying the Cube Data

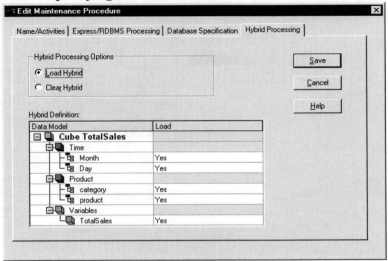

This procedure must then be saved, so it can be reused later. You can create as many *maintenance procedures* as you like, each performing its own unique set of tasks.

In Figure 6.40, we can see that we have created two projects called *easy* and *easyinc*. Each project has its own maintenance procedure called *loading*. By clicking on the procedure, its details are shown in the right window. This is also the place where you can edit or delete this procedure. You can also jump directly to this window by selecting *Express Database Maintenance* from the list of options under project on the strip menu.

Finally you will be given the option of placing this maintenance task on the *Batch Manager* job queue so that it can be actioned immediately. The Batch Manager software is provided with Oracle Express and is completely separate from the Job Queue facility, which we discussed earlier in Oracle Enterprise Manager. Oracle Express will place the job on its own queue, and then you can wait for it to finish. You won't receive any notification in Relational Access manager that the job has finished, therefore, it is suggested that you start the Batch Manager GUI which can be found in the Oracle Express Folder.

Figure 6.40 List of Maintenance Tasks

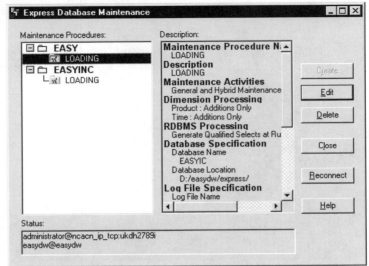

When the Batch Manager first starts, you are presented with a blank screen. Select *Jobs* from the strip menu at the top, and then select *Monitor*. Now select your Express Server from the list of possible servers, and the current state of your jobs will be shown, as per Figure 6.41.

In this example, we can see that our job to load the data has completed. If you select that job, then you can click on the *view log* button to see what Express did to complete this task.

The operation of loading the Express database for the first time may be time-consuming. The batch manager will show the status of the job as running if the operation has not completed. Please be patient, and, before long, your Express database will be ready to be queried.

One of the nice features of the Batch Manager is that the job will remain on the queue until it is deleted, so you can always refer back to see how the batch job executed. Also, should you need to run the job again, then you can restart it from here by clicking on the *Restart* button.

Once all of the data have been loaded into the database, you are now ready to start analyzing it using other Express tools.

Figure 6.41 Oracle Express Batch Manager Job

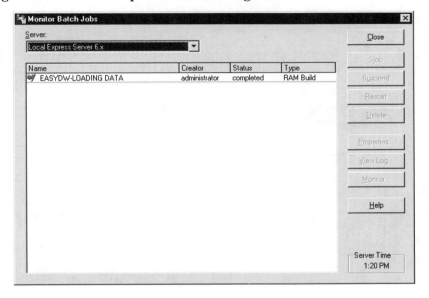

6.3.3   Analyzing the Oracle Express Database

One of the tools you can use to query your database is Oracle Express Analyzer. But before you jump straight in and try to create a report, take a moment to understand how this tool works, because it may behave a bit differently than you expected.

If you are expecting the traditional type of query tool, which has some type of language that you use to construct a report, then you will be disappointed. This is not how Express Analyzer works. Every report that you create is called a *briefing*, and, if you think of the briefing as pages in a document that you read, it will help you understand how to analyze your Express database.

Rather than construct a query, you lay out your report on pages using a layout editor. Using simple drag-and-drop techniques and clicking on tool icons, you create the report, and then you run it.

When you first start Express Analyzer, it asks you what you want to do, such as run an application or briefing or create or edit a briefing. If you decide to edit or create a new briefing, then the screen in Figure 6.42 will appear after you have specified the data file containing your briefing and have logged onto the Oracle Express server.

Figure 6.42 Oracle Express Analyzer

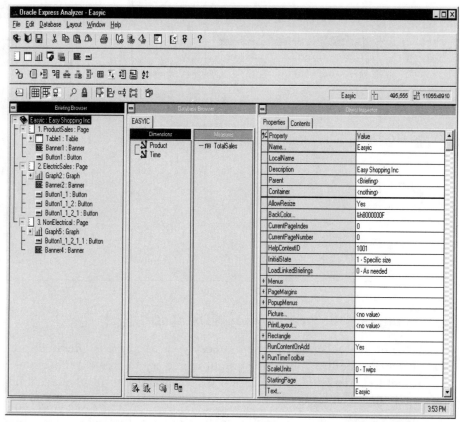

When Express Analyzer first starts, all that will be shown are the toolbars and the briefing browser window, which is the one on the left. In this example, we have asked for the database browser and Object inspector windows to be present, which are selected from *window* on the strip menu.

The first step is to select a page in the briefing browser window; if one does not exist, then select the page icon and drag it over to the briefing browser window, and a blank briefing page will appear.

It is on this blank page where we lay out our report. Figure 6.43 illustrates a very simple briefing page that looks exactly as the user will see it. The heading of Electrical Sales by Quarter was created by clicking on the banner icon and then dragging it over to the briefing page. Place it in the desired location on the page, and then click on the right mouse button to change its properties such as heading and fill-color.

Figure 6.43 Briefing Page

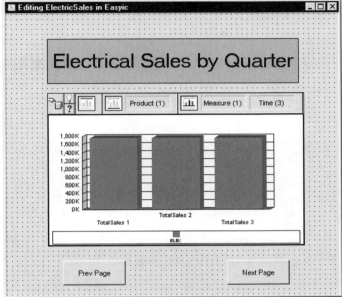

The data for the report is obtained by selecting one of the measures from the database browser window and dragging it over onto the page. In our example, there is only one measure, but normally there would be quite a variety to choose from. The data can be displayed in either a tabular or graphical form. At the moment, the report will show all data, but you can customize it to your own requirements. For example, this report will show only sales of electrical items.

Double-clicking on any of the dimensions such as product and time, shown in Figure 6.43, will display the selector window, where you can specify what data are to be displayed. In Figure 6.44, we can see the various options that are available, such as all data and range.

Figure 6.44 Selecting Data to Display

Therefore, to display only electrical data, click on the *List* icon, then the screen shown in Figure 6.45 will appear, which will list all of the data. From here, you then select which data are to be available for reporting purposes. In our example, we will remove all product categories except electrical.

Figure 6.45 Selecting Data to Display

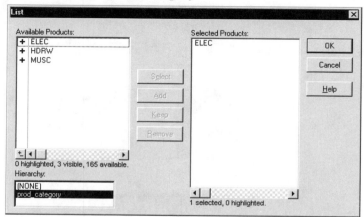

In this brief example here, we have but skimmed the surface as to how you can decide which data a user may see. For instance, they could see only values that exceed a certain value or match a given set of characters.

So far, we have only placed a heading and data on our briefing page, but if we look at our example in Figure 6.43, you will see that there are also *buttons* to navigate the pages. These buttons are not essential because you can navigate using another technique, but here they serve to illustrate that you can make your report look as familiar as every other report. There is a button icon in Express Analyzer that is dragged onto the *Briefing* editor and then modified to suit your needs.

You continue to make as many pages in your briefing as needed and place upon those pages as many tables, pictures, and text as is required. For example, every page may contain the company logo and a standard set of navigation buttons. It should also be stated that we have only illustrated a very simple example, and you can produce quite complex tables and graphs.

The saved briefing can be run at any time by selecting *Run* from the *File* menu. In Figures 6.46 and 6.47, we can see two of the pages in our briefing report. Note that at the top of the screen, there are video-style buttons to navigate between pages, or you can select the page from the drop-down list.

Figure 6.46 Sample Briefing Report

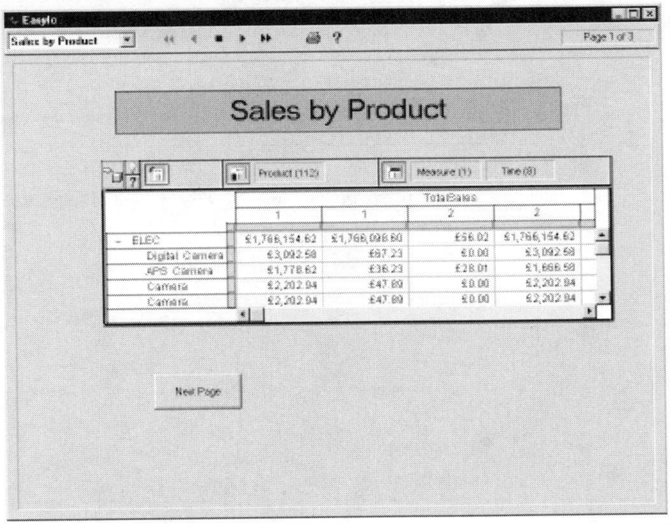

A user who is running this briefing can drill the data up and down as required. For example, in Figure 6.46 we can see the sales of our electrical products broken down by individual products. In Figure 6.47, we have a graphical representation of the data displayed by quarter.

An important design point to note here is how your dimensions are named. By default, Express Analyzer will use the actual dimension values; therefore, it may be necessary to customize your labels so that they mean something to the readers of this report.

The time taken to create a briefing report is not very long. All the hard work was performed in the Relational Access Administrator, where the relationships between the data were defined. Now you do not have to worry about the data; instead, your concerns are around presentation in terms of how the briefing looks and what data it is showing.

Figure 6.47 Sample Briefing Report

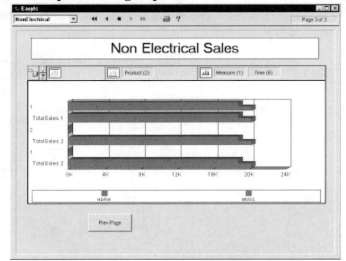

Hopefully, now you will see that Oracle Express is an excellent reporting tool and is ideal for providing reports to senior management or non-computer-literate users. In Chapter 8, we will see how we can use our Intranet to publish these briefings, thus making them even more accessible. Imagine the benefit to the CEO of the company or any member of the staff, being able to connect to the company intranet anywhere in the world and obtain the latest data via their browser.

6.4   TIME SERIES

Oracle8 introduced several options supporting specific applications, one of which was called Time Series. These options were at one time called cartridges and also included image and audio. Time Series has been included in this chapter because, if you have time-based data and need to perform certain types of analysis upon it, it could be very useful to your organization.

Oracle 8*i* Time Series, provides a mechanism to easily store and manage time-based data. As you are reading this, you are probably thinking to yourself that a lot of data is time-based. So why would you need to purchase this option? Well, Oracle Time Series is ideally suited to manage data such as stock prices, and once it has been defined for Time Series use, you can then perform analysis upon that data—such as "tell me the highest and lowest price during the day," and "What was the average trading volume over the past week?"

In order to use Oracle Time Series, your data must be stored in one of the following:

- Index-organized table
- Nested index-organized table
- Table

To help you to try and better understand how to use Oracle Time Series, let us describe it in the context of our Easy Shopping Inc. example. However, before you start, it is very important to ensure that your dates will be displayed in the correct format. This is achieved by setting the following parameter, which could also be included in your initialization file so that it becomes the default for your database.

```
ALTER SESSION SET NLS_DATE_FORMAT = 'MM/DD/YYYY HH24:MI:SS';
```

In our Easy Shopping Inc. example, we are storing time-based data because we record the exact time at which an item is sold. Therefore, let us see how we can use Oracle Time Series to analyze our data to determine if there are any specific times when products are purchased.

Hint: Script files containing examples with syntax very similar to these examples can be found in the time series demo directory

---

6.4.1   Creating and Populating the Time Series Table

Oracle Time Series needs to have the data in its own table or indexed-only tables; therefore the first step is to create the table where the data will reside. Fortunately, Oracle Time Series comes with a number of PL/SQL packages that we can call, facilitating very easy creation of all the tables and metadata that it requires. Therefore, it is recommended that you use the following approach to set up the environment.

In the following example, we have created a simple table that will tell us the value of products sold at each time. Everything that we need is placed inside a group, which is created using the *Begin_Create_Ts_Group* package, and here our group is called *easyinc_ts*. The parameter with a value of *flat* indicates that this will be a flat table.

Using the routine *Set_Flat_Attributes,* we define what this time series will be based on, which is product data. Note that we do not have to define a timestamp-based column because it knows that we must have one of these. Then for every numerical value that we require, we use the *Add_Number_Column* package to declare the item. In this example, we have defined only one value called *totalsales.* When the definition of the time series group is complete, it is closed by calling the *End_Create_Ts_Group* routine.

```
connect easydw/easydw@easydw;

DECLARE
BEGIN

 ORDSYS.TSTools.Begin_Create_Ts_Group('easyinc_ts','flat');
 ORDSYS.TSTools.Set_Flat_Attributes(tsname_colname =>
                             'product',tsname_length => 7);
 ORDSYS.TSTools.Add_Number_Column('totalsales',9,3);
 ORDSYS.TSTools.End_Create_Ts_Group;

exception
  when others then
    begin
     ORDSYS.TSTools.Cancel_Create_Ts_Group;
     raise;
    end;
END;
/
```

Executing these PL/SQL statements has resulted in all the tables that we need to manage our time series:

- EASYINC_TS_MAP
- EASYINC_TS_TAB
- EASYINC_TS_CAL

The table EASYINC_TS_TAB will contain the actual data points, and its format follows.

```
SVRMGR> DESCRIBE EASYINC_TS_TAB
Column Name                      Null?     Type
------------------------------   --------  ----
PRODUCT                          NOT NULL  VARCHAR2(7)
TSTAMP                           NOT NULL  DATE
TOTALSALES                                 NUMBER(9,3)
```

Now that we have our table, we need to populate it with data from our fact table called PURCHASES. Fortunately, our data is very small in volume and does not require any special manipulation to present it in the correct format. Therefore, we can populate our time series table using the following very simple query:

```
INSERT INTO easyinc_ts_tab
 SELECT product_id, time_key ,
  SUM(purchase_price) FROM purchases
        GROUP BY time_key, product_id ;
```

Unfortunately, in the real world, it probably won't be this easy to populate your data. Therefore, you would normally prepare an external load file and then populate the time series table using tools like SQL*Loader, which is described in Chapter 4.

For those of you who already have tables that you would like to perform Time Series analysis on. There is also a retrofit mode, for mapping existing tables for use by Oracle Time Series.

6.4.2   Calendars

It is also very helpful if you know whether your time series can be considered a regular or an irregular time series. An irregular time series is one when it is not known when the data will arrive. For example, if you were monitoring Internet activity by the second, you cannot be sure that someone will be accessing your system all of the time. Therefore, there may be seconds when you have no time data.

A regular time series is one when you know that the data will be sampled at a predefined time, such as every minute. For example, you may quote the price for a stock every minute during trading hours.

If your time series is regular, then you can also define a calendar that allows you to map time to the data. This may sound strange at first, but by using the calendar, you can say which days and hours a store is open for trading, thus preventing invalid time data from being loaded into your system. When a calendar is created you must specify the:

- Frequency of the calendar, i.e. hourly, daily, etc.

    1= second, 2 = minute, 3 = hour, 4 =day, 5= week,

    6=month, 7=quarter , 8=year

- Pattern that describes the valid periods

  For example, if the calendar is hourly, you can set the hours to "1" when the store is open for business; once the pattern has been defined for the frequency of the calendar, it will automatically be repeated for the duration of all time data.

- Exceptions such as days when you do not trade

  For example, for Christmas day, the exception is entered as a date.

Calendars are objects and are typically stored in tables, and this table will have been created for you when you created the time series group in the previous section. By default, the name of the calendar table will be *Timeseries name* _CAL, and here we can see the format of our calendar table, EASYINC_TS-CAL.

The calendar table has to be populated with information about each of the calendars that we are interested in. Although there won't typically be many records in the calendar table, once created, it will help us to perform various types of analysis on our data.

Below we can see the format of our calendar table.

```
SVRMGR> DESCRIBE EASYINC_TS_CAL
Column Name                            Null?      Type
------------------------------------  --------   ----
CALTYPE                                           NUMBER(38)
NAME                                  NOT NULL   VARCHAR2(256)
FREQUENCY                                         NUMBER(38)
PATTERN                                           ADT(36)
MINDATE                                           DATE
MAXDATE                                           DATE
OFFEXCEPTIONS                                     RAW(2000)
ONEXCEPTIONS                                      RAW(2000)
```

Now you can populate the calendar. We will set up the calendar for daily, weekly, and minute data. First we call our calendar DAILY, but we could name it whatever we like. Its frequency has to be set to "4" to denote that it is a daily calendar. The pattern bits of (0,1,1,1,1,1,1) tell us that, since the 04-JAN-1998 is a Sunday, the first day is not a valid day, but the other days are valid trading days. The valid ranges for this calendar are 01-JAN-1998 until 01-JAN-2000, and we have also stated in the exceptions area that we do not do business on the 25th or 26th of December.

```
INSERT INTO easyinc_ts_cal VALUES(
   ordsys.ordtCalendar(
   0,          -- Calendar type (0 = standard)
   'DAILY',      -- Name of this calendar
   4,          -- 4 = frequency code for daily
   ORDSYS.ORDTPattern( -- Pattern definition (required)
    ORDSYS.ORDTPatternBits(0,1,1,1,1,1,1),
     TO_DATE('04-JAN-1998','DD-MON-YYYY')),
   TO_DATE('01-JAN-1998','DD-MON-YYYY'), -- Mindate
   TO_DATE('01-JAN-2000','DD-MON-YYYY'), -- Maxdate
   ordsys.ordtExceptions(TO_DATE('25-DEC-1998',
       'DD-MON-YYYY'),TO_DATE('26-DEC-1998','DD-MON
       YYYY')),NULL) );
commit;
```

The definition of our hourly calendar is almost identical to the monthly calendar. In this instance, our frequency must be set to "3" and the bit patterns tell us that, for the 24 hours in the day, we do not do business between 0300 and 0900.

```
INSERT INTO easyinc_ts_cal VALUES(
   ordsys.ordtCalendar(
   0,          -- Calendar type (0 = standard)
   'HOURLY',      -- Name of this calendar
   3,          -- 3 = frequency code for hourly
   ORDSYS.ORDTPattern( -- Pattern definition (required)
   ORDSYS.ORDTPatternBits(1,1,0,0,0,0,0,0,0,1,1,1,1,1,1,1,1,1,1,1,1,1,1,1),
     TO_DATE('04-JAN-1998','DD-MON-YYYY')),
   TO_DATE('01-JAN-1998','DD-MON-YYYY'), -- Mindate
   TO_DATE('01-JAN-2000','DD-MON-YYYY'), -- Maxdate
   NULL, NULL)-- No off- or on-exceptions );
commit;
```

In this example for a minute calendar, since all minutes are valid trading time, we can set the pattern bits to a single "1" which will be repeated for all values.

```
INSERT INTO easyinc_ts_cal VALUES(
   ordsys.ordtCalendar(
   0,          -- Calendar type (0 = standard)
   'MINUTE',      -- Name of this calendar
   2,          -- 2 = frequency code for minute
   ORDSYS.ORDTPattern( -- Pattern definition (required)
    ORDSYS.ORDTPatternBits(1),
     TO_DATE('04-JAN-1998','DD-MON-YYYY')),
   TO_DATE('01-JAN-1998','DD-MON-YYYY'), -- Mindate
   TO_DATE('01-JAN-2000','DD-MON-YYYY'), -- Maxdate
   NULL, NULL)    -- No off- or on-exceptions );
commit;
```

Mapping the Calendar Data to Time Series Data

Once the calendars exist, we now need to map the data to the calendar, which is achieved using a special table that was created when we defined our Time Series group. By default, this table will be called timeseries name _map, and, therefore, for our Easy Shopping example, it is called EASYINC_TS_MAP. Its contents are shown below.

```
SVRMGR> DESCRIBE EASYINC_TS_MAP
Column Name                             Null?      Type
--------------------------------        --------   ----
PRODUCT                                 NOT NULL   VARCHAR2(7)
CALNAME                                            VARCHAR2(256)
```

As you can see, it is a very simple table comprising only the product identifiers and the calendar name.

Populating our mapping table is straightforward, because all we need is a list of the distinct product identifiers held in our table. We can then say which calendars we want to associate with that data.

```
INSERT INTO easyinc_ts_map (product )
  SELECT DISTINCT product FROM easyinc_ts_tab ;

UPDATE easyinc_ts_map SET calname = 'MINUTE';
```

Validate the Calendar

Before we perform any analysis on our data, it is important to check that the calendars contain correct data. The following procedure shows the results of running this package against our data.

```
SET SERVEROUTPUT ON

DECLARE
  tstCal ordsys.ordtcalendar;
  dummyVal integer;
  validFlag integer;
BEGIN

  -- Select a calendar into tstCal
  select value(cal) into tstCal
  from EASYINC_TS_CAL cal
  where cal.name = 'MINUTE';

  -- Display the calendar
```

```
    select ordsys.timeseries.display(tstCal)
          into dummyVal from dual;
    dbms_output.new_line;

    validFlag := ORDSYS.CALENDAR.IsValidCal(tstCal);

    if (validFlag = 1) then
      dbms_output.put_line('MINUTE calendar is valid.');
    else
      dbms_output.put_line('MINUTE calendar is NOT valid.');
      dbms_output.put_line
            ('Use ValidateCal to determine inconsistency.');
    end if;

END;
/
Calendar Name = MINUTE
 Frequency = 2 (minute)
 MinDate = 01-JAN-1998 00:00:00
 MaxDate = 01-JAN-2000 00:00:00
 patBits: 1
 patAnchor = 04-JAN-1998 00:00:00
 onExceptions :    Atomic NULL

 offExceptions :    Atomic NULL

MINUTE calendar is valid.
```

Deleting a Time Series

If at any time we need to remove our time series, the package Drop_Ts_group_all can be used; as shown below. Doing so will remove all of the tables associated with a given time series.

```
DECLARE
BEGIN
 ORDSYS.TSTools.Drop_Ts_Group_All('easyinc_ts');
 EXCEPTION
  When others then
    raise;
END;
/
```

6.4.4   Perform Time Series Analysis

Now that everything is set up, we are ready to query our data. Oracle Time Series comes with a very comprehensive set of functions that includes:

- cumulative average, maximum, minimum , product, and sum
- moving average and sum
- first, last, lead, and lag
- scaling function (interpolate, split, avgerage, minimum, maximum, count, first minimum, first maximum, and sum)

These functions are embedded in SQL, so they are easy to use once you get the hang of the SQL needed to use them. Now is also the time to dust off those college mathematics books to remind you of when you need functions like these. Here we have only skimmed the surface of what is possible with Oracle Time Series, and it is highly recommended that you read the documentation to see all the functions that are offered.

Cumulative Average

Suppose we are interested in the average sales per hour of our products. We can obtain this by using the function Cumulative Average (CAVG) as shown below. Note how we only get data only for the hours when this product was purchased and now we can see how popular times are lunch and tea time.

```
SELECT TO_CHAR(tstamp) TimeofDay, value
 FROM easyinc_ts  ets,
  TABLE (CAST(ORDSYS.TimeSeries.ExtractTable(
        ORDSYS.TimeSeries.Cavg(ets.totalsales,
          to_date('01-JAN-1999','DD-MON-YYYY'),
          to_date('31-JAN-1999','DD-MON-YYYY'))
    ) AS ORDSYS.ORDTNumTab)) t
  WHERE ets.product='SP1001';


TIMEOFDAY                     VALUE
--------------------    ----------
01-JAN-1999 11:05:00       1694.59
01-JAN-1999 12:05:00         861.3
01-JAN-1999 13:05:00    707.043333
01-JAN-1999 14:05:00       629.915
01-JAN-1999 15:05:00       757.542
01-JAN-1999 16:05:00    697.706667
02-JAN-1999 17:10:00    602.035714
02-JAN-1999 18:10:00      530.2825
8 rows selected.
```

Time Series Functions

In the example shown below, we have calculated the average, variance, and standard deviation for total sales for the product SP1001 for the entire series of data that is held for this item.

```
SELECT ORDSYS.TimeSeries.TSAvg(totalsales),
    ORDSYS.TimeSeries.TSVariance(totalsales),
    ORDSYS.TimeSeries.TSStdDev(totalsales)
 FROM easyinc_ts
 WHERE product='SP1001';


ORDSYS.TIM ORDSYS.TIM ORDSYS.TIM
---------- ---------- ----------
656.537778 482066.306 694.309949
1 row selected.
```

Cumulative Sum

Other functions available to us include a cumulative sum, and here we have asked for product SP1001, but only for the month of January.

```
SELECT TO_CHAR(tstamp) TimeofDay, value
 FROM easyinc_ts   ets,
TABLE (CAST(ORDSYS.TimeSeries.ExtractTable(
        ORDSYS.TimeSeries.Csum(ets.totalsales,
            to_date('01-JAN-1999','DD-MON-YYYY'),
            to_date('31-JAN-1999','DD-MON-YYYY'))
    ) AS ORDSYS.ORDTNumTab)) t
  WHERE ets.product='SP1001';


TIMEOFDAY               VALUE
-------------------- ----------
01-JAN-1999 11:05:00  1694.59
01-JAN-1999 12:05:00   1722.6
01-JAN-1999 13:05:00  2121.13
01-JAN-1999 14:05:00  2519.66
01-JAN-1999 15:05:00  3787.71
01-JAN-1999 16:05:00  4186.24
02-JAN-1999 17:10:00  4214.25
02-JAN-1999 18:10:00  4242.26
8 rows selected.
```

Scaleup

So far, all of our reports have been reporting at the minute level, but suppose we wanted to roll that data up to report the average sales by day. This is possible using the function *ScaleupAvg*.

If we look carefully at this query, you will see that we reference two tables, the detail table and the calendar table. Since we want to roll up to the day level, we select the DAILY calendar in our query.

```
-- Query by Day
SELECT to_char(tstamp) Day, value
FROM easyinc_ts ets, easyinc_ts_cal cal,
TABLE (CAST(ORDSYS.TimeSeries.ExtractTable(
     ORDSYS.TimeScale.ScaleupAvg(ets.totalsales,VALUE(cal))
   ) AS ORDSYS.ORDTNumTab)) t
  WHERE ets.product='SP1001' AND cal.name ='DAILY';

DAY                     VALUE
-------------------- ----------
01-JAN-1999 00:00:00  697.706667
02-JAN-1999 00:00:00       28.01
 ..... some data removed
```

But suppose we wanted to report monthly. When we first set up this environment, we didn't define a monthly calendar. But if we create one now and run our report again to reference the monthly calendar, we can now get the results by month instead of by day.

```
-- add the monthly calendar
INSERT INTO easyinc_ts_cal VALUES(
   ordsys.ordtCalendar(
    0,           -- Calendar type (0 = standard)
    'MONTHLY',      -- Name of this calendar
    6,           -- 6 = frequency code for monthly
    ORDSYS.ORDTPattern( -- Pattern definition (required)
     ORDSYS.ORDTPatternBits(1),
       TO_DATE('04-JAN-1998','DD-MON-YYYY')),
    TO_DATE('01-JAN-1998','DD-MON-YYYY'), -- Mindate
    TO_DATE('01-JAN-2000','DD-MON-YYYY'), -- Maxdate
    NULL, NULL)    -- No off- or on-exceptions );
commit;

-- Query by Month

SELECT to_char(tstamp) Day, value
FROM easyinc_ts ets, easyinc_ts_cal cal,
TABLE (CAST(ORDSYS.TimeSeries.ExtractTable(
     ORDSYS.TimeScale.ScaleupAvg(ets.totalsales,VALUE(cal))
   ) AS ORDSYS.ORDTNumTab)) t
WHERE ets.product='SP1001' AND cal.name ='MONTHLY';
```

```
DAY                     VALUE
------------------- ----------
04-DEC-1998 00:00:00  530.2825
04-JAN-1999 00:00:00   1666.58
2 rows selected.
```

Hopefully, this brief introduction to Oracle Time Series has given you some idea of how you can analyze your data using these functions.

7 Managing the Warehouse

7.1 WHAT HAS TO BE MANAGED

Once the warehouse has been created and is populated with data, it is very important to ensure that it is correctly managed. In this chapter, we will described some of the management tasks and provide advice on how to execute them.

Once again, we will make use of the GUI tools provided in Oracle Enterprise Manager (OEM) to manage our database. There are alternative methods to this approach, but we are sure you will agree that, using OEM makes managing the database considerably easier. However, it should be pointed out that, if the management of your warehouse is complex, especially if it is complicated by issues such as jobs being dependent on one another. Then you may find that Oracle Enterprise Manager is not suitable and will prefer to use one of the many other tools available in the marketplace. For example, summaries cannot be refreshed until the new data has been loaded and it is coming from two different sources. Rather than compare a number of tools, we will consider only Oracle Enterprise Manager.

7.2 MANAGING USING ORACLE ENTERPRISE MANAGER

Although it is very easy to use Oracle Enterprise Manager, at the time of writing, the initial setup may not seem straightforward. Therefore, it is strongly recommended that you follow the steps precisely and read the instructions before commencing setup. There are a number of steps that must be followed, and they are described in the installation guide.

Once it has been configured, Oracle Enterprise Manager can be used to manage any database, located anywhere on the wide area network. Therefore, from this one tool, you can manage your entire system, no matter where the components might be. This is an extremely powerful capability and you should remember that what we are describing here can be used not only for the data warehouse but also for any databases on your network.

7.2.1   The Console

All work is performed from the Oracle Enterprise Manager console. A typical console is shown in Figure 7.1. By default, when it starts, the console is divided into four windows:

- Navigation area (top left)
- Groups that visually display the environment (top right)
- Job area (bottom left)
- Events (bottom right)

Figure 7.1 Oracle Enterprise Manager Console

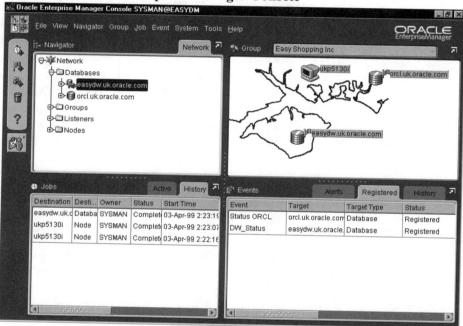

The *Navigation* window is probably the most important area on the screen because it is from here that numerous operations are started. By default, there are four subject areas: databases, groups, listeners, and nodes.

When you start the console for the first time, or whenever anything changes in your environment, the information shown here should be refreshed. This is achieved by selecting *Discover Nodes* from the *Navigator* option on the top strip menu. You will be prompted for the nodes to be searched, and, provided the Oracle Agent process is running on those nodes, it will interrogate your system and advise the console of the databases and listeners that are running. Therefore, you don't have to specify anything. In our example here, we can see that it has detected two databases on our node "ukp5130i," the default instance ORCL and our data warehouse EASYDW.

Figure 7.2 Navigation Window

In Figure 7.2, the navigation window has been expanded. In the databases section, it lists every database, irrespective of the node on which it resides. To see on which system a database resides, you have to expand the *Nodes* area and then see which databases are on that node. In our example, it is easy because we only have only one node if we had many nodes running many databases, however, the view would be more complex. This is when the group feature that is described shortly becomes very useful.

Hint: Many maintenance tasks, such as removing a group, are achieved by selecting the item in the navigation window and then selecting the action from the strip menu.

Any one of these four windows can become the main window by clicking on the ![icon] icon, which can be found in the top right corner just above the window. To return to the four-pane view, click on the ![icon] icon. All four windows do not have to be displayed. You can choose which ones by clicking on *View* in the strip menu and selecting which ones are to be displayed. Alternatively, in the top left-hand corner, there is a group of four icons which you can click on to hide and display the relevant windows.

From the navigation window, we can perform a number of tasks with respect to databases. By double-clicking on the database name, it will expand to display its various components.

Here is another setup step that has to be completed to avoid specifying the database user name and password every time access to the database is required. These values can be retained by the console by clicking on *System* in the strip menu and then clicking on *Preferences*. Doing so displays the seven screen shown in Figure 7.3.

Figure 7.3 Setting User Credentials

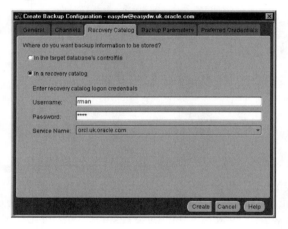

Here we can specify for every database and node the user name and password required for access. Although it is very convenient to place this information here, it could provide an opportunity for a breach in security, because once a user has logged on to the console, he would have access to everything.

Therefore, provided appropriate security restrictions are placed on who can log onto the console, which is achieved by Oracle Enterprise Manager requiring its own user name and password, security should not be an issue. In fact, most DBAs will probably welcome not having to enter the user name and password every time.

So far we have only viewed the information displayed here, but there is a lot more that we can do. From the *Navigation* window, if we were to select a database and then click on the right mouse button (for left-handed people, use the left mouse button), the screen in Figure 7.4 would appear with all these options. Now we can manage our database by starting and stopping the instance directly from here without having to go to SQL or the Instance Manager GUI.

Figure 7.4 Database Options

Take note: At the bottom of this drop-down list, there is the ability to perform other management tasks such as using backup, restore, and import and export. This is the only place where some of these options can be started.

7.2.2   Why Create Groups

In the top right window in Figure 7.1, we have created a group called Easy Shopping Inc. This was achieved by clicking on *Group* in the strip menu and then selecting *Create Group*. You will be prompted, as per Figure 7.5, for a group name, the location of a bitmap image, and whether large or small images are required.

Earlier, we spoke of the issues surrounding managing multiple databases, and one solution to this problem is to be able to see a graphical representation of your environment. The purpose of a group is to allow you to visually represent an environment. It doesn't have to be the entire environment; it could be just a part of it. Within the display, you can select any of the objects from the navigation window to be included.

Figure 7.5 Creating a Group

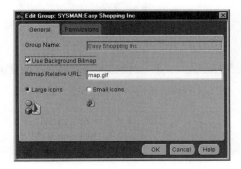

Therefore, the group name describes the environment, and the image is required so that you can overlay the objects onto a useful picture. In Figure 7.6, we can see our group called Easy Shopping Inc., which represents our warehouse.

The underlying graphic is a map of the area in the UK where the warehouse is located. To add items to the group, you simply drag them from the *Navigation* window to the group window. Referring to Figure 7.6, we have dragged the EASYDW database, the ORCL database, and the machine UKP5130. They have been placed on the map to represent where they physically reside; of course, the choice is yours where to place them.

You may be saying to yourself, "This all looks very pretty, but what is the point apart from graphically showing the system?" In the next section, we will describe events, and when events are combined with the group picture, a very powerful management environment is now available.

You can create as many groups as you like, and they are displayed by selecting the one you require from the drop-down list, which is located immediately above the group window.

Figure 7.6 Group—Easy Shopping Inc.

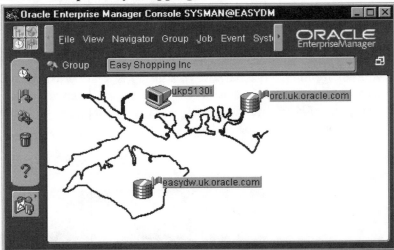

7.2.3   Using Events

One of the problems for anyone managing a database is knowing when certain events occur. For example, suppose the database instance suddenly decides to go down. Wouldn't you like to know immediately that it has happened rather than wait for the calls from your users, who are complaining that the system is no longer available?

Within the console, you can define events that will allow you to monitor your data warehouse and be notified when certain events occur. An event is created by clicking on *Event* in the strip menu and then clicking on *Create Event*. At this point, the screen shown in Figure 7.7 will appear.

Referring to Figure 7.7, we have given our event a name, "Warehouse Status," and also added some further comment. This particular event is a database event, but we could select others from the drop-down list, such as node, in the section marked "Destination Type." Next we select the EASYDW database from the list on the right side and, using the arrow buttons, move it over to the left side. The frequency of monitoring can also be changed, if required. Then we must click on the other tabs at the top of the window to complete the event definition.

Figure 7.7 Creating an Event

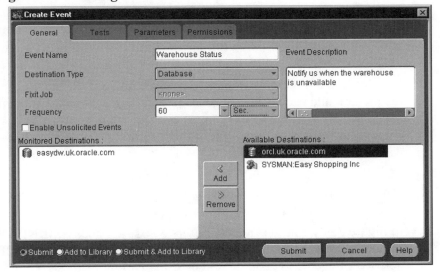

Clicking on the table *Tests* displays the screen in Figure 7.8, where we select the event of interest. In this example, we have selected DatabaseUpDown, so that we are notified whenever the database goes up or down.

Figure 7.8 Selecting Events to Monitor

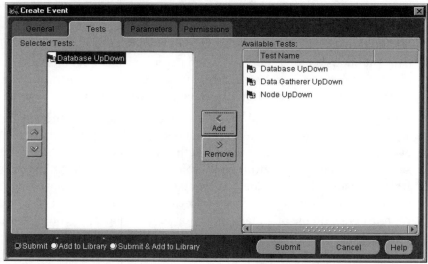

This event has no parameters for us to specify, so the next step is to state who should be notified when this event occurs. It is not mandatory to notify anyone; you could define the event, and then, provided the database has been dragged over to the group, the status of the event will register there.

For example, in Figure 7.6, the two databases EASYDW and ORCL reside in the picture, and each database has a colored flag against it (which unfortunately, is very difficult to show in a black-and-white book!). The EASYDW database is showing a green flag to denote that it is open, and the ORCL database has a red flag against it, to show that it is currently closed.

This is one of the powerful visual features of creating a group, because you can instantly look at the picture and see the state of your system. It is an example of your own customized message board.

In Figure 7.9, we have stated that users SYSMAN and ADMINISTRATOR should be notified whenever this event occurs. Administration staff can be notified of events via paging and/or E-mail. Both of these options can be configured within the console.

Figure 7.9 Advising Users of an Event

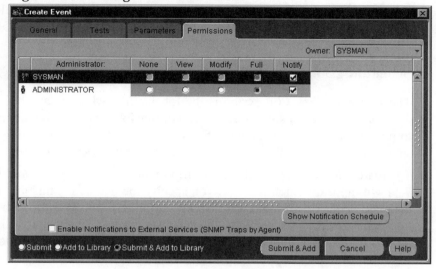

By selecting *System* from the strip menu and then *Preferences* and clicking on the *Schedule* tab, the screen in Figure 7.10 will appear.

Once again, this is difficult to see in a black-and-white book, but here you specify how you are to be notified for each hour of the day. Since we know that lunch is always taken at 1 P.M., during this period and on Saturday, we have stated that we should be paged whenever this event occurs. However, during the working day, the preferred contact method is E-mail.

Figure 7.10 Notification Schedule for Events

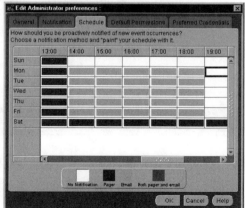

Here we have just scratched the surface of what is possible with events. But hopefully it will encourage you to investigate these further and implement them as part of your data warehouse management procedures.

7.2.4   Scheduling Jobs

The fourth window to describe is the job facility, which is another useful component of the console. Here you can define jobs that must be run in order to manage your data warehouse. These jobs can be placed in a library and scheduled automatically by the console to run at the specified time.

To create a job, select *Job* from the strip menu and then *Create Job*. Figure 7.11 will appear, which is where you specify the details for this job. In this example, we are creating a job that will automatically close the data warehouse at 7 P.M. First we name the job and state upon which database it is to be performed. Although this example features a database task, other options are available from the drop-down list on destination type.

Figure 7.11 Creating a Job

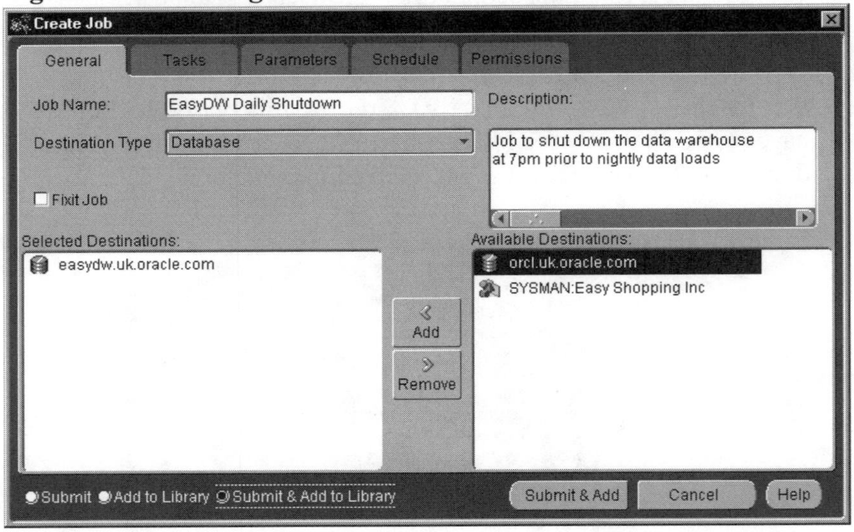

All jobs may be kept in the job library for reuse. Therefore, if you wish to retain the job, now is a good time to click on the button at the bottom of the window to *Submit and Add Job to the Library*. Choosing this option at this time will merely enable that option and change the submit button to *Submit*

and Add. It is not until you click the *Submit and Add* button that the job will be submitted onto the job queue.

To move onto the next screen, click on the *Tasks* tab to select the action that is to be performed. You can see in Figure 7.12 that many tasks are available. In this example, we have selected shut down database.

Once the task has been chosen, click on the *Parameters* tab to see if any parameters are needed for this task. In Figure 7.13, we can see that, for closing the database, it asks us how we want to close the database. We have selected the *Immediate* mode.

Also note here that we have the ability to specify a different user name and password to perform this operation from the default one that we set up earlier. Since closing the database requires a powerful user name, we have changed it to use the system user name for this task.

Figure 7.12 Selecting Task for a Job

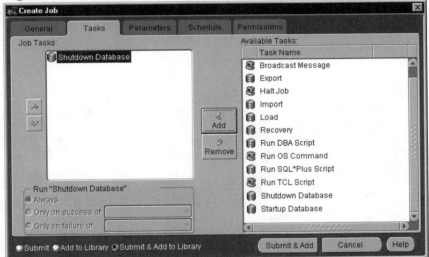

The definition of the job is almost complete. We must now click on the *Schedule* tab to state when this job is to be run.

Figure 7.13 Parameters for a Job

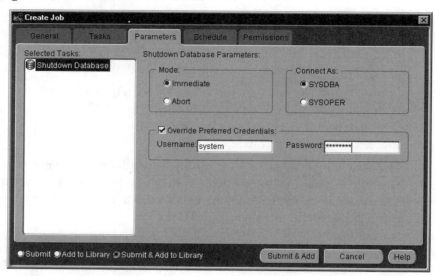

Referring to Figure 7.14, we have stated that this job is run on Monday through Friday, starting from May 3rd at 7:00 P.M.

Figure 7.14 Scheduling a Job

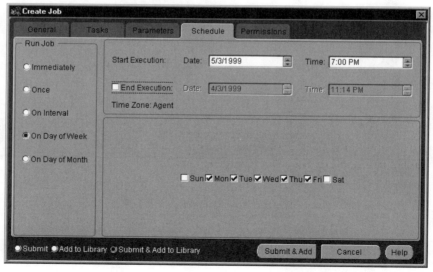

Finally, click on the *Permissions* tab to state who, if anyone, should be notified when this job is run. Then click on the *Submit* button to place this job on the queue to be run.

Assuming you have clicked on the *Active* tab, which monitors current jobs, you can monitor the job's progress once the job appears in the queue, shown in Figure 7.15.

Figure 7.15 Watching a Job Run

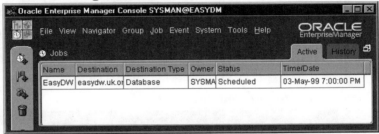

In the example in Figure 7.15, the status is scheduled because the job is pending. If it was actually running, the status would be shown as active. Once the job has completed, it will disappear from the active window. Click on the *History* tab to see whether it succeeded or failed.

Double-clicking on the job will display the screen shown in Figure 7.16, which is where we can see the details of the job. In Figure 7.16, we can see that the job completed successfully.

Figure 7.16 Logging from the Job

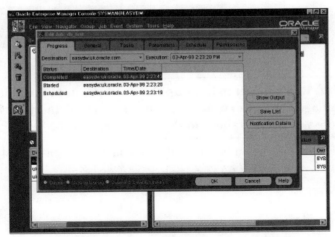

To see the results from the job, we must click on the *Show Output* button. In this example, we have simply queried the database, so the results of the SQL query are shown in Figure 7.17. However, typically when managing our data warehouse we would see the log from the job.

It is important to remember that, although we have shown database events and jobs, we could be running a job that simply involves an operating system task that needs to be performed for managing our warehouse, such as ensuring that files are copied from one system to another prior to loading or scheduling the data loading tasks or refreshing our materialized views.

The number of jobs we can submit here is quite extensive, and, once they are in the library, we have a comprehensive set of tasks that are safe and that can never be lost.

Figure 7.17 Output from the Job

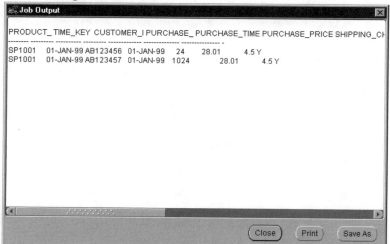

Hint: Don't forget to back up the database used the hold the Enterprise Manager repository, or you could lose all of the jobs in the library if there was ever a failure of the database.

The job library can be found by clicking on *Job* on the strip menu and then clicking on *Job Library*.

7.2.5   Launching Applications

The console is not only for monitoring databases and nodes; we can also launch database applications from here. The licensed options will determine the applications that are available. In Figure 7.18, we can see one of the techniques used to launch an application. Here we have selected the database from the *Navigation* window. By clicking on the right mouse button, the available tools are displayed such as shut down the database.

Figure 7.18 Starting Applications from the Console

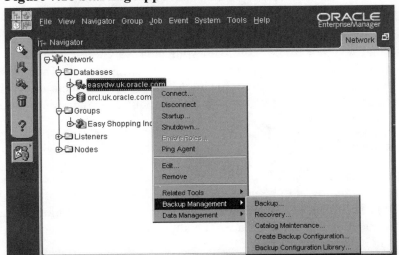

Farther down the list, related tools will provide access to the standard tools such as Instance, Schema, and Storage Manager. In this example, we have clicked on Backup Management, giving us access to the Backup and Recovery tools. To perform an export or import of the data, the Data Management option must be selected.

An alternative method for starting the default applications such as SQL*Plus Worksheet is to click on the icon , which is located halfway down on the right-hand side. Applications can also be started from the strip menu under the *Tools* section.

Hopefully, you are now beginning to appreciate how to manage your data warehouse using Oracle Enterprise Manager.

7.3   BACKUP & RECOVERY

One of the most important management tasks for any database is taking back-ups of the data. It may seem obvious, but you will be surprised how many companies jeopardize their business by infrequently taking backups or by not taking care of their backup tapes.

The problems with backing up a data warehouse are slightly different a backing up a typical production system. Since warehouses usually receive large loads of data, typically overnight, we have to schedule the backup along with this work. Plus we have the added complication of deciding how to back up the database.

Why is this a problem? Well, normally, a database is backed up in its entirety, but that may not be possible with your data warehouse, especially if it is particularly large (terabyte size or hundreds of gigabytes). Therefore, alternative practices are required, meaning careful management of the backup tapes or you could find yourself unable to rebuild the data warehouse.

7.3.1   Recovery Catalog

When creating a backup configuration, there is a tab to specify whether a *recovery catalog* is to be used. The *recovery catalog* is an extremely useful feature in Oracle 8*i* because it allows you to store information about all of your backups in a central place. The alternative is to store backup information in its own control file.

Figure 7.19 Recovery Catalog

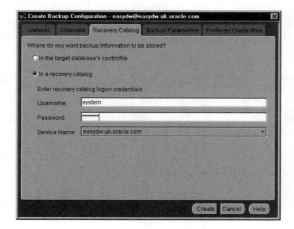

In our example in Figure 7.19, we have stated that the recovery catalog is to be used. It can be found in the database "orcl.us.oracle.com," and we must supply a user name and password to access that information.

The recovery catalog should always be placed in a different database then the data warehouse. Also, don't forget that the recovery catalog must also be backed up regularly because is stored inside a database.

Before you can use a recovery catalog, some setup steps are required. This involves creating the catalog inside a database. First, it is recommended that a tablespace be created specifically for the recovery catalog data. In our example, we will use the OEM_REPOSITORY tablespace.

It is probably a good idea to create a new user specifically for using the catalog. Below, we have created a user called "rman" and granted it the appropriate privileges.

```
CREATE USER rman IDENTIFIED BY rman
 TEMPORARY TABLESPACE temp
 DEFAULT TABLESPACE oem_repository;

GRANT recovery_catalog_owner TO rman;
GRANT connect,resource TO rman;
```

The next step is to actually create the recovery catalog, which is achieved by running the rman utility. As soon as the rman prompt appears, connect to the database that will hold the catalog. Since you are using the syntax *Connect catalog*, an error message will appear that the catalog does not exist. Ignore this message. Then issue the *Create Catalog* command. Once complete, you are now ready to use the catalog.

```
rman

RMAN> connect catalog rman/rman;

RMAN> create catalog tablespace oem_repository;
```

Before a database can be included in the recovery catalog, it must be registered. Therefore, while using the backup tools, you may see the message shown in Figure 7.20.

Do not be alarmed by the message. Simply click on the *Register* button, and the database will automatically be registered in the catalog.

Figure 7.20 Registering Database in Recovery Catalog

Once the database has been registered in the recovery catalog, the catalog can then be used to report information about the backups that have been taken. At the time of writing the rman utility does not have a GUI interface and must be run from the operating system command line. In Figure 7.21, we see how to connect to the recovery catalog from Windows NT.

Figure 7.21 Connecting to the Recovery Catalog

```
E:\>rman

Recovery Manager: Release 8.1.5.0.0 - Production

RMAN> connect target easydw/easydw@easydw;

RMAN-06005: connected to target database: EASYDW (DBID=3064347757)

RMAN> connect catalog rman/rman@orcl;

RMAN-06008: connected to recovery catalog database

RMAN>
```

When connecting to the recovery catalog, you must specify the *target* database, which is the database to be backed up and then the database where the recovery catalog is held. Once inside the rman utility, you can do many things apart from backing up the database. Assuming that we have already taken some backups we can obtain information such as tablespaces in the database to be backed up as shown in Figure 7.22 using the *report schema* command.

Or we could find out what is in those backup files and when they were taken by issuing a *List Backup* command, an example of which is shown in Figure 7.23. In this figure, we can see some of the files that are included in the backup that was taken on the April 11th.

Figure 7.22 Creating a Backup Configuration

```
Command Prompt - rman                                              _□×

RMAN> report schema;

RMAN-03022: compiling command: report
Report of database schema
File K-bytes      Tablespace          RB segs Name

1      57168 SYSTEM                   YES     E:\ORACLE\ORADATA\EASYDW\SYSTEM01.D
BF
2      16384 RBS                      YES     E:\ORACLE\ORADATA\EASYDW\RBS01.DBF
3       3072 USERS                    NO      E:\ORACLE\ORADATA\EASYDW\USERS01.DB
F
4      10240 TEMP                     NO      E:\ORACLE\ORADATA\EASYDW\EASY_TEMP.
F
5       5120 INDX                     NO      E:\ORACLE\ORADATA\EASYDW\INDX.F
6       5120 OEM_REPOSITORY           NO      E:\ORACLE\ORADATA\EASYDW\OEMREP01.D
BF
7       8192 UNDO                     NO      E:\ORACLE\ORADATA\EASYDW\EASY_UNDO.
F
8       6144 SUMMARY                  NO      E:\ORACLE\ORADATA\EASYDW\EASY_SUMM.
F
9       5120 DIMENSIONS               NO      E:\EASYDW\DIMENSIONS.D
10      5120 EASYDW_DEFAULT           NO      E:\ORACLE\ORADATA\EASYDW\EASYDW_DEF
AULT.F
1
```

The *List* command can be used to report various backup information. The Oracle 8*i* backup and recovery manual should be consulted for more detailed information.

Figure 7.23 What Is in a Backup

```
Command Prompt - rman                                              _□×
Key      Recid      Stamp      LV Set Stamp  Set Count  Completion Time

187      2          362485874  0  362485686  2          11-APR-99

     List of Backup Pieces
     Key      Pc# Cp# Status        Completion Time       Piece Name

     189      1   1   AVAILABLE     11-APR-99             E:\DW_BACKUP\EASYDW_B_02A
PM5TM_2_1

     List of Datafiles Included
     File Name                                    LV Type Ckp SCN  Ckp Time

     1    E:\ORACLE\ORADATA\EASYDW\SYSTEM01.DBF    0  Full 117336   11-APR-99
     2    E:\ORACLE\ORADATA\EASYDW\RBS01.DBF       0  Full 117336   11-APR-99
     3    E:\ORACLE\ORADATA\EASYDW\USERS01.DBF     0  Full 117336   11-APR-99
     4    E:\ORACLE\ORADATA\EASYDW\EASY_TEMP.F     0  Full 117336   11-APR-99
     5    E:\ORACLE\ORADATA\EASYDW\INDX.F          0  Full 117336   11-APR-99
     6    E:\ORACLE\ORADATA\EASYDW\OEMREP01.DBF    0  Full 117336   11-APR-99
     7    E:\ORACLE\ORADATA\EASYDW\EASY_UNDO.F     0  Full 117336   11-APR-99
     8    E:\ORACLE\ORADATA\EASYDW\EASY_SUMM.F     0  Full 117336   11-APR-99
     9    E:\EASYDW\DIMENSIONS.D                   0  Full 117336   11-APR-99
     10   E:\ORACLE\ORADATA\EASYDW\EASYDW_DEFAULT.F 0 Full 117336   11-APR-99
     11   E:\EASYDW\PURCHASESJAN99.F               0  Full 117336   11-APR-99
```

Another useful command is *report*. Some of the options are listed in Figure 7.24.

In this figure, we have asked if there are any orphan backups, obsolete backups, and backups that need more than seven days of Achive logs. Once again, there are many options available with the report command and it is suggested that you consult the Oracle 8*i* backup and recovery manual for detailed information.

Figure 7.24 The Report Facility in rman

```
Command Prompt - rman                                          _ □ ✕
RMAN> report obsolete orphan;

RMAN-03022: compiling command: report
Report of obsolete backups and copies
Type                    Key    Completion Time    Filename/Handle
───────────────────────────────────────────────────────────────────
Backup Set              150    09-APR-99
Backup Piece            151    09-APR-99          E:\DW_BACKUP\EASYDW_B_01APFSSO_1_
1

RMAN> report obsolete redundancy = 2;

RMAN-03022: compiling command: report
RMAN-06147: no obsolete backups found

RMAN> report need backup days =7 database;

RMAN-03022: compiling command: report
Report of files whose recovery needs more than 7 days of archived logs
File Days  Name
──── ───── ──────────────────────────────────────────────────────────

RMAN>
RMAN>
```

Although this has been a brief introduction to the recovery catalog, hopefully you can begin to see some of the benefits of using it, especially being able to see which backups exist. Using this information, you will see later how automatic recovery is possible, although, for our data warehouse, we may prefer to do it manually.

7.3.2   Backup

In this section, we will discuss the various techniques you can use to back up your data warehouse. However, it is important to realize that, if your data warehouse is very large, taking a full backup of it may be almost impossible due to time and other constraints. Therefore, the techniques used for extremely large data warehouses could differ significantly from those described here.

Prior to Oracle 8*i* backups were usually taken using the Operating System Backup Utility by copying all the relevant files. Now you can consider using Oracle 8*i* Backup Manager, which can be started by selecting the database from the navigation window, right-clicking on the database, and then selecting *Backup Management*. A list of tools is provided that includes both backup and recovery; however, start by selecting "Create Backup Configuration."

Figure 7.25 Creating a Backup Configuration

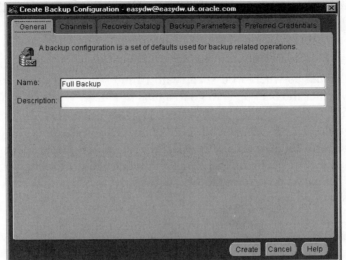

You can create as many backup configurations as are required for your system. The purpose of this step is to specify where the backup is to be placed and how it is to be named. Figure 7.25 illustrates the first step in this wizard where the name of this backup configuration is specified.

Figure 7.26 Creating a Backup Configuration

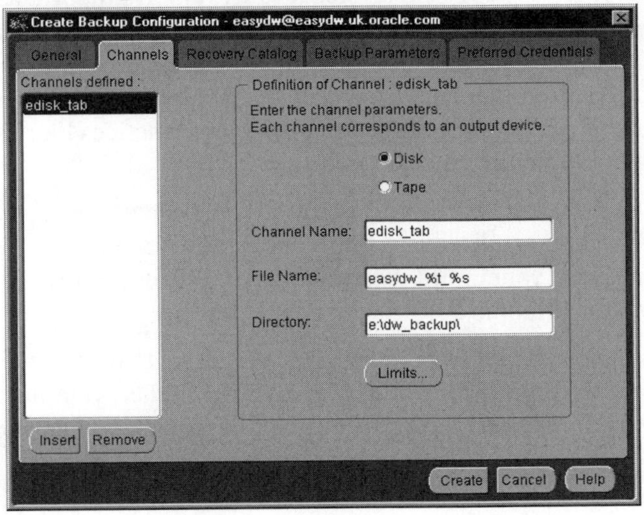

From here you now click on the various tabs to set up the options. It is not necessary to visit all of the screens, but you will have to click on *channels,* shown in Figure 7.26 which is where you define where the backup file is to be placed and how it is to be named.

Once again, you can create as many channels as you require. Think of the channel as where you specify all of the physical output attributes, such as whether the backup is to go to a tape or a disk. When it comes to naming the file, various options are available so that unique file names can be created. In Figure 7.26, we have chosen "%s" which returns only the backup set number. Another useful parameter is "%u" which generates an eight character name comprising the backup set number and the time the backup was taken. There is no browse capability for the directory name; therefore, ensure that it is spelled correctly.

Hint: The directory for the backup must end in a "\" or "/" depending on your hardware platform.

A complete list of all of the options can be found in the Oracle 8*i* backup and recovery manual. If you are backing up frequently, it is very important to name your backup files very carefully; otherwise, you could find that you are unable to recognize a backup file.

In this example, the backup will go to disk, but, in a data warehouse, it will have to go to tape. Therefore, it is extremely important to ensure that the physical labels placed on the tapes match the contents. Too many times the authors have experienced problems where it is impossible to recreate the database from the backups because the labels on the tapes do not match the actual tape contents. Sloppy management practices like this could mean that you lose your entire data warehouse.

Whenever you take a full backup of the system, do not discard the previous full backup set, because, if there is a problem with the current backup, you would lose your entire data warehouse. Therefore, save as many full backup sets as is possible before you recycle the tapes.

There are several other tabs that can be selected. If the default user for this database cannot connect as that SYSDBA, then you must click on the *Preferred Credentials* tab to specify a different user name and password.

Full Backups

The size of your data warehouse will determine how frequently a full backup is taken. Even if your warehouse is huge, a back up should always be taken periodically. However, if your warehouse is in the terabyte category, then you may prefer to back up the database in parallel using the operating system backup utility, because this approach will be considerably faster than the method described here.

One of the tools provided in Oracle Enterprise Manager is a backup utility, which includes a "backup wizard" where you can mean:

- define predefined backup strateg*y*
- customize your own strategy

Predefined Backup Strategy

The first example shown here illustrates how to set up a *predefined backup strategy*. The first question asked by the wizard, illustrated in Figure 7.27, is how frequently the backup is to be performed and when it is to be run.

Figure 7.27 Backup Frequency

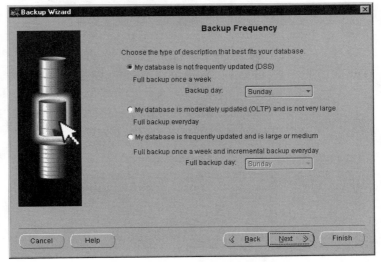

For those readers unfamiliar with creating backup procedures, the wizard advises on when backups should be taken based on the type of applications using this database. You can see that, for a data warehouse, it is suggesting once a week and picks Sunday, which it expects to be a quiet day, suitable for running backups. Of course, you can change the frequency and day.

The next screen presented by the wizard asks at what time the backup will be run. A review of the options are displayed in Figure 7.28. This is where you specify which backup configuration is to be used, which determines where the backup is to be stored and what the backup medium will be such as tape or disk.

Figure 7.28 Backup Configuration Selection

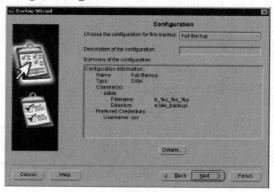

Now we have to specify against which database the backup will be run. In Figure 7.29, we have selected our data warehouse database EASYDW.

The definition of the backup procedure is almost complete. In Figure 7.30, we can see all of the options that we have selected. We now review these and press OK if they are correct. To change any of the values, press the *Back* key to return to the appropriate screen, and make the necessary modifications.

Figure 7.29 Selecting the Database

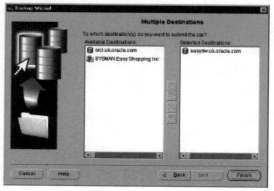

Figure 7.30 Reviewing the Backup Procedure

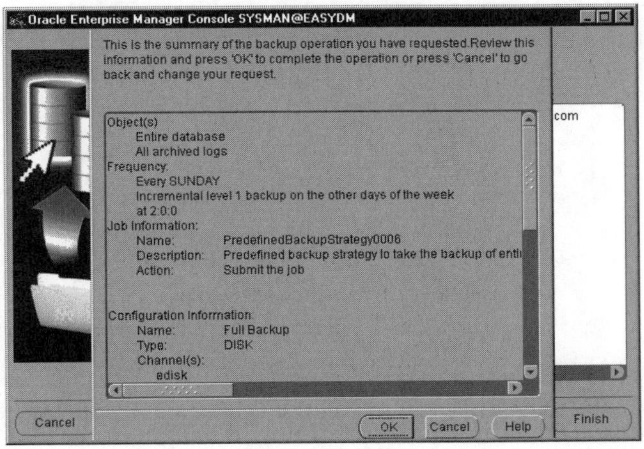

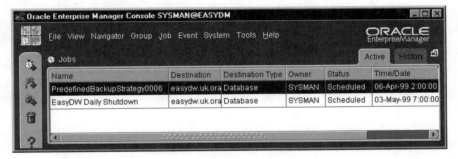

Once the definition of the backup is complete, it will be placed on the console job queue, as illustrated in Figure 7.31, until it is time for it to run.

Figure 7.31 Backing up Job on the Console Job Queue

Custom Backup Strategy

An alternative to the predefined backup is to create a *custom backup strategy*, which is very similar to the predefined strategy. The job will reside in the job library, if required, so that it can be invoked easily and scheduled for regular use, as per any other job in the library.

The first question asked by the wizard is the type of backup that you require, as illustrated in Figure 7.32.

Figure 7.32 Type of Custom Backup

If *Entire Database* is selected, you will then have the choice of either backing up the entire database or taking an incremental backup. An incremental back up could be of interest to data warehouse users because it allows you to back up only the data that has changed instead of the entire data warehouse.

Keep in mind that, depending on whether archive log is enabled, it will determine the types of back up options available. In Figure 7.32, we have more options because archive log mode is enabled. Enabling archive logging means that all changes to the database are journaled into the archive log.

The steps in a custom backup are very similar to those we have seen previously: you select the type of backup, the channel, when it is to be run, and then name it as shown in Figure 7.33. This is when you have the option of including this job in the job library.

Figure 7.33 Including Backup Job in Library

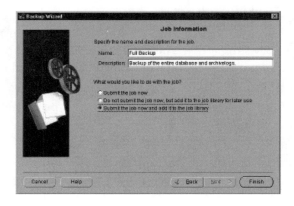

The job will now run automatically and is available for future use via the job library.

Incremental Backups

We mentioned earlier that a type of backup very useful in the data warehouse is the incremental backup. The screens presented for an incremental backup are very similar to those for a full backup except that the screen in Figure 7.34 will appear.

Here you must specify the incremental backup level. It is extremely important to select the correct level, otherwise you may get a full backup by mistake.

To clarify how the backup level is specified, let us refer to Figure 7.35. A complete backup is taken on Sunday; this is our Level 0. At close of business on Monday, a Level 2 incremental backup is taken, which backs up all the changes since Sunday. On Tuesday, another Level 2 incremental backup is taken which will contain all the changes to the database since Monday. On Wednesday, a Level 1 incremental backup is taken. Since 1 is greater than zero but less than 2, all the changes since Sunday will be placed in this backup file. On Thursday, a Level 2 backup is taken, so the most recent backup with a value less than or equal to 2 is the Level 1 backup from Wednesday; therefore, this backup will contain all the changes since Wednesday.

Figure 7.34 Incremental Backup Level

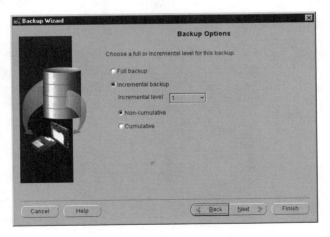

Using this approach may, at first, seem complicated, but when automatic recovery is used, the recovery manager will decide for itself which complete and incremental backups are needed to recover the database.

Figure 7.35 Selecting an Incremental Backup

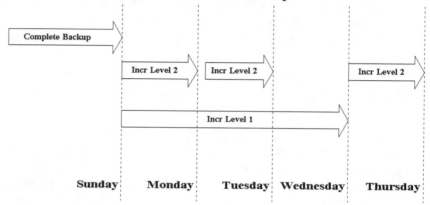

Tablespace Backup

Another technique for backing up the database that would be very useful in a data warehouse is a tablespace backup. Using this technique, you have the ability to back up a specific tablespace, which, in a data warehouse could make for a very nice backup strategy.

In Figure 7.36, we see one of the screens from the backup wizard asking us which tablespaces we want to back up. In our example, we have selected the two tablespaces that contain the January data.

Figure 7.36 Selecting a Tablespace to Back Up

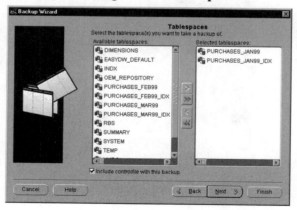

Here is a good example of where designing the database for management should be considered during the initial construction process. If we can group our updates to the database by date, and we know that after a given point in time, there will be no changes made within this tablespace, then, if you set the tablespace to be read-only and then back it up, we can rest assured that we have captured the data in that tablespace. Since it will never change, we won't have to back it up again.

Changing the status of a tablespace to read-only is very simple. You can either enter the SQL command, shown in Figure 7.37, or, use the Storage Manager GUI, shown in Figure 7.37, select the tablespace, and then click on the box at the bottom of the screen marked *Read Only*. Finally, clicking on the *Apply* button will make this a read-only tablespace. You can change it back to a read-write tablespace at any time.

Figure 7.37 Making a Tablespace Read-Only

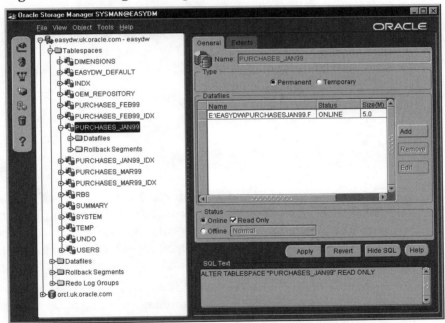

Of course, it makes sense to periodically take full backups, just in case there are any problems with the backup files you have taken. Taking only tablespaces is okay, but it still makes it possible for somebody to accidentally overwrite the tape containing all of the data for a given month.

Backup File Sizes

When a database is being built, designers are constantly aware of the size of the database. However, that information seems to get lost when people start thinking about backing up the database. Everyone tends to say "Well it's 300 gigabytes so it will take x minutes to back up." What they forget to add is that the backup file will need y gigabytes of space.

In the examples shown here, we have used disks to store our backups. For a real data warehouse, however, you will be storing them on tape, so don't forget how many tapes you will require—especially for the backup strategy you will be implementing. It has been known for sites to actually run out of tapes!

Our Easy Shopping database is very small, and it occupies around 210mb on an NT system. In Figure 7.38, we can see the different sizes for the various backup files.

Figure 7.38 Backup File Sizes

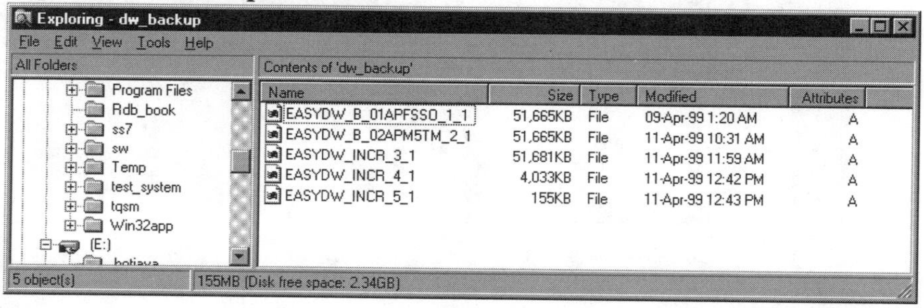

A full backup occupies just under 52 mb which is about 25% of the full size of the database. Therefore, you can see that you can save a significant amount of storage space by using the backup provided by Oracle 8*i* . If a backup was taken using the Operating System backup utility, which may or may not compress the file, then 210 mb of storage would be needed, instead of 51.6 mb.

The even smaller files shown in Figure 7.38 are the incremental and tablespace backups, and here we can see the big advantage of using this utility. Admittedly, only a few changes were made to the database. But you can see that even for the incremental backups, the size of the file ranged from 150K to 4 mb, which is a big difference from the requirements for a full backup.

By taking incremental backups, you can make backups of your warehouse more frequently and not have to worry about when you are going to find the time to back up the entire warehouse.

One final reminder on this topic: during the testing of the data warehouse, don't forget to test your backup procedures and obtain some estimates of possible run times for backups. Then you can discuss your requirements with the operations department so that your management tasks can be included with all of the other work that has to be done.

7.3.3   Restore

Restoring a database from a backup is a task that most DBA's probably fear. They are always concerned that the backup may fail, leaving them with no database. Unfortunately, unless you test every backup, you can never be sure that a backup file will actually work. If you can, it is a good idea to periodically restore your backup files onto a test system so that you know that the files and your procedures are good.

Hint: If you are restoring during a serious database problem, try to restore to another location so that, if the restore operation fails, you still have the original database.

One of the first problems you encounter when restoring a database is knowing which and what backup files to use. If you have been using the recovery catalog, then it is very simple; otherwise, you will have to check your records to determine the correct backup file.

Don't forget that restoring a database could require a number of backup files such as full and incremental backup files. However, this is when the Recovery Wizard is extremely useful, especially if you want to recover to the latest point in time.

The Recovery Wizard can be started in a number of ways:

- By selecting it from "Tools" on the strip menu
- By using the right mouse button when selecting "database" from the navigation window
- By checking on the database tool icon

Irrespective of the method chosen, the Recovery Wizard will start, the screen in Figure 7.39 will appear, and you will be asked for the type of restoration that is required.

In Figure 7.39, we have the option of restoring the entire database, which is what the example here will show, or restoring specific tablespaces or data files. Recovery can be to a specific point in time, such as to Monday at 11:30 A.M. Usually this type of recovery is unnecessary. If a specific problem corrupted the database, however, then you may want to restore to just prior to the job running against the database.

Figure 7.39 Selecting Type of Restore

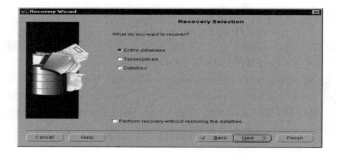

Next it will ask where the files are to be restored to, as illustrated in Figure 7.40.

Figure 7.40 Location of Data Files

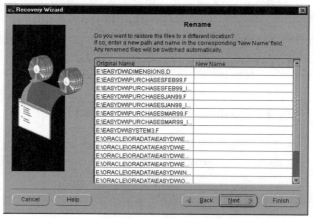

Depending on the reason for the restore, you may want them to go to another location, which can be specified here. The other advantage of this screen is that it provides an opportunity to check which files are going to be restored.

The next step illustrates the reason why you should be familiar with your restoration procedure, because the recovery configuration screen will appear, as shown in Figure 7.41. The wizard automatically selects a configuration. Since backup ones are the ones that exist, the full backup one is selected.

Figure 7.41 Recovery Configuration

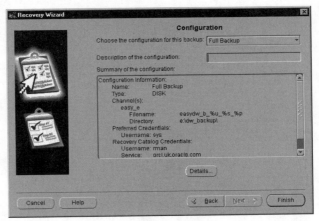

Using this configuration, the wizard knows where the backup files are located and is given the information to access the recovery catalog. If you had never run this procedure before, this could certainly alarm you and seriously delay the restoration process while you check manuals and maybe even telephone support to gain advice. This screen is only confusing the first time you run the restoration wizard, next time, it will make sense!

You will now have to respond to other screens to check what is to be restored. Finally, a job to perform the restore will be submitted to the Enterprise Manager job queue. You can now monitor the job from the console.

When the job is finished, you can check the restore by viewing the log from the job, which is available from the Job sections of the console under Job History. If you double-click on the job of interest, the various stages of the job are displayed. If you then double-click on the line that says "completed," the log of the job will be displayed, as shown in Figure 7.42

Figure 7.42 Recovery Log

In this example of a full recovery, we can see only a portion of the log, but note that, because we were using the recovery catalog, the utility automatically worked out which backup files were required. This example used three and then applied them.

Although we have illustrated how to recover a full database, the procedure is almost the same for a tablespace or data file recovery.

Hopefully this section has given you some idea how to backup and recovery an Oracle 8*i* data warehouse. This is such an extensive subject that it is highly recommended that you read the Oracle 8*i* backup and recovery manual for detailed information on functionality and many more ideas on how to design, create, and run backup-and-recovery operations.

7.3.4   **Disaster/Recovery**

The problem with planning for a disaster is that many people think that it is something that will never happen to them. Consequently, it may be given a low priority on the "Jobs To Do" list, or perhaps something is done, but only minimal effort is put in to the process.

When we talk about disaster/recovery we are referring to a catastrophic failure, such as building catches fire or a bomb destroys the building. Other problems such as a hardware failure caused by a disk crash should be recoverable from your standard restore procedures. Disaster/Recovery is different because it may mean setting up your computer systems at an entirely different site, which presents a whole new set of problems.

One of the main issues with the data warehouse is its sheer size. Hopefully, at least one recent set of backup tapes are kept off-site and those kept on-site are held in a fireproof safe. Once you know that you have a good set of backup tapes to restore the database, your procedures should take into account the size of the database and the hardware required to rebuild it.

The importance of your data warehouse to the business may determine whether it is even recreated at your new temporary location. It may be that you decide that the business can do without the warehouse until your regular site is available again. Great care should be taken if you make this decision, because it may take much longer than you think to return to normal working conditions. Chances are that if you have a major failure, especially something that relates to a building, it could be many months before you return.

Some readers may be reading this text and saying to themselves, "why bother." Well, you should speak to companies that have had to undergo major disasters to realize the importance of planning for these events. Catastrophic failures are more common than you think. In the last few years, there have been earthquakes, floods, terrorist bombs, and fires. Today, so many organizations rely upon the data in their systems that losing that data could mean the end of the company or a serious downturn in profits that could take years to recover from. If you are making key business decisions from warehouse data, then ask yourself if you can live without it.

So what else can be done to assist with disaster recovery. One solution is to maintain a copy of your data warehouse at another site. This is probably only feasible for small data warehouses or data marts. Using the Oracle 8*i* Managed Standby facility, you can have Oracle 8*i* automatically maintain a copy of the database at another site. Therefore, when a failure occurs, you can switch to this database at a moment's notice.

Managed Standby is ideal for recovering quickly from other types of failure, such as hardware-related failures. Because the hardware failure will probably be restricted to one system, you can switch your system to the site containing the copy of the database, and the users will only see a minor interruption to service.

7.4   REORGANIZING THE WAREHOUSE

Reorganizing a database, irrespective of whether it is a data warehouse or a database used for transaction-processing-style systems, is not a task to be undertaken lightly. Unfortunately, in a data warehouse, the time required to reorganize can become a serious issue due to the high data volumes involved. Therefore it shouldn't be necessary to reorganize the database entirely, but minor changes may be necessary.

7.4.1   Why Reorganize?

Reorganizations can occur for a variety of reasons, such as:

- The business needs change
- A flaw in the database design
- A regular archiving of data
- The government changes the rules

A change in the business requirements from the system is almost impossible to predict, and one solution to the problem may be to create a data mart rather than restructure the entire data warehouse.

A fundamental flaw in the database design can be overcome by carefully reviewing the database design and, if necessary, asking for an external review by an experienced data warehouse designer. One of the problems with data warehouses is that what may seem a good design at the outset may prove unsuitable in the long term due to the large volumes of data involved. Therefore, try to minimize the likelihood of this occurring by using techniques such as partitioning.

7.4.2   **Partition Maintenance**

Some of the structure changes required by the data warehouse can be achieved using partition operations. For example, when you first create the database, you probably have little or no historic data to populate it. Therefore, for the first 18 to 24 months, you happily add new data every month until the required system limits are met. Then, when the data warehouse is full, every month you would have to drop old data to make room for new data. Without partitions you would have to scan the data and manually delete it, which is very time-consuming. The fast alternative to this problem is to drop the partition containing the old data and create a new partition for the new data, as illustrated in Figure 7.43

Figure 7.43 Partition Maintenance

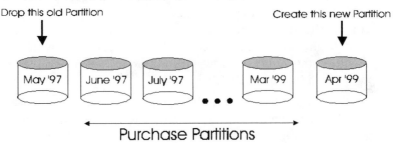

The SQL commands to perform the tasks shown in Figure 7.43 are shown below. First we drop the old partition for May 1997 sales.

```
ALTER TABLE easydw.purchases
 DROP PARTITION purchases_may97 ;
```

Next we create the new partition for April 1999 sales. The first step is to create the tablespace where the data will reside.

```
CREATE TABLESPACE purchases_apr99
 datafile 'E:\EASYDW\PURCHASESapr99.f'
size 5m reuse autoextend on default storage
(initial 16k next 16k pctincrease 0 maxextents unlimited);
```

The final step is to alter the table definition to reference the new tablespace that we have just created. That is, we add the partition to the table.

```
ALTER TABLE easydw.purchases
 ADD PARTITION purchases_apr99
```

```
values less than (TO_DATE('01-05-1999', 'DD-MM-YYYY'))
pctfree 0 pctused 99
storage (initial 64k next 16k pctincrease 0)
tablespace purchases_apr99 ;
```

However, this technique is applicable only if the data is partitioned on a date. Therefore, if you decide upon another partitioning scheme such as a code, then this type of maintenance operation would not be possible.

Another partition operation that you can perform that may prove useful is merging *two partitions* or *splitting a partition* if a partition becomes too large.

From a maintenance perspective, Oracle 8*i* features like Summary Management are aware of partitions, which can be very useful. Suppose you are maintaining a rolling summary of sales and would like to report on all sales but the database can hold only 18 months of data. If you create a summary (materialized view) that is fast refreshable, then you can drop the partition without affecting the summary data. When data arrives for the new partition, it will be included with the existing data. Therefore, provided you never have to rebuild the summary, you will be able to report using data over a wider period than the summary.

In the example discussed in this section we have shown only the table, but don't forget that partitions are used on indexes, so you will have to create the partitions that it requires.

7.4.3   Index Changes

Probably one of the aspects of the design that will be changed is the indexes. New ones will be created, and existing ones will be modified. In a data warehouse, there is a temptation to create more indexes because of the lack of updates to the system. However, you should consider the impact all of these indexes will have on the data load time.

If you need to rebuild an index for any reason, then it is suggested that you use the ALTER INDEX REBUILD statement, which should offer better performance than dropping and recreating the index. The only exception to this rule is if you have a global index on a partition table and one of the partitions is dropped. In the case of a global index, all partitions will be marked "unusable," forcing an index rebuild. Therefore, to incur only a single pass on the data, drop the index, and then create it again. Executing index operations in parallel is described in section 7.6.

> **Hint: By partitioning the data, you can perform maintenance on index partitions.**

7.5   REFRESHING THE WAREHOUSE

An extremely important management task is refreshing the warehouse with the latest data. This is a management task that is usually performed overnight with the data presented in batches. As was described earlier, frequently the data has to be cleaned and transformed before it can be loaded. We have already seen the various techniques that can be used for loading the new data into the warehouse. In this section, refreshing data refers to:

- loading the new data
- updating the materialized views

Throughout this book, we have seen extensive use of Oracle Enterprise Manager for managing and controlling many of our management tasks. Depending on how complex your tasks are and on the data dependencies, you may prefer to use your own techniques. Otherwise, you could place the jobs on the console job queue and come in the next day to see that everything has run smoothly.

For example, it is not uncommon to receive data loads from various sources at different times. If there is dependencies between the data, then you may have to control that within your own management suites.

Once the data has been loaded into the warehouse, then the refreshing of the summarized data (materialized views) must now take place. Depending on how many summaries you have created, this could also take a significant amount of time.

The refreshing of the materialized views could certainly be performed using a job on the console. In fact, you could refresh all of the summaries by calling a package called *dbms_mview.refresh_all_mview*s. Alternatively, you could use the *dbms_mview.refresh_dependen*t option to request that it refresh only summaries dependent on these tables. Or you can call the refresh package and specify which summaries are to be refreshed. Specific details on how to refresh summaries is described in Chapter 3.

7.6   PARALLEL MANAGEMENT TASKS

Throughout this book, the typically large size of the data warehouse means that tasks can take a very long time to complete. So far, we have considered some techniques for improving performance, but there is a very useful one that has only been briefly mentioned, and that is the ability to run operations in *parallel*.

Normally, an SQL statement is executed by a single process, but imagine the performance gains we could achieve if we could split that SQL statement into a number of processes running alongside one another. Provided you are using Oracle 8*i* Enterprise Edition, this capability is available to you. One very important point to mention is that, to use some of these parallel commands, you do not have to purchase the Oracle Parallel Server option.

With every release, Oracle increases the number of operations and commands that can be run in parallel. At the time of writing, they are:

- table scan
- create table as select
- create and rebuild indexes
- partitions; rebuild index, move and split
- update, delete, insert, select
- joins—hash, nested loop, and sort merge
- select distinct
- group by, order by, not in
- union all
- aggregates
- constraint enable
- cube and roll up
- star transformation

7.6.1   How Many Parallel Processes?

The syntax required to execute in parallel varies according to the task being performed. If we first consider a simple parallel SQL statement, such as rebuilding an index, the first thing to determine is what Oracle refers to as the "degree of parallelism." This is the value specified with the PARALLEL clause, which defines the number of parallel execution processes that will be used to perform this task. Using this approach, it is possible to use a different number of servers for each task. Obviously, parallel tasks are suited for when Oracle can run the processes on multiple cpu's. In Figure 7.44, we can see how an SQL command is decomposed to run via four parallel execution servers that will each read a specific partition.

Figure 7.44 Degree of Parallelism

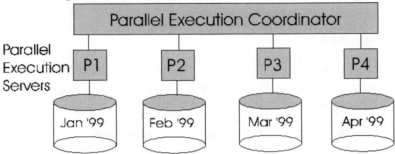

To parallel the operation shown in Figure 7.44, you specify the degree of parallelism by using the PARALLEL 4 clause in SQL, or you could do it via the hint PARALLEL (purchases, 4). The PARALLEL clause can be used on many SQL statements; therefore, you should check the SQL reference manual to determine its position within the statement.

Hint: When accessing partitions, specify the PARALLEL clause to correspond to the number of partitions that will be accessed.

7.6.2   **Parallel DML and Parallel DDL**

Another operation that can be paralleled that is of great interest to the person managing the data warehouse is parallel DML or DDL. You can make one of these commands be performed in parallel by either including the PARALLEL clause in the statement, such as CREATE INDEX, or by specifying:

```
ALTER SESSION FORCE PARALLEL DML
```

There are various rules regarding what can be run in parallel. For example, you can specify the PARALLEL clause when creating an index, irrespective of whether it is partitioned or a non-partitioned index. The Oracle 8*i* Concepts manual contains all the details regarding what is possible.

Referring to our Easy Shopping example, suppose we had to create some new indexes. We could improve the index creation time if multiple processors were available just by adding the PARALLEL clause to the index definition as shown below.

```
CREATE INDEX easydw.purchase_product_index ON purchases
 (product_id )
 local
 pctfree 5 tablespace indx
 storage (initial 64k next 64k pctincrease 0)
 PARALLEL 6 ;
```

In this example, we have stated that six parallel processes should be used. Suppose later we needed to rebuild another index that is partitioned. The original index definition is shown below.

```
CREATE BITMAP INDEX easydw.purchase_time_index ON purchases
 (time_key )
 local
 (partition indexJan99 tablespace purchases_jan99_idx,
 partition indexFeb99 tablespace purchases_feb99_idx,
 partition indexMar99 tablespace purchases_mar99 );
```

Imagine that some new data was added, and we knew that it affected only the indexFeb99 partition. Rather than rebuild the entire index, we can rebuild the specific partition as follows:

```
ALTER INDEX easydw.purchase_time_index
  REBUILD PARTITION indexFeb99 PARALLEL 6;
```

By now, you should be able to appreciate some of the benefits of managing the database using parallel operations. This is a useful technique to use to improve the performance of your index build time. However, when you are using the ALTER INDEX REBUILD statement, you can only specify the PARALLEL clause if the index isn't partitioned. To rebuild a partitioned index in parallel, you must use the ALTER INDEX REBUILD PARTITION .

7.7   TUNING THE WAREHOUSE

One should not forget that a data warehouse needs to be tuned just like any other database, although you may be tuning for reasons such as:

- Improving data load time
- Improving query response
- Refreshing data performance
- Improving time to perform management tasks

When people think of tuning, their first thoughts are likely to be improving query performance. Traditional techniques used to resolve this problem include creating indexes and placing data in the buffer so that it is faster to read. In a data warehouse, the index is still extremely important, but placing the data in the buffer is unlikely to help, due to the huge volumes of data typically being searched in a data warehouse.

Therefore, one of the best techniques to use to improve query performance is to create summary tables (known in Oracle 8*i* as a materialized view). Provided the query is used several times, if a materialized view is created that precalculates the query, then the optimizer will execute the query by retrieving the results form the summary table rather than the detail table. If your detail table is large, this can represent a very significant improvement in query response time.

7.7.1   Summary Advisor

To assist with the management of summary data, there is a Summary Advisor package that you can use. One of the problems with using summary tables is that you either need to know the queries in advance so that you can create suitable summary tables. Since many of us will not know what the queries will be, we can use Oracle Trace to monitor query usage, and then use the information that it gathers as input to the Summary Advisor to recommend which summaries to create.

The Summary Advisor is part of Summary Management, available in the Enterprise Edition of Oracle 8*i*. Within the advisor, there are some very useful packages for anyone responsible for managing summaries in the warehouse. They provide the ability to:

- Recommend summaries, with or without a workload
- Estimate the size of a summary
- Report summary usage

Setting up the Advisor

To use the advisor functions, you must first set up some dimensions. Below we have created three dimensions on Customer, Product, and Time. You must also ensure that all the tables in your database have been analyzed using the ANALYZE command. This step is very important because the data collected by the ANALYZE is required by the advisor.

```
CREATE DIMENSION customer
 LEVEL customer IS customer.customer_id
 LEVEL town   IS customer.town
 LEVEL region IS customer.county
HIERARCHY customer_zone
 ( customer CHILD OF
 town   CHILD OF
 region ) ;

CREATE DIMENSION product
 LEVEL product IS product.product_id
 LEVEL category IS product.category
 HIERARCHY products
 (product CHILD OF category)
 ATTRIBUTE product DETERMINES product.product_name;

CREATE DIMENSION time
LEVEL time   IS time.time_key
LEVEL month   IS time.month
LEVEL quarter  IS time.quarter
LEVEL year   IS time.year
HIERARCHY calendar_rollup (
 time CHILD OF
 month  CHILD OF
 quarter CHILD OF
 year   );
```

Hint: Even if you are not using dimensions and create them only for the advisor, defines ones that make sense for your application, and you should see better recommendations from the advisor.

Recommending Summaries to Create

You are now ready to recommend the summaries that are required in your data warehouse. The warehouse advisor can be run with or without a workload. If you do not supply a workload, then it creates its own hypothetical workload. The recommendations created by the advisor package *dbms_olap.recommend_mv* are stored in the database in a table called *mview$recommendations*. Here we see an example of calling the summary advisor without a workload using the following four parameters:

```
EXECUTE dbms_olap.recommend_mv ('purchases',1000000,
NULL,10);
```

- Fact table
- Space available for summaries
- Summary retention list
- Percentage of existing summaries to keep

Once the recommendations are available, at the time of writing, you can either query the table directly or use the package *demo_sumadv.prettyprint_recommendations* to display the results as shown below.

```
SET SERVEROUTPUT ON SIZE 900000
EXECUTE demo_sumadv.prettyprint_recommendations;

Recommendation Number = 1
Recommended Action is CREATE new summary:
SELECT CUSTOMER.TOWN, CUSTOMER.COUNTY, PRODUCT.CATEGORY,
    TIME.TIME_KEY, TIME.MONTH, TIME.QUARTER, TIME.YEAR ,
    COUNT(*), SUM(PURCHASES.PURCHASE_PRICE),
    COUNT(PURCHASES.PURCHASE_PRICE),SUM(PURCHASES.PURCHASE_TIME),
    COUNT(PURCHASES.PURCHASE_TIME),SUM(PURCHASES.SHIPPING_CHARGE)
    ,COUNT(PURCHASES.SHIPPING_CHARGE)
FROM EASYDW.PURCHASES, EASYDW.CUSTOMER,
        EASYDW.PRODUCT, EASYDW.TIME
WHERE PURCHASES.CUSTOMER_ID = CUSTOMER.CUSTOMER_ID AND
        PURCHASES.PRODUCT_ID = PRODUCT.PRODUCT_ID AND
        PURCHASES.TIME_KEY = TIME.TIME_KEY
GROUP BY CUSTOMER.TOWN, CUSTOMER.COUNTY, PRODUCT.CATEGORY,
        TIME.TIME_KEY, TIME.MONTH, TIME.QUARTER, TIME.YEAR
Storage in bytes is 11466
Percent performance gain is 22.5798797201405
Benefit-to-cost ratio is .00196929005059659
```

This package can be found in the SQL file called *sadvdemo.sql* which is located in the \rdbms\demo\summgmt directory. The output from the package is the same, irrespective of whether the summary recommendations come from a real workload or a hypothetical one. At the time of writing, you will have to take this statement and edit it to produce the CREATE MATERIALIZED VIEW statement, which will actually create the summary.

The storage in bytes is an estimate from the advisor as to how much space this summary will occupy. The *performance gain* is the incremental improvement in performance expected from using this materialized view. The *benefit to cost ratio* is calculated based on the size of the detail table compared to the size in bytes of the materialized view.

Collecting a Workload with Oracle Trace

The recommendations made by the advisor will improve significantly if it can reference a workload. At the time of writing, a workload can be collected only by Oracle Trace. If you have purchased the Tuning pack for Oracle Enterprise Manager, then you can create and format workloads using this friendly interface. Once the Enterprise Manager console has been started, you can start this GUI by selecting the database from the navigation window, right-clicking on the mouse to get a list of options, and selecting *Related Tools* followed by Oracle Trace.

Using Trace terminology, a *collection* must be created to obtain the workload, which is achieved using the collection wizard. The screens shown in Figure 7.45 is the summary screen, which is where you first select the type of data that is to be collected. Then some nice screens will be presented where you name the collection file and specify when it is to be run.

Figure 7.45 Oracle Trace—Creating a Collection

One of the nice aspects to using the GUI is that it will format the data automatically. In the next section, you will see the manual process for achieving this. Figure 7.46 illustrates how you use the Oracle Trace wizard to specify where the data is to be loaded.

Figure 7.46 Oracle Trace—Formatting the Data

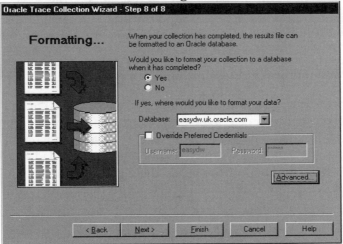

The collections will automatically be scheduled onto the Enterprise Manager Console, and, once it has completed, you can run the summary advisor to recommend which summaries to create. At any time you can see the state of your collection by referring to the main screen in Oracle Trace, which is illustrated in Figure 7.47. In this example, we can see that, for our database EASYDW, the collection is still running and has not yet been formatted.

Figure 7.47 Oracle Trace—Monitoring a Collection

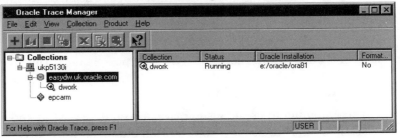

Collecting a Workload without Oracle Trace GUI

It is still possible to collect a workload without using the GUI just described; however, it is a more involved process. Trace collection is turned on by enabling the following parameters in your init.ora file.

```
oracle_trace_enable=true                ! turns on trace collecting
oracle_trace_facility_name=oraclesm     ! following used for
oracle_trace_collection_size=0          ! summary management
oracle_trace_collection_path=e:\Oracle\Ora81\Otrace\Admin\cdf
oracle_trace_collection_name=oraclesm
```

You then access your database as per normal, and, the first time a query is issued, it is recorded in the trace collection file. In addition, it also records every time a summary is used. Therefore, you can monitor your data warehouse for whatever period of time is suitable. Provided you don't monitor for too long, the data collection file should not grow too large.

When you have finished collecting data, restart the instance with the parameter *oracle_trace_enable=false*, which turns off Trace. Two files are needed by the format utility, oraclesm.dat and oraclesm.cdf. Format this data into your data warehouse, as shown below, using the *otrcfmt* command.

```
otrcfmt oraclesm.cdf easydw/easydw easydw
```

Hint: Don't forget to delete your oraclesm.cdf and .dat files before your next data collection.

Once the workload information is in the data warehouse, you can now call the summary advisor again, as shown below, and ask it to recommend which summaries to keep, retain and create. Here we are using the workload, so the package is suffixed with _w.

```
EXECUTE dbms_olap.recommend_mv_w ('purchases',10000, NULL,25);
```

Estimating the Size of a Summary

If you are going to create a summary, it would be nice to know how much space it is likely to occupy. You can find out this information by calling the package *dbms_olap.estimate_summary_size,* as shown below.

This package is very easy to use: simply pass in the SQL statement only for the SELECT expression of the materialized view.

```
SET SERVEROUTPUT on

DECLARE
no_of_rows NUMBER;
mv_size   NUMBER;
BEGIN
no_of_rows :=555;
mv_size :=5555;

DBMS_OLAP.estimate_summary_size ('purchases_by_county',
 'SELECT SUM(purchase_price), county
 FROM PURCHASES pv, CUSTOMER ct
 WHERE pv.customer_id = ct.customer_id
 GROUP BY county' , no_of_rows, mv_size );

DBMS_OUTPUT.put_line ( 'SELECT on Purchases GROUP by County ');
DBMS_OUTPUT.put_line ( 'No of Rows: ' || no_of_rows );
DBMS_OUTPUT.put_line ( 'Size of Summary (bytes): ' || mv_size);
DBMS_OUTPUT.put_line ( '');
END;
/

SELECT on Purchases GROUP by County
No of Rows: 3
Size of Materialized view (bytes): 96
```

In this example, it reports how many rows and the expected summary size. Also note that, in this example, we have used DBMS_OUTPUT.put_line to display the results from the package.

Monitoring Summary Usage

Another important question the DBA will ask is which summaries are being used? A major problem for the administration group is knowing when it is safe to remove a summary from the data warehouse. If you have been monitoring your summary usage by collecting workload information via Oracle Trace, then look for a package available in the summary advisor called *dbms_olap.evaluate_utilization_w*. When this package is run as shown below, it analyzes the workload information and places details of summary usage in the table MVIEW$_EVALUATIONS. Querying this table as shown below, you can see exactly which summaries are in use and how often they were used.

```
EXECUTE dbms_olap.evaluate_utilization_w ();

SELECT * FROM mview$_evaluations;
```

OWNER	SUMMARY_NAME	RANK	STORAGE	FREQ	CUMULATIVE	BENEFIT
EASYDW	PURCHASE_BY_COUNTY	1	340	20	18002	52.947
EASYDW	MONTHLY_CUSTOMER_SUM	2	196020	11	9345	35.532
EASYDW	SALES_BY_MONTH	3	380	2	7856	23.361

3 rows selected.

7.7.2   Tuning Tools

There are many tuning tools available to tune an Oracle database, available from both Oracle and third-party software suppliers. If you purchase the optional Tuning pack for Oracle Enterprise Manager, then the following tools will be available to you:

- *Oracle Expert*—creates a database design
- *SQL Analyze*—tunes SQL statements
- *Tablespace Manager*—manages tablespaces useful for space usage
- *AutoAnalyze*—automatically keeps statistics accurate
- *Index Tuning Wizard*—recommends indexes

Some other useful tuning tools are in the Diagnostics Pack, include:

- *Performance Manager*—shows how database is being used
- *TopSessions*—displays user's database usage

Just because the database is being used as a data warehouse should be no excuse to forget to tune it. However, if you are familiar with tuning OLTP systems, then the techniques used will be slightly different, although the end result is the same: faster query response.

Tuning is a bit of a black art, and it is impossible in just a few pages, to tell you how to tune a data warehouse. Instead, the authors suggest that you become familiar with the tuning tools available to you and determine what information you need to know. For instance, how much I/O was used to perform this query. Then determine how, if at all possible, you can obtain that data from your tuning tool.

Practice this technique in a controlled environment on a small system before you attempt to analyze a production system. Keep practicing to improve your confidence, and then, when you really do have to tune, it shouldn't be such an ordeal. There are many books available on Oracle tuning, and all should provide useful advice on tuning your data warehouse.

Plan Stability

One of the significant advantages for using a relational database is that you don't have to tell the database how to access the data when a query is defined. Instead, the query optimizer determines the most efficient query execution path. Usually the optimizer selects the best strategy, but problems can occur when new releases of the software are installed or when the database cardinality statistics change, because the optimizer may choose a different strategy. Therefore, there is a risk that your query could suddenly take much longer to complete. One solution to this problem is to use a hint, but this means amending the code, which may not be possible.

To overcome this problem, Oracle 8*i* introduced a new feature called *plan stability*. This allows you to create a stored outline for a specific SQL statement or all SQL statements. When the plan stability feature is enabled, your query is compared with the one stored in the outline. If it matches exactly, then the strategy for the outline is used in preference.

Therefore, if you are concerned about strategies changing, especially as a result of a software upgrade, then consider creating some outlines for your important queries. Once they have been created and stored in the database, you do not have to use them. Instead, you could keep them there in case of emergency and turn them on only when required.

7.8 OTHER MANAGEMENT ISSUES

We have already seen a number of management tasks. The ones specified here are by no means a definitive list, and there may very well be ones that are not mentioned here that may be applicable in your environment. There are also some additional tasks mentioned here that you may also like to consider.

7.8.1 Building a Test System

When you suggest the construction of a test system, it is not uncommon for many people to throw their hands up in the air and say, "impossible." But you should stop for a moment and consider the implication on your business if you don't have a test system. When a test system exists, it can be used for a variety of reasons, such as:

- Testing new software releases

- Timing data loads
- Evaluating management task times
- Practicing management tasks
- Testing scripts before executing in production
- Assessing impact of maintenance tasks e.g. index rebuild
- Determining query response times

Many people think that a test system has to be identical to the production system, but, in a warehouse, that is usually impossible. Therefore, what is required is a cut-down version of the warehouse that is representative of your real warehouse. Ideally, numbers obtained from it should scale easily so that you can determine what the effect would be on your production warehouse.

Data inside the warehouse should, whenever possible, be representative of the real data. It may be that, to obtain the desired effect, you may have to extract data from the real warehouse and then load it into the test warehouse, and this may be done every time the test warehouse is required.

Let us now discuss the various uses for a test system to understand why it is needed.

Testing New Software

Once a database becomes a critical component in the business and the information supplied from it, is used to make critical business decisions, no one wants to jeopardize the business by introducing new software that may have software problems. Therefore, if you have a test system, you can check that all of the important parts of the database software that you use are the same. The range of items to test could be extensive. For example, you will want to check that queries use the same optimizer strategy as before. If they have changed, then you should make use of the Plan Stability feature to ensure consistency of query response times.

However, you should always ensure when using outlines that performance will not degrade when a new version of Oracle is installed—it could improve due to an optimizer change so always check for the current strategy.

Another important check to make is that key features that you rely on still function the same. For example, if you rely heavily on partition operations to maintain the data in your warehouse, then check that they still work.

Utilities you rely on should also be checked to see that no changes have occurred that cause them to change their behavior.

If a script is created that contains all of these important tasks, then each time you upgrade the software, you have only to run the scripts and check the results. Therefore, considerable effort will be required to construct the scripts the first time. Once completed, however, they can be run repeatedly and you will know that everything that is important to your environment will have been checked.

Timing data loads

The test system provides an ideal opportunity to determine the load time for data and to practice any data cleaning that may be required. The fastest way to load data into an Oracle 8*i* data warehouse is using the utility SQL*Loader via the direct path method.

Hint: Don't forget to check the logs from any SQL*Loader jobs in case any problems occurred during the run, such as constraints not being enabled.

Evaluating/Practice Management Tasks

Now is also an ideal opportunity to practice and try out all of those management tasks before it is done in production. When it comes to testing backup and recovery processes, time will be saved by using very small databases initially and then moving on to the full size once you are sure that all of the procedures are working correctly.

Determine Query Response Times

The test system provides an ideal opportunity to see the data warehouse in use before all the users are given access. Even with a limited user audience, you will be surprised that you will find queries that do not perform well. Therefore, you now have time to diagnose the cause of the poor performance and resolve the problem by adding a new index, for example, or creating a materialized view to make the query perform faster.

In a test environment, it is unlikely that you will see an exact reproduction of usage of the data warehouse. Nevertheless, problems will still surface, and it is easier to fix them now, before the pressure comes with users demanding reports yesterday!

7.8.2   Maintaining Security

One should not forget the security of the data in a data warehouse. In many respects, warehouse data should probably be more secure than production data because its value to your competitors could be enormous. Imagine if one of your users started earning spare cash by running reports against your data or if an employee left the company with information from the data warehouse. If you are laughing at the last statement, please don't, because although it is very rare, it actually does happen.

The level of security in your data warehouse will depend on what you think is appropriate for your system. Some sites may prefer to have the warehouse open as far as reading data is concerned, but restricts management tasks such as creating summary data to the administration team.

We have already seen in Chapter 2 how we can protect individual tables by specifying explicitly who may access the tables using the GRANT and REVOKE commands.

Another technique is to create a ROLE, assigning privileges to that role, and then granting that role to a user. Roles can be created via SQL or by using the friendly GUI Security Manager, which is provided as part of Oracle Enterprise Manager.

Figure 7.48 Creating a Role

In Figure 7.48, we are creating a role called EASY_USER, and here we are specifying which tables in the database this user can access. Security isn't limited only to tables; you can place security on a wide range of database objects. For those of you who do not want to use the GUI interface, the SQL box at the bottom of Figure 7.48 shows the commands to implement this role.

Once the role has been defined, you can then allocate this role to a user, as shown in Figure 7.49. Roles are an extremely powerful feature in Oracle and can save you an immense amount of time not having to allocate lots of privileges to a user.

Figure 7.49 Allocating a Role to a User

7.8.3   Monitoring Space Usage

A very important piece of information for the DBA to know is how much space is available in the data warehouse. One technique to avoid running out of space is to create the data files with autoextend and to define an unlimited number of extents. However, this won't help you if the disk actually fills up.

Therefore, as part of your routine monitoring of the data warehouse, you should check for free space. This could be done using the Tablespace Manager GUI in the Enterprise Manager in the Tuning pack, or you may prefer to simply query the Oracle metadata for this information.

Inside the Oracle database, there are a significant number of system tables that contain very useful information about this database. Within the Oracle documentation, you can find a detailed explanation of all of these tables and the information they provide. In fact, some DBAs will tell you that this is the only way to manage your database and that they wouldn't dream of using one of the GUIs. The technique you use is a matter of preference; if you don't like writing SQL, then join the GUI gang.

Here is a sample of a report that queries the tables DBA_FREE-SPACE and DBA_DATA_FILES to advise on space usage. Although it looks like a very nice report, you should see the SQL required to generate it!

```
             Free Space in the Database

                  No of Max Free
Tablespace Name              Size (K)  Free (K)  % Used Free  Exts  Ext (K)
-------------------------  ----------  --------  -----------  ----  ----------
DIMENSIONS                      5,120     4,976         2.81     1     4,976
EASYDW_DEFAULT                  5,120     4,592        10.31     1     4,592
IF1                             1,024       976         4.69     2       944
IF2                             1,024       976         4.69     1       976
IF3                             1,024       976         4.69     1       976
INDEXES                         1,312       224        82.93     7        32
INDX                            5,120     3,632        29.06     1     3,632
OEM_REPOSITORY                 56,320    22,768        59.57     1    22,768
PURCHASES_FEB99                 5,120     4,704         8.13     1     4,704
PURCHASES_FEB99_IDX             3,072     3,024         1.56     1     3,024
PURCHASES_JAN99                 5,120     4,704         8.13     1     4,704
PURCHASES_JAN99_IDX             3,072     3,024         1.56     1     3,024
PURCHASES_MAR99                 5,120     5,008         2.19     1     5,008
PURCHASES_MAR99_IDX             1,024     1,008         1.56     1     1,008
RBS                            16,384    11,248        31.35     1    11,248
SUMM                            2,048     2,032          .78    47     1,136
SUMMARY                         6,144     6,128          .26     1     6,128
SYSTEM                         68,208     5,408        92.07     6     4,992
TEMP                           10,240     9,792         4.38     1     9,792
UNDO                            3,072     1,200        60.94     1     1,200
USERS                           3,072     1,392        54.69     1     1,392
                           ----------  --------
TOTAL                         207,760    97,792
```

This has been a long chapter, but hopefully you will now begin to appreciate what is involved in managing a database. Many of the tasks described here apply equally to a traditional OLTP database. It's often the size of the data warehouse that makes the task different.

Remember that it is better to manage now than not at all. Failure to back up the database or monitor space usage could have disastrous results, usually when you can least afford the time.

8 Warehousing and the Internet

8.1 OVERVIEW

You may be starting to read this chapter and wonder what the Internet has to do with data warehousing. Most of us, when we first think of the Internet, probably think about checking out a company's product or placing an order, so what does that have to do with our data warehouse?

One of the problems is that the Internet has become a term that people use, but it has several interpretations. The *Internet* is the global connection of public computers, but sat behind the Internet is a company *Intranet,* and this is the part of the Internet that we are interested in.

Those organizations that have a presence on the Internet most likely have built up an internal Web site for use by employees only, which is known as an intranet. Here they can place sensitive information, knowing that the firewall between their intranet and the global Internet keeps that information secure. There are a number of companies that only have intranets, and they find this a very useful means of communication. It is also worth remembering that an intranet does not have to be connected to the Internet, thus it can be completely independent.

So what does a company place on its intranet? Well the possibilities are endless:

- press releases
- product information
- software to download
- telephone lists
- site information
- employee details
- sales information
- historical data
- trends and analysis
- many different types of reports and documents

At first glance, this list looks like a typical Internet site, but its the last items—sales information, historical data, and trends and analysis—that differentiate it from the normal Internet and indicate a role for our data warehouse.

Internal intranets are full of useful information and provide an excellent mechanism for communicating with your employees, no matter what office they may be located in. For example, before the intranet, if there was a report that an employee needed, she would have to request that report and then wait for the paper copy to arrive on her desk. Now the intranet changes all of that, because standard reports can be created and then published on the Intranet for staff to review, or they could create reports themselves using the tools described in this book.

Of course, if you are concerned about security, information can be protected so that only certain staff can review sensitive information. Aside from the internal security issues, the benefits of this approach can be significant. Now the report is available to everyone, no matter the location, once it has been run. No longer do you have to wait for it to arrive in the internal mail.

If you are working from a hotel, home, or dialing in from some location, you can still review the report. You could even consider converting the report into a spreadsheet so that it can be downloaded and manipulated locally.

Other ways that you can use the intranet against your warehouse is to have reports that a user can request via the intranet, or the user could even interact directly to specify the report he requires and wait for the results to return. Hopefully, now you are beginning to appreciate how the intranet can help solve your report publishing and distribution problems and provide a mechanism for your users to have access to the very latest information.

For example, suppose you have a static report. You could automatically re-generate that report, say, every hour and publish it on the Web or refresh it on demand as users request it. On-line interaction with reports has traditionally not been feasible with a data warehouse because queries can take hours to run. But now, with features like Summary Management, a query that used to take hours can be reduced to seconds.

Before you can start using the intranet with your data warehouse, you must first have an intranet in place. The first section of this chapter will discuss how to set up a simple a Web server. We will not discuss how to set up a firewall and other security issues because they are outside the scope of this book.

Instead, we will first see how to set up Oracle's Web Application Server ,which is the product we will use here to display our web pages. Then we will see how we can take information from our data warehouse and publish it on the intranet. You can use any web server product to set up your intranet; however, you should check that it will support your tools.

One final point: the terms web, intranet and Internet all mean the same thing in the context of this text, and that is a web-based system.

8.2   ORACLE APPLICATION SERVER

Before we see how we can use our intranet with the data warehouse, we will first discuss what is involved in setting up a *Web server*. Here we will review Oracle Application Server version 4. You could use another Web server, although the procedures would be different. If you use Oracle Application Server, then your Web environment can be built using components such as the PL/SQL cartridge. If you used Microsoft Internet Information Server, then the application would be built using active server pages and access to the database would be via ODBC.

The *Web server* is a very important piece of software, because this is where you define, configure, and run your intranet. Unlike other software, it doesn't have to reside where your data warehouse is located. Therefore, it could be on the machine where the warehouse is running, or it could be running on another machine that could even be running a different operating system from the one that you are using for the data warehouse.

Also, your intranet will probably have many Web servers, especially if you are a global organization. For example, there could be Web servers at your offices in London, Paris, New York, and Boston

Figure 8.1 illustrates the architecture used in a Web environment in a simple form. That is, a *Browser* constructs the initial request, which is passed to the Web server, which then passes it on to the Web agent or cartridge. The HTTP listener receives the request and passes it to the Web request broker, which invokes the appropriate cartridge that talks to the data warehouse. The data warehouse responds with the requested information in HTML, which is passed back through the various components and displayed on your browser.

Figure 8.1 Web Architecture

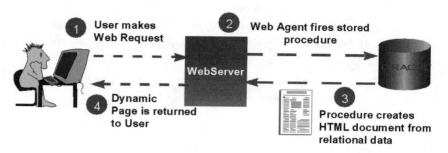

At first glance, this may seem rather involved, but the software handles all of the complexities, and there is usually a simple configuration process so that setup takes a minimal amount of time.

The architecture in Figure 8.1 works fine if everything is on the same machine, but what if your data warehouse is on a Unix box, for instance, but you want your Web server to run on Windows NT? The solution to this problem is to use the Web cartridge. In Figure 8.2, we can see how the machine where the Web server is running is not important because we are using client-server computing to manage our environment.

Figure 8.2 Using a Web Server on a Different Machine

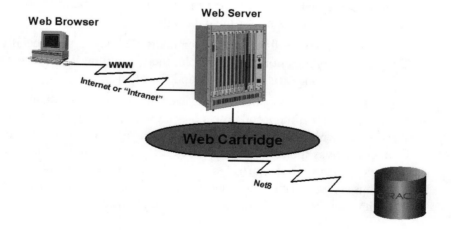

8.2.1   **Getting Started**

If you do not already have the Oracle Web Application Server running within your organization, then one must be set up and running. Readers may skip this section if one already exists; otherwise, a short overview of set up is included here.

Once the software has been installed, the setup steps must be followed exactly as per the installation guide; otherwise, your Web server will not run correctly.

Hint: Make sure that the Oracle Web Node Manager has been started, or your browser will fail to connect to the Web server.

The nice about configuring your Web server is that it is all done through your browser. Therefore, you simply start your browser, specify the URL as your *nodename : port number,* where the port number is usually "8888" for the administration process. The port number is extremely important when you are trying to administer the database because it is the one that determines that you see the administration screen in Figure 8.3 and not the standard home page. By default, the node manager port is "888," and the administration port is "8889," but this can be changed during installation.

Before the screen in Figure 8.3 appears, you will be asked to enter a user name and password. This will be the one that was specified during installation. By default, the user name is "admin."

Figure 8.3 OAS Administration

It is important to remember this screen, because, from here, you can perform tasks such as manage your Web environment, view the on-line documentation, and run the supplied demos to see some of the capabilities of Oracle Web Application Server.

To configure our Web server, click the mouse on *OAS Manager,* and the screen in Figure 8.4 will appear. The first step we need to complete is starting all of the components used by the Web server. This is achieved by selecting *All* in the right window and then clicking on the *Play* button in the window above. A new window will appear which displays the status of the operation.

Using the video-style control box shown in Figure 8.4, you can also stop any of these components by clicking on the *Stop* button. Once again, another window will appear showing the status of the operation. With all these extra windows appearing, always click the *OK* button at the bottom of the display to ensure that the window disappears when you have checked that there were no errors.

Figure 8.4 Starting the Components

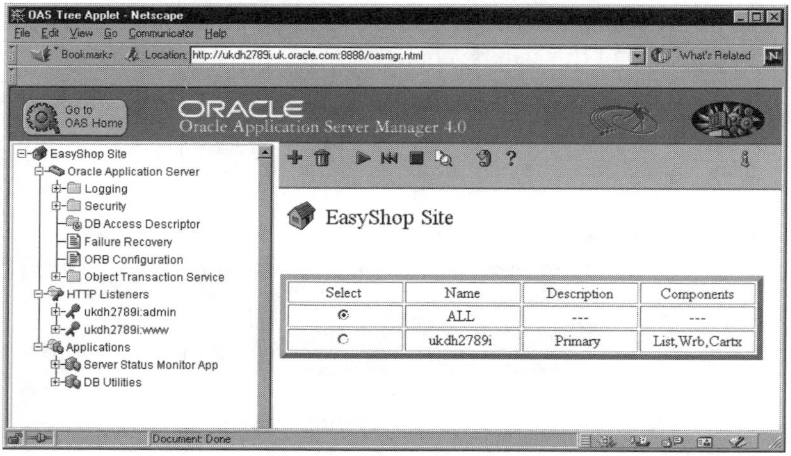

To check that all of the components have been started correctly, click on the name of your Web server site, which is shown in the left navigation window. In our example, it is called "EasyShop." Then select one of the components such as HTTP Listeners, as illustrated in Figure 8.5.

Figure 8.5 Status of the Components

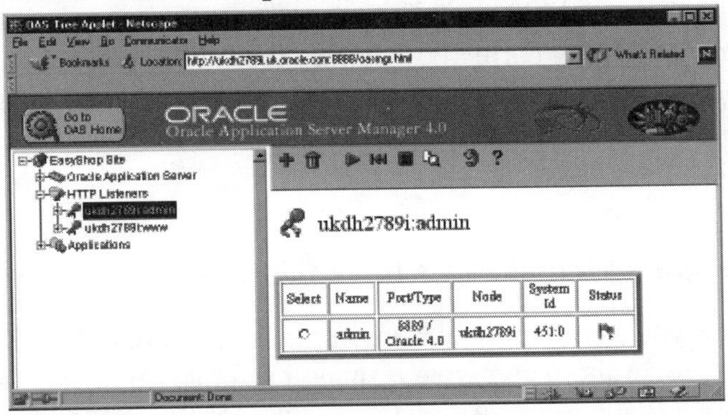

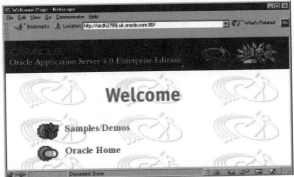

The right window will then show the status of the component by a red or green flag in the status column. Our flag is green, which means everything is working correctly.

Hint: If the status flag for an application is red, it could just mean that the application has not yet been used, because they start automatically when they are first requested.

8.2.2   Testing the Environment

Before proceeding, it's a good idea to check that your Web server is working correctly. When it was installed, two HTTP listeners were created to listen for requests. The way they work is that they are assigned a port number, where "80" is the port for general access, and "8888" is the port to administer the database. If you install the utilities, port "8889" will be used.

Figure 8.6 Default Screen

Therefore, to access the default document in the general area, you would enter the following URL into your browser *http://computer_name:80* and if everything is working correctly, then the screen in Figure 8.6 will appear. If it isn't working, then check that all the components have been started correctly, as described in the previous section, and also double-check that your network is working correctly.

8.2.3   Mapping Virtual Paths to Real Computer Directories

Once you know that your environment is sound, the next step you would probably want to complete is mapping actual directories on the computer to the *virtual paths* or *virtual directories* that a user specifies in a URL. If you have ever wondered how a URL such as "http://ukdh2789i.uk.oracle.com/easydw/Jan99.html" finds the document in your system, then now all will become clear. If we look closer at this URL, the part, "ukdh2789i.uk.oracle.com" refers to the name of our computer and the domain. And the part EASYDW refers to an actual directory on our computer that has been defined as part of the setup. You can create as many of these *virtual paths* as you need by using the administration tool, selecting the www HTTP listener, and then select *Directory* from the list of options, as shown in the left window in Figure 8.7.

Figure 8.7 Creating a Virtual Path

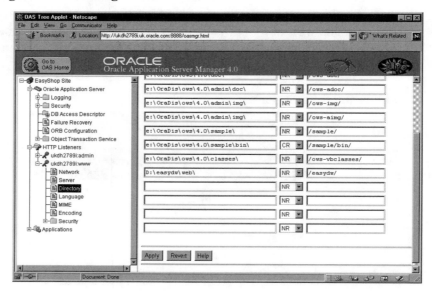

Your virtual path is specified in the right window. Referring to Figure 8.7, we can see that, on the right side, we specify the virtual location EASYDW and then, on the left side, we specify actually where it exists, which, in this case, on the Windows NT machine, is D:\easydw\web.

Therefore, every time the user includes the virtual path EASYDW in this URL, the Web server translates this to the directory D:\easydw\web. You can and will create many of these virtual locations , so get to know this place. You will be visiting it quite a bit in the early stages of your Web development.

Hint: Don't forget to terminate each definition with a forward or backward slash as appropriate.

8.2.4 Security

One of the areas that often concerns people with the Internet is security. There are a number of issues here, such as:

- Can the public see our Web site?
- Should everyone in the company see all of the information?
- Are certain pages available only to specific users?
- Can only specific groups gain access to a given area?

  When we are publishing data from the warehouse, it is quite likely that we may want only people from a certain department or specific users to see that information. Fortunately, Oracle Application Server allows us to protect our data in the following different ways:

- By using a domain name
- By using a user name
- By using an IP address
- By using certificates

Irrespective of the technique chosen to protect data, the process is almost the same; therefore, here we shall show how to protect our data by user. You can, of course, use any number of these different techniques. One final point to remember is that we are not describing here a totally secure Web site. You can identify one of these because the URL will begin HTTPs rather than HTTP.

Referring to our EASYDW example, suppose we have created a report for the CEO of the company that only he and his fellow senior executives may view. First we create a directory on the system and then map a virtual location to that directory, as we saw in the previous section. Now we will protect this virtual location so that anyone who requires access will have to specify a user name and a password.

This level of security protection is achieved by displaying the Administration window in our browser, selecting HTTP listeners, selecting the generic "www" listener, and expanding the navigator until we find the *Security* section. When the security section is expanded, you can see the various types of security available. We want to pick *Basic,* which will bring up the screen shown in Figure 8.8.

Basic security is enabled by naming a *user* along with their password. In Figure 8.8, we have created a user called "Lilian." Note that the password box is blank; it will always show as blank, even though a password exists for this user.

Figure 8.8 Basic Security Users and Groups

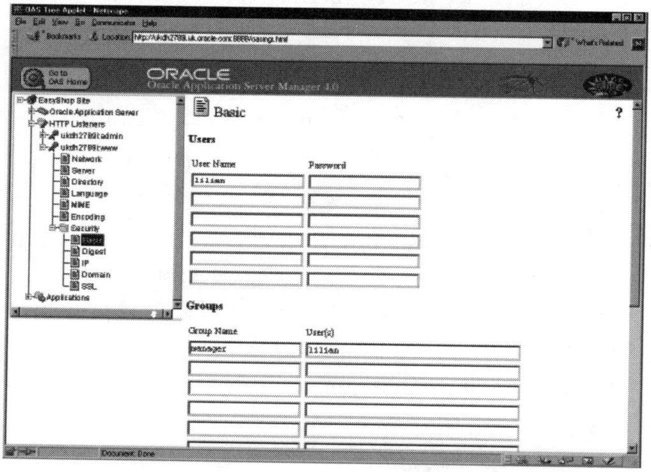

A user is then assigned to a *group,* and we have said that "Lilian" belongs to the manager group. In Figure 8.9, we can see the remainder of the basic security screen where groups are assigned to a *realm.* In our example, our manager group is assigned to the realm "easymgr."

Figure 8.9 Basic Security Groups and Realms

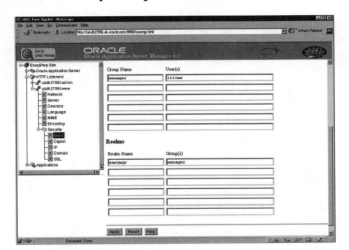

By having these three different categories, it then makes it very easy to grant data access to an entire group.

When you are finished setting up the users, groups, and realms, click on the *Apply* button to save your changes, and then click on *Security* in the left navigation window and Figure 8.10 will appear.

This is the place where you map security to a *virtual location*. Therefore, referring to our example, we can see that for the virtual location EASYDW, which we just created, we have stated that:

- Users have read access
- Users use the basic security method
- Realm "easymgr" has access to this location
- group manager has access to this location

There are some other security options that may be specified, but they are not required for this example and, therefore, can be ignored.

Figure 8.10 Securing a Directory

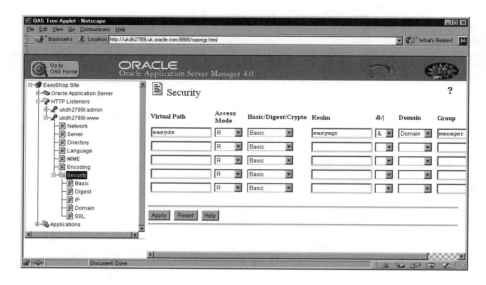

Now our page is secure, and, whenever anyone tries to access a document at that location, before the information is displayed they will see the box displayed in Figure 8.11.

Figure 8.11 User Name Required to View Web Page

Hopefully you will agree that it has been very easy to secure our data. What is also nice is that the process of asking and checking the user name and password is dealt with by the Oracle Application Server software and is outside of your HTML document. Therefore, you do not have to code any complex security checks into your application.

Figure 8.11 illustrates the simple box that is displayed requesting your user name and password. Failure to enter the correct information will prevent you from continuing further.

If this box looks familiar, it should, because when you first started the Administration utility you would have seen a box identical to this where you entered the user name *admin* and its password, which then displayed the administration window.

8.3   TOOLS FOR CREATING WEB DOCUMENTS

Now that we know that our Web server is working correctly, you can now start creating your Web documents. There are various methods that you can use, such as:

- HTML, the language used by browsers
- Java, for writing powerful applications
- JavaScript, a Java look-alike embedded in HTML
- Web Authoring Tools, to create HTML

In the examples shown here, we will hand craft the language by entering it ourselves, but it doesn't have to be this way. There are a number of tools available to facilitate easy Web document creation, especially when it comes to writing HTML.

Tools such as Adobe PageMill, Microsoft Front Page, or Netscape Composer enable you to work with a WYSIWYG (what you see is what you get) tool to lay out your Web page. Then, when you are satisfied with its content, you can automatically generate the HTML needed to produce the Web page and publish it on your Web site.

8.3.1   HTML

HTML, which stands for Hypertext Markup Language, is the language used by a browser such as Netscape Navigator to produce the Web pages that you have seen on Internet sites. HTML has evolved over the years into quite a powerful language, and first we will see how we can use it to create static Web documents and then progress on to more dynamic Web documents where the data displayed depends on what you requested.

The simple Web page you can create is a static Web document, which contains information that can be changed only by recreating the HTML statements. Therefore, every time you request the page, you will see the same information.

The HTML language uses what are known as *tags,* and most tags have an opening and closing version. For example, you start a document using the tab <HTML> and you define the end of the document using the tag </HTML>. Tags can be nested, and many tags have parameters. For example, to include a graphic using the <IMG> tag, inside the tag we would add the parameter SRC= to advise which graphic file to use. If you are used to writing any type of computer language, then you will very quickly understand HTML.

One important point that you should remember when writing HTML is that it is an evolving language. Therefore, be careful when choosing new statements if your organization doesn't update its browser software regularly. Otherwise, you could find that either no one can read your Web page or that, you force a company-wide upgrade, which probably will not make you very popular with the IT department.

For those of you who are not familiar with HTML, Figure 8.12 shows a simple static page for our Easy Shopping Inc. example.

Here we have:

- Changed the background color to white <BODY BGCOLOR=>
- Aligned the text <P ALIGN=CENTER>
- Included a graphic <IMG>
- Included headings <H1> and <H2>
- Generated a bulleted list <UL> and <LI>
- Drawn a blank line <HR>
- Constructed a table <TABLE>
- Given the reader the chance to send us E-mail <A HREF= >

Figure 8.12 Simple Static Web Page

In Figure 8.13, we can see the HTML that was used to generate this page, which was created using a standard text editor. The file was saved in the same directory that is pointed to by our virtual location, EASYDW, using an extension of HTML. We called it index.html.

Therefore, when the browser is giving the URL of

```
http://ukdh2789i.uk.oracle.com/easydw/index.html
```

It goes to the directory pointed to by EASYDW and looks for a file called index.html. These tags are then translated into the display you see in Figure 8.12, using the tags shown in Figure 8.13.

Figure 8.13 HTML for our Simple Static Web Page

```
<HTML>
<TITLE>Easy Shopping Inc Home Page </TITLE>
<BODY BGCOLOR="#FFFFFF">

<H1 ALIGN=CENTER> Easy Shopping Inc</H1>
<IMG ALIGN="right" SIZE = 10% SRC="shop2.gif">

<P ALIGN=CENTER>
Welcome to the Home Page for Easy Shopping Inc.
<BR><BR>
<P ALIGN=LEFT>We want to ensure that every customer
<UL TYPE=SQUARE>
<LI>has a pleasant experience shopping with us
<LI>always pays the best rice
<LI>never has to wait more than 3 days for their goods
   to be delivered
</UL>

<HR SIZE=5 WIDTH=75% ALIGN=CENTER>
<H2 ALIGN=CENTER>Store Locations</H2>
<TABLE>
```

```
<TABLE BORDER>
<TR><TH>Store </TH><TH>Location</TH><TH>Telephone </
        TH></TR>
<TR><TD>Southampton</TD><TD>High St</TD><TD>(703) 897
        1234 </TD></TR>
<TR><TD>Nashua</TD><TD>The Mall</TD><TD>(603) 234
        5678</TD> </TR>
</TABLE>
<BR><BR>
If you need further information contact
<A HREF="mailto:custserv@easyinc.com"> customer
        services. </A>
</BODY>
</HTML>
```

Hint: The spelling on many of the parameters will be the American version such as COLOR= rather than COLOR=. Therefore, if a parameter isn't working, verify your spelling.

Figure 8.12 illustrates the difference between a dynamic and static Web page, because the list of store locations is explicitly written in HTML. Referring to the example, if you look at the <TABLE> tag and then the line entries for the table, defined using the tags <TR> and <TD>, you can see that each store has its own entry in the table. While this approach is fine, it still means that somebody has to update information if a new store is opened or an existing one closes.

In the early days of the Internet, it was quite common to visit a Web page and view potentially out-of-date information. Today, we will create a dynamic Web page where the list of store locations is retrieved from our data warehouse, thus ensuring that we always display the latest store information.

The HTML language is very extensive in the facilities that it offers and is continually evolving, which is very important because the demands being placed on it grow every day. As more and more businesses start to use the Internet as a place of commerce, the HTML language must provide the commands to enable you to easily run your business.

Therefore, it must be no surprise that other languages are trying to provide an alternative approach to writing Web-based applications, and one of the main contenders is Java.

8.3.2   Java

Java is a language developed by Sun MicroSystems, which is taking the computer world by storm because it is such a versatile language. It's designed for the challenges of building applications of the 90s and the next millennium, especially for the Internet or company intranet. While HTML is ideal for presenting information over the Web, such as product details, company data, etc. JAVA has to be the language of choice when you start to write applications that involve transactions such as buying or selling goods or managing your bank account or portfolio of stocks.

Unlike conventional programming languages, Java can be used in several ways. For example, you can write a stand-alone Java program, or what is known as a Java applet. It is Java *applets* that are of interest to the Web-user, because an applet is a self-contained program that is embedded in your HTML document. Provided your browser supports Java, when you request the Web page, the applet is automatically downloaded to your computer and executed there. Java applets are ideal to use when there is to be a high level of interaction with your users.

Using this approach, the person reading the Web page doesn't have to copy the Java applet; rather, it is done automatically for them. Whenever the applet is updated by the owner, you will always receive the latest copy. Another important benefit of writing Java applications is that they will execute on any computer, regardless of the operating system, provided it has a Java-capable browser.

However, the real power to the application developer is in the Java language itself. It is extremely comprehensive and, of course, includes all the commands to interact with your user via typical GUI mechanisms such as windows and buttons.

You have probably visited many Web sites and may not have realized that the power behind the page comes from a Java applet. Earlier, in Chapter 6, we discussed Oracle Time Series. A demo is available that illustrates some of the features Time Series has to offer. All the information that you see on the screen is displayed by a Java applet, which is responsible for:

- asking the user for data
- obtaining the information from the database
- displaying the data
- providing windows GUI-style interface native to the machine

However, the HTML required to embed this applet is as simple as that shown in the example below. First we use the <APPLET> tag to define the characteristics of the applet, and then we pass in some parameters identifying where the database to be used is located, the instance name, which is ORCL and the location on our Web server where other files can be found. Now whenever we call this Web document, our Java program will be run.

```
<HTML>
<HEAD> <TITLE> Java Applet in HTML </TITLE> </HEAD>
<BODY>
TSDemoApplet will appear below in a Java enabled
  browser.<BR>
<APPLET
 ARCHIVE = "jbcl.zip,chart.zip"
 CODEBASE = "."
 CODE   = "airdemo.class"
 NAME   = "TestApplet"
 WIDTH = 640
 HEIGHT = 510
 HSPACE = 0
 VSPACE = 20
 ALIGN = middle
>
<PARAM NAME = "ConnectString" VALUE =
  "jdbc:oracle:thin:@ukdh2789i:1521:orcl">
<PARAM NAME = "XMLConnectString" VALUE = "http://
ukdh2789i.uk.oracle.com/xml/plsql
        ordsys.ordtxml.OracleTimeSeries">
</APPLET>
</BODY>
</HTML>
```

Hopefully now you can begin to appreciate how your web pages can come alive. From your Java applet you can obtain any data from your warehouse and return it to your users. Thus enabling them to see the latest position and potentially in some unusual format.

Java and Oracle 8*i*

When it comes to using Java against your Oracle 8*i* database, a number of options are available to you. On the server, Oracle 8*i* provides *Java Servers,* and you have the choice of using:

- Oracle JServer VM (Java Virtual Machine)
- Java cartridge in Oracle Application Server

If you choose to use Oracle JServer VM, then database programmers will be able to write database-stored procedures, triggers, and object-relational methods in Java. They would then invoke that Java procedure using the same technique as for a PL/SQL procedure.

A Java developer can write what is known as an *Enterprise Java Bean,* which is a server-side reusable piece of Java code. For those people developing distributed systems, CORBA servers in Java can be implemented.

Alternatively, you can install the Java cartridge as part of your Oracle Application Server environment, and then you can develop Java applications using:

- JCORBA interface, for developing CORBA servers
- JWeb, for generating static web pages in Java

On the *client* side, you can use:

- JDBC (Java Database Connectivity)
- SQLJ (SQL embedded inside Java)
- JDeveloper, a development environment for creating Java applications

If all of this seems a bit confusing, then hopefully Figure 8.14 clarifies what you need to use Java against in your Oracle 8*i* database.

Figure 8.14 The Java Programming APIs

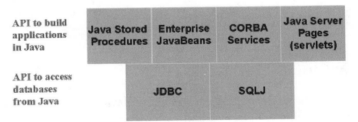

With Oracle 8*i,* your Java programs can be stored inside the database, so you never need to worry about where they being stored. Therefore, you can share them across all applications, and you can store either the Java source or a Java archive file, which has a file extension of .jar.

In Figure 8.15, we can see how a Java-stored procedure is held in the database alongside PL/SQL procedures, and then we can see how it is invoked from the client using different methods.

Figure 8.15 Using Java-Stored Procedures

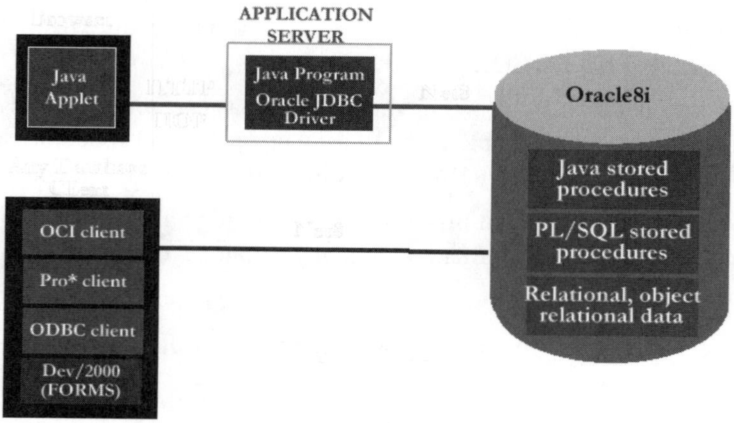

We have but skimmed the surface here of what is possible with Java and Oracle 8*i*. Since Java is a real programming language, there is very little that cannot be achieved inside a Java application. Therefore, as soon as you want to do anything fairly complex, it makes sense to write that application in Java if it is going to be used on a Web-based system.

It is highly recommended that you discover as much as you can about Java before you use it against your warehouse. This way, you won't be disappointed with the results.

8.3.3   JavaScript

An alternative to writing Java is to use JavaScript in your HTML. JavaScript was created by Netscape and provides many of the features found in Java without the need to learn the Java language. It should also be noted at this point that Java and JavaScript are quite different.

However, on the surface it may appear that they offer similar functionality because, using JavaScript, you can create a Web page that interacts with your user by asking for input and then determining what is displayed next according to their requests. You can also display dialog boxes, start new windows, and access data in your database. But Java is a very comprehensive programming language offering much more; therefore, depending on your requirements, JavaScript may not always be able to perform the tasks asked of it.

8.3.4   Web Authoring Tools

There are a number of tools available to help you create Web documents. Popular ones like Microsoft Front Page, Netscape Composer, and Adobe Page Mill are primarily designed for creating static Web pages. Which one you choose will depend on your own needs. Of course, you can still create the source document by hand. For Java developers, Oracle provides the JDeveloper tool.

8.4   PUBLISHING REPORTS ON THE INTRANET

Now that we have set up our Web server and seen some of the tools available to us to interact with our users. Let us now see how we can publish data in our warehouse on the Intranet without having to write any HTML or Java application code.

All of the tools illustrated here show you how to generate documents containing data from your data warehouse, although with some of these tools you can automatically regenerate the Web page at some specified interval to obtain the latest position. In Section 8.4, we will see how to access our data warehouse directly and report the latest information from the data warehouse.

Figure 8.16 Specify the SQL Query

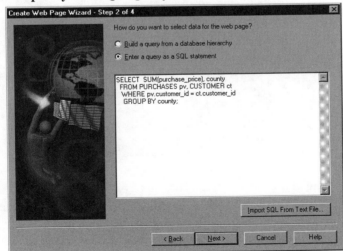

8.4.1   Oracle Web Publishing Assistant

Oracle Web Publishing Assistant is a tool that helps you create static Web pages containing information from your Oracle 8*i* database and is installed when you install Oracle 8*i* on an NT machine. Once created, the information does not have to stay constant because you can schedule the pages to be rebuilt automatically with the latest data. Therefore, it is not the same as a true dynamic page where, at the point in time when you query the database, you are guaranteed to see the latest information. Instead, you view the state as of the last refresh period. What is attractive about this process is that you do not have to re-create the document manually because the assistant will do that for you.

When the tool first starts, the screen in Figure 8.20 will appear. By clicking on the + button, which creates a new Web-page, and then providing your user name and password to log on to the data warehouse, the screen in Figure 8.16 will appear. Here you have the choice of either directly writing the SQL to query the database, as shown below, or picking the tables and columns, as shown in Figure 8.17.

Figure 8.17 Select the Columns and Tables

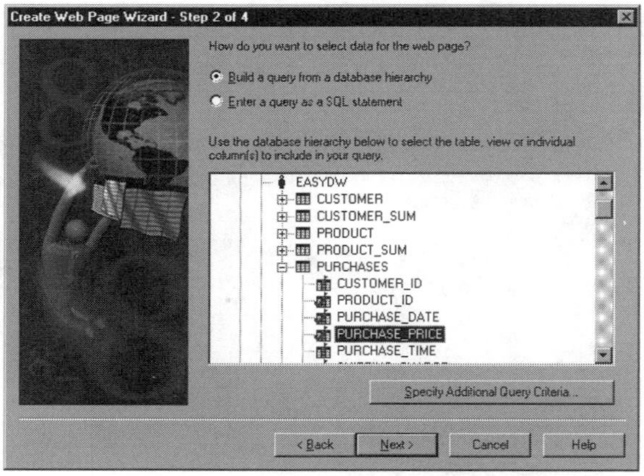

Note how all of the tables are displayed, including our summary or materialized views, which we created earlier. To include specific columns, simply expand each table, and click on the column so that a tick mark appears to include it in the report. In Figure 8.17, we can see that we have selected that only the columns product_id, purchase date and purchase price be displayed from the purchases table.

Once the query has been defined, we must now specify how often the Web page is to be updated. In Figure 8.18, we can see the various options. For this Web page, we have asked that it be refreshed every hour, but you have a wide range of time intervals ranging from one minute to "Do it manually."

Figure 8.18 Specifying Frequency for Web Page Refreshing

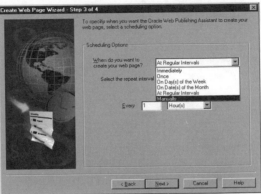

In our example for our EASY Shopping data warehouse, we have stated that this Web page is to be updated every hour. Therefore, once an hour this tool will regenerate the Web page, create a new version, and store it in the location indicated by Figure 8.19.

In Figure 8.18, we specify the physical location of the document. Virtual paths must not be used here. We have decided to call this page productsales.htm. Since you are likely to create many documents, try to choose some meaningful names for the documents to make them easier to manage.

Hint: The location for the HTML document is specified using an actual location and not a URL address.

Figure 8.19 Naming the Web Page

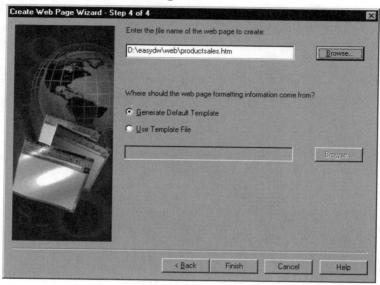

As each Web page is created, it will be listed in the main window of Oracle Web Publishing Assistant, which is illustrated in Figure 8.20. Here we can see that currently we have created two Web pages for our Easy Shopping data warehouse, called "product sales" and "customer sales."

Figure 8.20 Web Publishing Assistant Web Pages

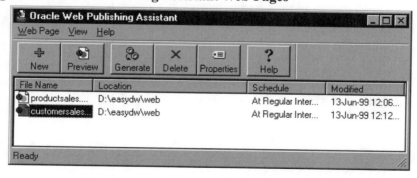

From this window, we can also see how often the Web page is refreshed and the date and time of the last refresh.

We can also:

- Change the refresh interval
- Delete a Web page

- Request an automatic regeneration of a Web page
- Preview a Web page
- Create new Web pages

In Figure 8.21, we can now see the Web page created by this tool. It should be noted that this one is not very exciting, but if we were to replace the default template with one that incorporated standard information and graphics, then this page would appear just like any of the Web pages on our Web site. Alternatively, if the page was never to be refreshed again, then we could edit the source directly to suit out own requirements.

Figure 8.21 Web Page Created by Web Publishing Assistant

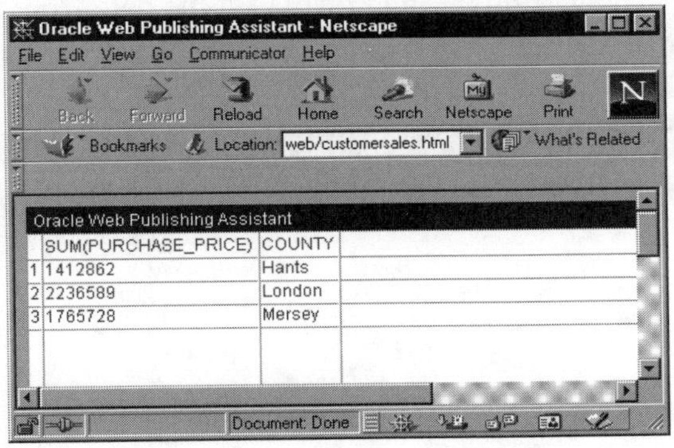

Oracle Web Publishing Assistant may be a simple tool, but at least you can create reasonable quality documents quite quickly without knowing how to access your database from HTML.

8.4.2   Oracle Express Web Publisher

Provided with Oracle Express is a tool called Oracle Express Web Publisher, which allows you to create an Express *briefing* that can be viewed from your Web browser. Unfortunately, you cannot take a briefing created by Sales Analyzer and turn that into a Web document; instead, you must create a new briefing inside this tool.

When Oracle Express Web Publisher first starts, you must name a *Web site,* which is where your Web briefings will be stored. Next, select the Express database that you wish to report on. You are now ready to create a Web briefing.

If this is the first time that you have run Express Web Publisher, then you will have to create a new Web site by selecting *File* from the strip menu and then New Website. You can now add pages to your Web briefing by selecting *Insert* from the strip menu; then, select *WebBriefing* to create a briefing. Next, select *Insert Web Page,* and the box in Figure 8.22 will appear, where you specify the type of Web page you require.

There are several different types of Web page that you can create. The first one we will look at is the data view, where the wizard will automatically create a header, a footer, and display some data from the Express database.

Figure 8.22 Oracle Express Web Publisher

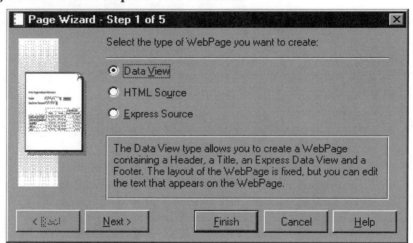

The first question asked by the wizard is to give your Web page a name, as illustrated in Figure 8.23. Choose something useful, because this name will appear in the navigation window and it should assist you in knowing what is on the page.

Figure 8.23 Naming the Express Document

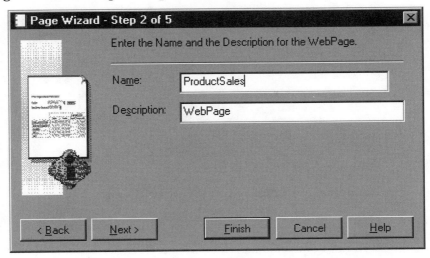

Now you can specify the text that is to appear as a heading, the title on the Web page, and as the footer, as shown in Figure 8.24.

Figure 8.24 Title, Header & Footer for Oracle Express

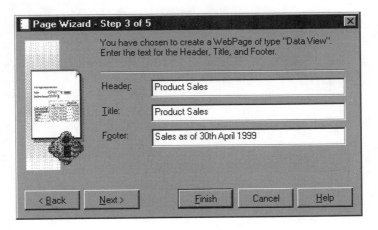

Figure 8.25 Oracle Express—Type of Report

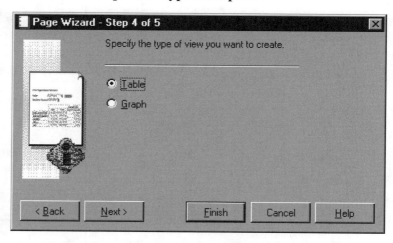

It must now seem almost a tradition to ask the user whether the data is to be presented in tabular or graphical form, as illustrated in Figure 8.25. Then you click on the *Finish* button, and the screen in Figure 8.26 will appear.

Figure 8.26 Oracle Express Web Report Example

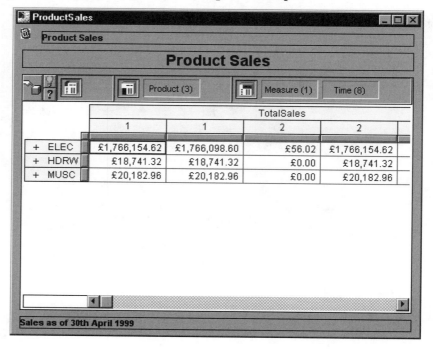

This will result in the box in Figure 8.26 appearing. However, when the screen is first displayed, it will be blank, so you will need to drag the attribute from the database window to this window, as we did before when creating reports in Express. This briefing will behave like the ones we saw earlier, so you can drill the data up and down to help with further analysis.

8.4.3   Oracle Reports for the Web

In Chapter 5, we discussed Oracle Reports. Here we will see how we can publish those reports on the Web, making them accessible to anyone via a Web browser. The Report Builder's Web Wizard makes it easy to generate HTML or Adobe Acrobat (PDF) files.

The Web Wizard, shown in Figure 8.27, is invoked by clicking the button on the *Live Previewer* toolbar

Figure 8.27 Oracle Reports Web Wizard

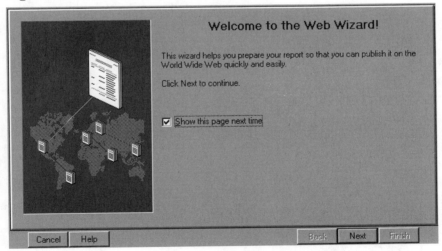

Bookmarks can be added to provide navigational capabilities to the output. They provide a hyperlinked table of contents of the report that allows users to navigate through the report easily.

In the example in Figure 8.28, bookmarks will be created for the month column, allowing users to go directly to the page containing the month they are interested in.

Figure 8.28 Creating a Bookmark

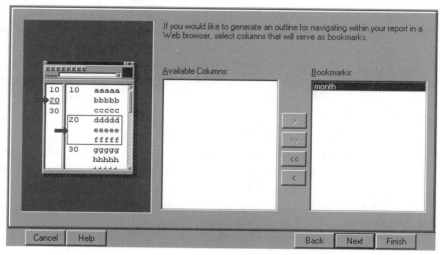

The output format is chosen, as shown in Figure 8.29. In this case, the report will be output in HTML format, but we could have chosen Adobe Acrobat (.pdf) format.

Figure 8.29 Output Format

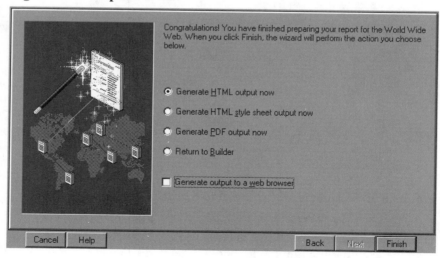

In Figure 8.30, we can see an example of the first page of the 1999 Sales by Product by Month report, previously created in Chapter 5, viewed using a

Netscape browser. The bookmarks on the left side can be used to quickly navigate to the page containing the sales for each month of the year.

Figure 8.30 Sample Web Report

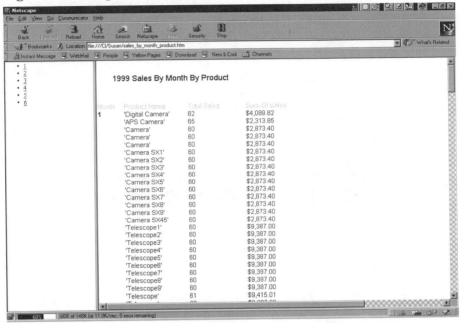

8.4.4   Discoverer

Unfortunately, at the time of writing, there are no tools available that can take a report produced by Discoverer and publish it on the Web.

8.5   INTERACTION WITH WAREHOUSE USERS

The real power of the intranet or Internet can be exploited with your data warehouse when you can access the data directly from your browser. Now we will look at what is involved in setting up our data warehouse to access it directly.

8.5.1   Database Access Descriptor

The first step is to define the DAD, which stands for *database access descriptor*. It is created from the administration area by selecting Oracle Application Server and then Database Access Descriptor. Here you give it a name and supply the user name and password that will be used to access the database, as illustrated in Figure 8.31.

If the database is remote, specify the connect string for that remote database, and then Oracle Application Server will automatically access that database and load into the appropriate information. In our example here, we specified that the database user is EASYDW. We haven't specified a connect string, because this database is local; instead, we use the EASYDW service name.

Figure 8.31 Create a Data Access Description

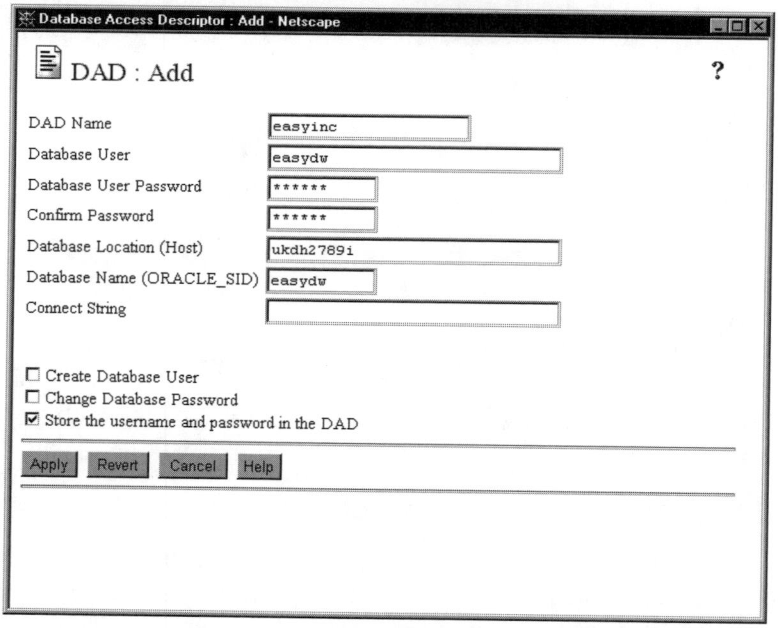

If your environment is configured such that the Web server is on one computer and the data warehouse is on another; it is not necessary to install Oracle 8*i* on the Web server machine. When Oracle Application Server was installed, it automatically added the components it requires to access the remote database. All you have to do is add an entry into the tnsnames.ora file to advise where this database is located, the protocol to use, and its instance name.

You can create as many DADs as you like. In Figure 8.32, we can see that we have created two DADs. If you are wondering why you may need multiple DADs, it is because they could be required if you want to access the database using different user names or if you have a number of different databases to access.

Figure 8.32 Database Access Descriptor

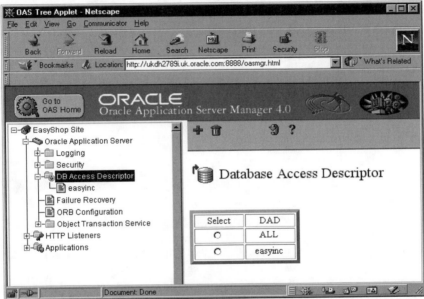

8.5.2   Database Transaction Control

If you want to have transaction control over database access once the DAD has been defined, you can set this by expanding *Applications* from the Administration menu, expanding *DB Utilities,* and then selecting *TX Property.* At this point, the screen in Figure 8.33 will appear. This is where you specify for each DAD that has been defined whether database transactions are allowed.

Figure 8.33 Database Transaction Control

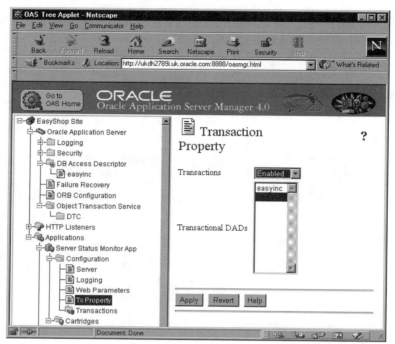

8.5.3   Using PL/SQL to Generate Web Pages

Many people prefer to write their own applications rather than use tools such as WebDB, which we will discuss shortly. PL/SQL is very popular among Oracle users for writing applications, and the good news is that you can create a PL/SQL procedure, which contains everything to interact with your users via the Internet.

This is achieved by loading into your database a set of packages that contains functions and procedures that can be called to generate HTML. In Figure 8.13, we created a static HTML page. Now we will see how to create the same Web page using PL/SQL.

We create a PL/SQL procedure that is compiled into the Oracle 8*i* data warehouse, which contains calls to functions that emulate the HTML commands. Therefore, instead of the tag <TITLE> we would use the function htp.title. Consequently, it is very easy to translate our HTML into the equivalent Oracle function calls. The procedure is stored in the database and then is called directly from your browser.

Below, we can see the PL/SQL procedure that performs part of the HTML in Figure 8.13

```
create or replace procedure easy_welcome as v_date date;
begin
 htp.htmlOpen;
 htp.headOpen;
 htp.title('Easy Shopping Inc Home Page');
 htp.headClose;
 htp.bodyOpen;
 htp.line;
 htp.img('/ows-img/shop2.gif');
 htp.header(1,'Easy Shopping Inc');
 htp.line;

 htp.paragraph;
 htp.print('Welcome to the Home Page for Easy Shopping
 Inc.');
 htp.br; htp.br;
 htp.print('We want to ensure that every customer:');
 htp.br;
 htp.print(' - has a pleasant experience shopping with us') ;
 htp.br;
 htp.print(' - always pays the best price') ; htp.br;
 htp.print(' - never has to wait more than 3 days for the
   goods to be delivered') ; htp.br; htp.br;

 htp.tableOpen;
 htp.tableRowOpen;
 htp.tableData( 'Store' );
 htp.tableData( 'Location' );
 htp.tableData( 'Telephone' );
 htp.tableRowClose;

 htp.tableRowOpen;
 htp.tableData( 'Southampton' );
 htp.tableData( 'High St' );
 htp.tableData( '(703) 897 1234' );
 htp.tableRowClose;

 htp.tableRowOpen;
 htp.tableData( 'Nashua' );
 htp.tableData( 'The Mall' );
 htp.tableData( '(603) 234 5678' );
 htp.tableRowClose;
 htp.tableClose;

 htp.bodyClose;
 htp.htmlClose;
 end;
```

We have just scratched the surface here on the functions that are provided. If you look at the examples provided with Oracle Application Server, they will show you how to create interactive forms, query your data warehouse, and display that data on the Web.

The URL required to invoke this procedure will vary from site to site, but in this instance it was "http://voyager/sample/plsql/easy_welcome," where "voyager" is the name of the computer; "sample" is a virtual location; "plsql" is a PL/SQL procedure; and "easy_welcome" is the name of the procedure created in the Oracle 8*i* data warehouse. In Figure 8.34, we can see the page generated by this PL/SQL procedure.

Figure 8.34 PL/SQL Procedure Generating a Web Page

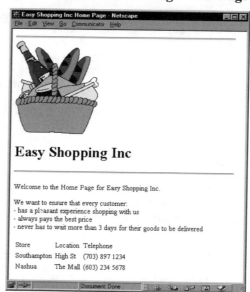

8.6   ORACLE WEBDB

There is a new facility available from Oracle 8*i* that can be used to Web-enable Oracle databases from 7.3.3 onward, called WebDB. It is installed separately and enables not only you to administer your database, but also to create a comprehensive Web-based reporting environment.

At the time of writing, you are not given the choice of which database is installed in. It currently uses the default instance. Once installed, there are a few minor extra manual setups that are required. As always, follow the installation instructions carefully. Then you are ready to start WebDB by entering the following URL into your browser. At this point, the screen in Figure 8.35 will appear.

```
http://ukp5130i.uk.oracle.com/WebDB/
```

Figure 8.35 Oracle WebDB Main Menu

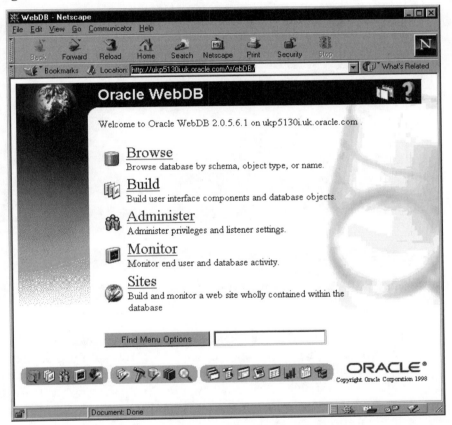

You will see that, from this main menu, we can look at our schema objects, administer the database, check up on users, and build ourselves a Web site. One of the really nice features of WebDB is that you do not have to install a Web server because it installs all of the software that you need to get started.

Before we see how to build an application containing reports from our data warehouse, let us briefly look at some of the other features that are available.

8.6.1   Schema Browser

The *schema browser* not only allows you to view the objects in your database but also to insert and amend data in the warehouse. Clicking on the word *Browse* in the main menu will result in the box in Figure 8.36 appearing. This is where you select the schema and objects to display.

Figure 8.36 Select Schema Objects

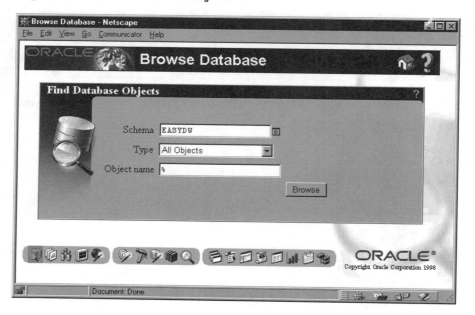

This screen is typical of the friendly environment that WebDB presents. First you select the schema. We have chosen EASYDW, but if you do not know its name, then click on the small page icon to the right of the input box, and a list of all of the available schemas will appear. You can then select any of these from the list, and it will save you typing in the entry. Then, if you are interested in a specific type of object, select it from the drop-down list. You can even restrict the items displayed to certain named objects. When you are done, click on the *Browse* button to display the screen in Figure 8.37. This is where we can see all of the tables and materialized views in our database.

Figure 8.37 List of Tables

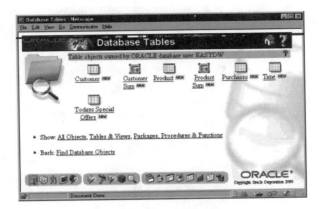

Note that, at the time of writing, a materialized view is displayed as a table and will not appear in the snapshot list. Now to look at, say, the data in our Special Offers table, click on the special offers icon. At this point, the window in Figure 8.38 will appear, which is where we specify what it is we want to see from the table and how it is to be presented.

You will see that there are lots of options here in Figure 8.38. Not only can we say that we only want the product id and offer date displayed, but we can also specify:

- How the columns are justified
- An optional WHERE clause
- How we want the data ordered
- Font size and color
- Output format
- Any columns that should be aggregated
- Columns to break the report on

Figure 8.38 Displaying Options

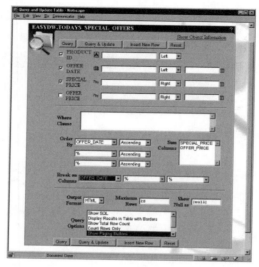

When we click on the *Query* button, the box in Figure 8.39 appears with our simple report. We can also see the contents of our materialized views from within WebDB by clicking on any of our materialized views, such as Customer_Sum and querying them as if they were tables.

Figure 8.39 Simple Report from WebDB

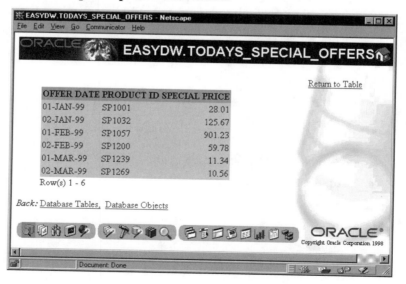

Hint: In this version of WebDB, you will be able to view only the contents of the materialized view if every computed column has been given a column alias.

Therefore, all computed columns in your materialized view must be defined as

```
SELECT SUM(purchase_price) AS total_sales .....
```

instead of

```
SELECT SUM(purchase_price), county
```

Another nice feature for the data warehouse user is that you can see the state of your materialized views. If you look carefully at the top right of the window in Figure 8.38, there is a highlighted option, *Show Object Information*. If you click on this, the box in Figure 8.40 will appear with the information that is held in the system metadata. This is where you can see information such as the query, which defines this materialized view and its current state.

Figure 8.40 Materialized View Metadata

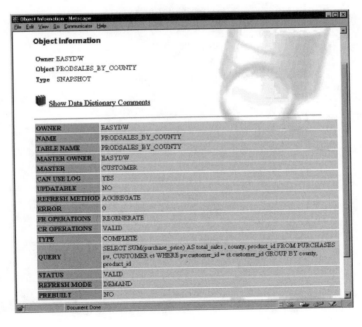

Note that the information presented here is likely to change. Therefore, when you try this with WebDB, don't be surprised if the information displayed is slightly different.

When you click on *Show Object Information* for a table, different information is displayed. One of the useful pieces of information displayed for the DBA managing the data warehouse, are the materialized views that have been defined on this table.

Referring to Figure 8.41, which shows an example of table metadata, we can see that, currently the *Customer* table has two materialized views created on it, *Customer_sum* and *Prodsales_by_County*. Clicking on either of those icons will display the information shown in Figure 8.40.

Figure 8.41 Table Metadata

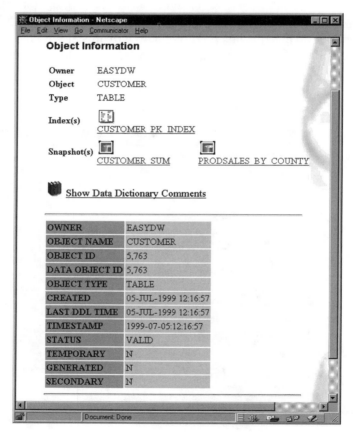

You can also use WebDB to create database objects. Unfortunately, at the time of writing, you cannot create materialized views using this interface.

8.6.2   Database Tools

Before we move on to building some reports against our data warehouse, WebDB has a lot to offer the DBA. For example, by clicking on *Monitor,* the screen in Figure 8.42 will appear enabling us to see the facilities available for monitoring our database usage.

Figure 8.42 Monitoring Tools

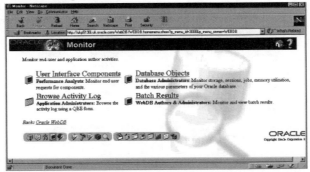

Alternatively, to see how our database is configured, click on *Database Objects*. At this point, Figure 8.43 will appear enabling us to see all of the information that can be presented about our data warehouse.

Figure 8.43 Database Information

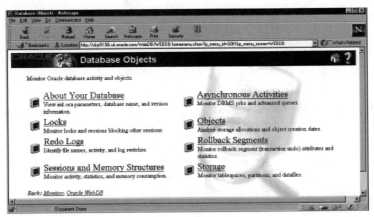

If we select *About Your Database* from the screen in Figure 8.43, then the screen in Figure 8.44 will appear. This is where we can see our init.ora parameter setting and other useful database information.

Figure 8.44 More Database Tools

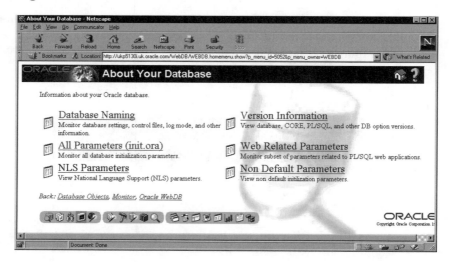

8.6.3   Creating a Menu

Menus enable users to navigate around within a Web site. These can be created by selecting *Build* from the main screen and then selecting *Menu*. You will now be inside the create menu wizard, where first you must specify into which schema the menu will reside, as illustrated in Figure 8.45.

Using these wizards, you must click on the arrow icons to move forward and backward.

Hint: While you are using the wizard, you may notice a "%" bar in the main box. This is advising how far through the menu creation process you are. Do not confuse this bar with the one displayed at the bottom of your browser, which advises how much of the Web page has been retrieved.

In this example, it is set at 20 percent. In the screen in Figure 8.45, it will increase or decrease appropriately as you move forward and backward between pages.

Figure 8.45 Name the Menu

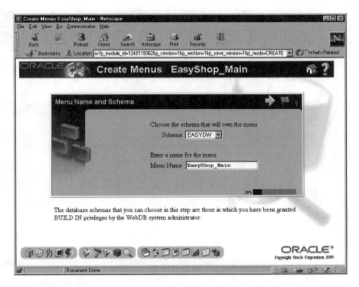

The next screen displayed by this wizard is shown in Figure 8.46, where you specify the title, header, and footer for the display. Use the *header* as a place where you can specify, say, some welcoming text to the page. In this example, we have specified the standard welcoming message from Easy Shopping Inc.

For the *footer,* we have put just the company name, but it could be a copyright notice or the date the page was last amended.

Hint: No spell-checker is available, so do check for spelling accuracy before you paste into these windows.

Moving on to the next screen, we can now specify the items that are to appear in the menu. In the example in Figure 8.47, we have specified four items to appear in the menu:

- Product list
- Store location
- Purchase goods
- Today's special offer

Figure 8.46 Headers and Footers for the Menu

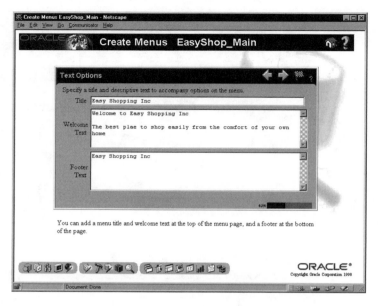

Figure 8.47 Specifying the Menu Items & URL

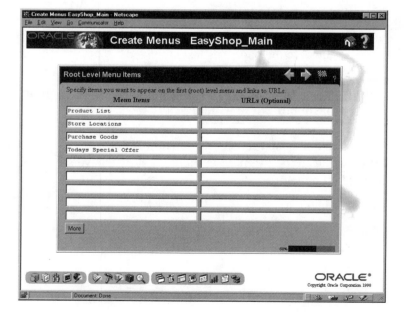

Note that, in Figure 8.47, we have not specified the URLs at this time. We will supply this detail later. This means that, if you have an idea of the menu structure you want to create, you can create it now. When the actual reports have been created, it is not difficult to return to this menu and update the URL entry or even add new menus.

We can now choose our fonts in the window in Figure 8.48 and also specify the template to be used for display purposes. In all of the examples shown in this chapter, we have used the default template; however, in practice, you would want to create one or more templates. WebDB will allow you to define many of them.

Figure 8.48 Specifying the Fonts and Template

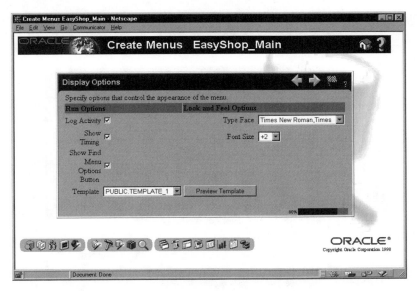

You will also find inside WebDB the ability to manage colors, fonts, and images that you want to display.

Now we click on *OK,* and a procedure is created inside our database containing our menu. Rather than run our menu directly, the screen in Figure 8.49 will appear. This is where we can see everything about our procedure, including when it was created plus a number of options such as *Edit* and *Run.* This is the standard screen that is used to administer an object in WebDB.

Figure 8.49 Managing the Menu

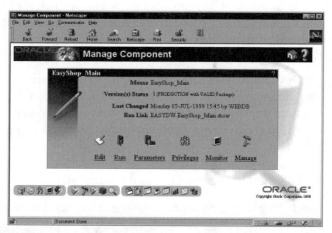

Figure 8.50 Menu from WebDB

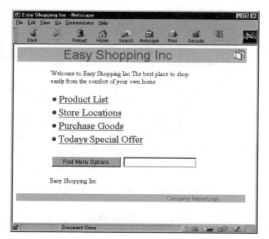

When we click on *Run*, our menu will now be displayed in our browser, as illustrated in Figure 8.50. Alternatively, we could run this menu directly from our browser be entering the URL

```
http://ukp5130i.uk.oracle.com/WebDB/EASYDW.EasyShop_Main.show
```

The naming convention for the URL is:

```
machine
        web site
                schema.procedure name
```

8.6.4   **Creating a Report**

Throughout this book, we have seen tools that help us build reports to query
our database, and WebDB is no exception in this area. Here we will see how
we can build a simple report and then link it into our menu that we created
previously.

Figure 8.51 Specifying the SQL Query

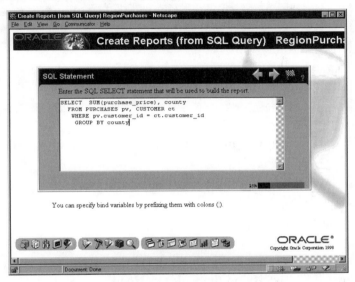

Reports are created by selecting *Build* from the main menu, then *User Interface,* and then *Reports*. A report can be created by using the wizard or directly
from a SQL query. Irrespective of the method chosen, you will step through a
number of screens that are easy to complete.

Hint: A report name cannot include a space.

Now in our example, we have chosen to specify the SQL query as illustrated
in Figure 8.51. You can cut and paste any valid SQL into this query box.
However, it is probably a good idea to check that the SQL works before you
include it here.

The next screen, Figure 8.52, is where we can name the columns and specify
our formatting options. A nice feature is that it gives us the opportunity to
specify the column names, so it is easy for us to substitute the aggregated
column SUM(purchase_price) with the heading Total Purchases.

Figure 8.52 Specifying the Column Headings

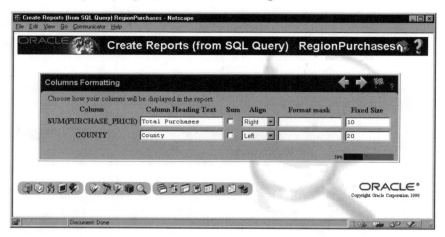

WebDB provides us with a variety of formatting options, as illustrated in Figure 8.53, such as:

- When line breaks are to occur
- How the data should be sorted
- What colors the background text should use
- Font size

Figure 8.53 Specifying the Column Headings

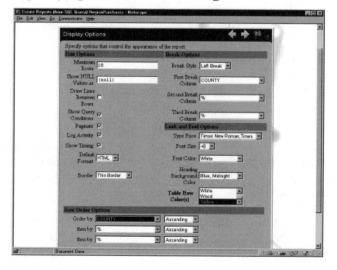

If this were a report where the user could specify a value, then the next screen will request how this data may be supplied.

Other screens allow us to specify:

- Titles
- Headers
- Footers
- PL/SQL procedures to execute before and after displaying the page

Our report is now complete. The screen in Figure 8.54 will appear, from which we can run the report. This is also the screen from which we can edit our report or perform other maintenance operations.

Figure 8.54 Managing the Component

When we run the report the screen in Figure 8.55 is displayed with the results obtained from our database.

Figure 8.55 Report from WebDB

One of the pieces of information that the report can display is the elapsed time. In this example, it took 5.34 seconds to execute this query. If you now take a look at Figure 8.56, you can see that the report took only 0.41 seconds to complete the second time. Why? Because the query rewrite feature was enabled, and materialized views existed that could satisfy the query.

Figure 8.56 Report Using Query Rewrite

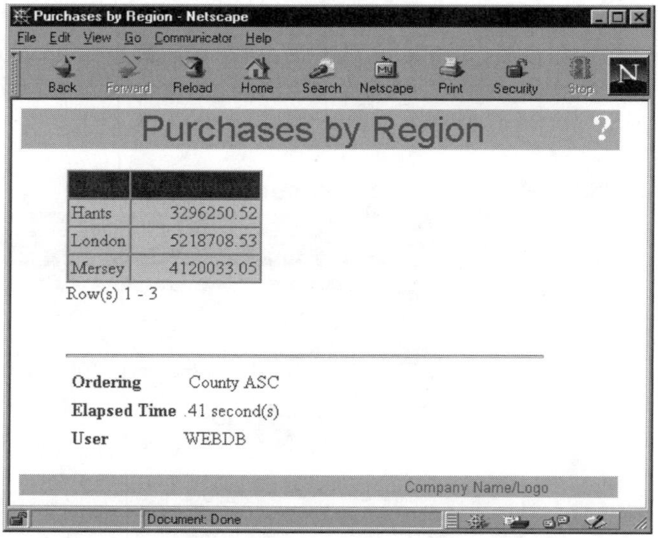

Therefore, behind the scenes, the query is automatically being rewritten to use the materialized view that satisfies this query, without the user having to do anything. The user constructed his query using WebDB, directing it at the ordinary tables in the data warehouse, and Oracle 8i has decided to ignore those tables and use the materialized views instead. Consequently, this query to the data warehouse has executed considerably faster, in only 0.41 seconds.

Finally, we need to add this report to our menu so that all of our users can run it and see results. We should also not forget that this is a dynamic report because we are retrieving the information directly from the database.

To include this report in our menu, first we request to edit our menu. The screen in Figure 8.57 will then appear. The technique used here to add an item to the menu is a little different than the wizard we discussed earlier. To add this report, click on *Add Child Menu* in the menu where you want to add the item. At this point, the screen in Figure 8.58 will appear.

Figure 8.57 Editing a Menu

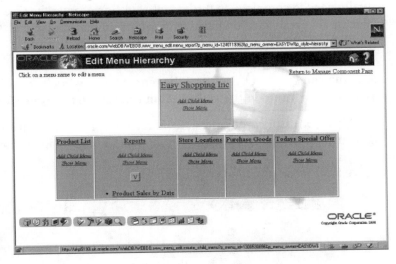

Figure 8.58 Adding an Item to the Menu

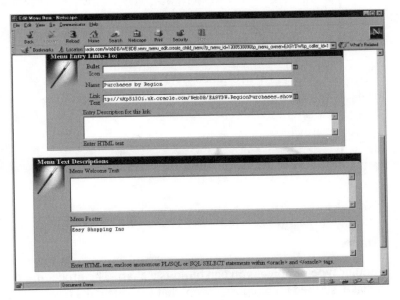

Although there is a lot of space in Figure 8.58, there is very little that you actually need to complete. In the box labeled *Name*, enter the title for the link, which, in this case, is "Purchases by Region." In the box labeled "Link Text," enter the URL used to run the report.

Hint: You can get the URL to run the report by copying it from the browser window when you run the report from the screen in Figure 8.55.

Now when you display your menu, the screen in Figure 8.59 will appear. Clicking on the report will display the one shown in Figure 8.55 or Figure 8.56.

Figure 8.59 Report Added to Menu

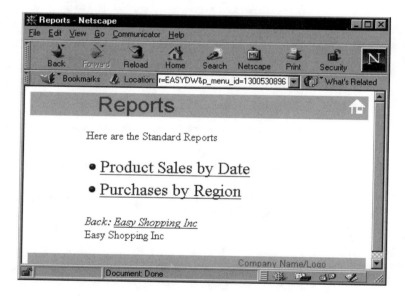

8.6.5   Charts

Another type of object you can build is a chart. The procedure is very similar to that described for a report, except that you select the *Chart* option. A sample chart is shown in Figure 8.60, which displays the total sales by day.

The questions used to generate this chart were almost identical to those shown for creating the report. This chart can also be added to our menu.

Figure 8.60 Chart from WebDB

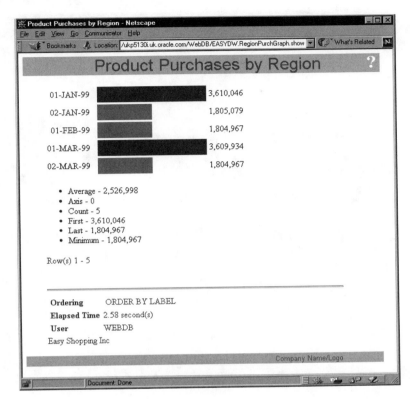

8.6.6   Using Calendars

Another nice feature in WebDB is the ability to produce a report where the output is in calendar format. Now, at first glance, this may seem a bit strange, but when you look at Figure 8.61, then you begin to realize the potential of this capability.

Every time we run this report, we are directly querying the database to see the total product sales by day, and then the value is placed against that date in the calendar. Referring to Figure 8.61, we can see the total sales for the 1st and 2nd of January. Now, although the user cannot see this, underneath there is a materialized view that ensures that this report is produced quickly.

The steps are almost identical to those for creating a report or chart, except for some additional options, such as specifying how long a calendar is to be produced.

Figure 8.61 Calendar Report from WebDB

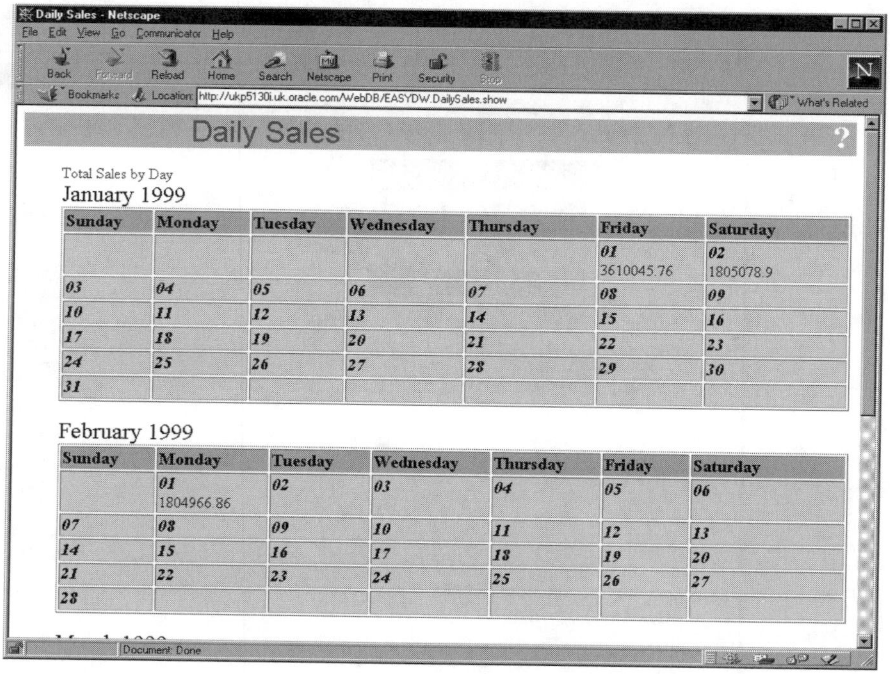

8.6.7   Dynamic Web Pages

WebDB will also enable you to create an HTML document that includes PL/SQL calls directly to the database. Here you are prompted to write HTML and write direct calls to the database. This could be one way of creating a very nice Web page in exactly the format that you require, showing the latest data in your data warehouse.

Figure 8.62 illustrates the window where you enter the HTML and PL/SQL. In this example, we are simply finding out the current number of orders in our Purchases table; however, imagine what you could do here if you are an experienced HTML programmer.

Figure 8.62 HTML for a Dynamic Web Page

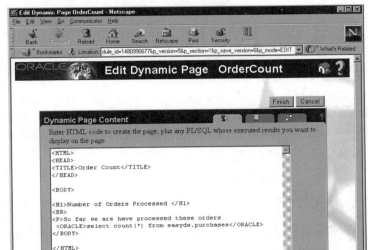

In Figure 8.63, we can see the actual Web page generated by the HTML entered in Figure 8.62.

Figure 8.63 Result of the HTML for a Dynamic Web Page

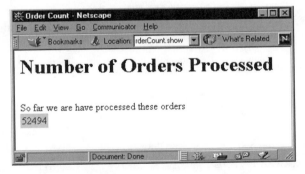

There are many other facilities available inside WebDB, such as the ability to create forms, frames, and hierarchy queries where you drill up and down. Explore all of the menus, and you will not be disappointed.

8.6.8   Management Tools

WebDB includes some very useful tools for managing the database and helping to understand what your users are doing. They can be found by selecting Monitor from the main menu. Among the options available are:

- User interface components
- Database objects

When *User Interface Components* is selected, the window in Figure 8.64 will appear. The selection that is of interest to us is *Request by Component Name*, because now we can see which are the most popular components being used by our users.

Figure 8.64 User Interface Components

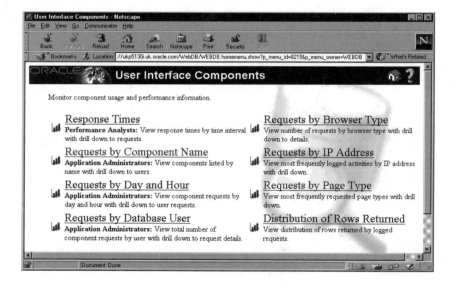

Therefore, after a day of usage, you could call up the screen shown in Figure 8.65, which advises which procedures our users have been invoking. Here we can see that our procedure *Productssalesbydate* has been used frequently.

Figure 8.65 Procedure Usage

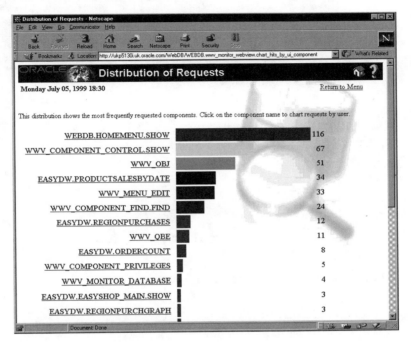

From these screens, some quite detailed information is available to the DBA on system usage. Unfortunately, it is outside the scope of this book to investigate this area further.

8.6.9   JavaScript

Earlier we discussed JavaScript. WebDB does not preclude you from creating your application using this approach. You can write JavaScript by selecting *Shared Components* and then completing the screen shown in Figure 8.66 with your JavaScript.

This is then stored in the database and can be run as per any of the other components we have created earlier by simply specifying its URL.

Figure 8.66 Defining JavaScript in WebDB

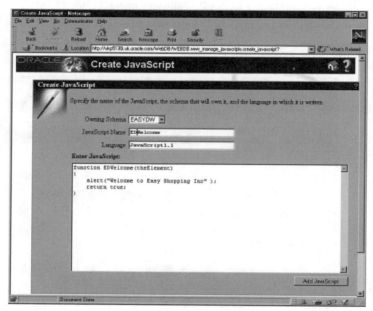

8.6.10   The Complete Application in WebDB

Hopefully, you now have some idea of how you can Web-enable your data warehouse using WebDB and very easily and quickly create an environment for your users that is easy to use and appears very professional.

In this chapter, we have created a number of components that we have linked together on our main menu. To run this application, all we have to enter for the URL for our browser is:

```
http://ukp5130i.uk.oracle.com/WebDB/EASYDW.EasyShop_Main.show
```

Doing so takes us to the procedure describing the main menu. When this is specified, the screen in Figure 8.67 will appear, from where we can run all of the components we have created against our data warehouse.

Figure 8.67 Our Easydw WebDB Application

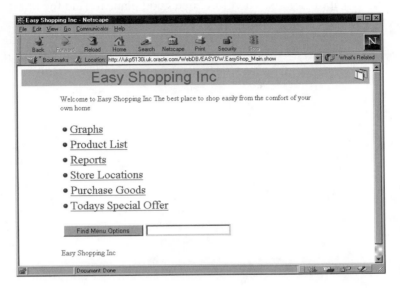

8.7 E-COMMERCE

The Internet is creating huge opportunities for some companies and is creating many new ones. New customers are being found and are also being taken away from other companies.

The data warehouse can be a key component in making your E-commerce business successfull. Why? Because it can help answer all those important questions to ensure that your business succeeds, such as:

- What products do people buy?
- When are these products sold—at what time of year and time of day?
- Is there a quiet time when systems can come off-line?
- Based on current sales, what do we predict our sales will be this time next year?
- How much will free shipping cost us?

Hopefully, this chapter has given you an insight into how you can use the Web with your data warehouse. There are many ways it can be exploited, and we have barely touched the surface here with respect to the tools and techniques that are available.

Oracle is also continually enhancing the tools to facilitate easier construction of Web applications. Therefore, one good place to find the latest information is at Oracle's Web site, at www.oracle.com.

Index